Conflicts in the Middle East since 1945

'The tone of the book is one of detachment based on a deep understanding of the situations in the Middle East . . . A masterly synthesis.'

The Old Radleian

'A rigorous but accessible overview.'

BBC History Magazine

This third edition of *Conflicts in the Middle East since 1945* analyses the nature of conflict in the Middle East, with its racial, ethnic, political, cultural, religious and economic factors. Throughout the book Peter Hinchcliffe and Beverley Milton-Edwards put the main conflicts into their wider context, with thematic debates on issues such as the emergence of radical Islam, the resolution of conflicts, diplomacy and peacemaking, and the role of the superpowers.

The book is brought fully up to date with events in the Middle East, covering, for instance, developments in 2006 in Iraq, where a democratically elected government is in place but the insurgency shows no sign of coming under control. The analysis of the Palestinian–Israeli conflict is also brought up to the present day, to include the election of the Hamas government and the 2006 conflict between Israel and Lebanon's Hizballah.

Including a newly updated bibliography and maps of the area, this is the perfect introduction for all students wishing to understand the complex situation in the Middle East, in its historical context.

Beverley Milton-Edwards is Professor in the School of Politics and Assistant Director for the Study of Ethnic Conflict at Queen's University, Belfast. She is the author of *Contemporary Politics in the Middle East* (1999) and, in this series, *Islamic Fundamentalism since 1945* (Routledge 2004).

Peter Hinchcliffe was Honorary Senior Research Fellow in the School of Politics at Queen's University, Belfast, and is an Honorary Fellow at the University of Edinburgh. He is co-author of *Jordan: A Hashemite Legacy* (Routledge 2000) with Beverley Milton-Edwards and a former British Ambassador to Kuwait and Jordan.

The Making of the Contemporary World
Edited by Eric J. Evans and Ruth Henig

The Making of the Contemporary World series provides challenging interpretations of contemporary issues and debates within strongly defined historical frameworks. The range of the series is global, with each volume drawing together material from a range of disciplines – including economics, politics and sociology. The books in this series present compact, indispensable introductions for students studying the modern world.

Conflicts in the Middle East since 1945

Third edition

**Beverley Milton-Edwards
and Peter Hinchcliffe**

Routledge
Taylor & Francis Group

LONDON AND NEW YORK

First published 2001 by Routledge
Reprinted 2002 (twice)

Second edition published 2004
Reprinted 2005, 2006

Third edition published 2008
Reprinted 2008
by Routledge
2 Park Square, Milton Park, Abingdon, Oxon OX14 4RN

Simultaneously published in the USA and Canada
by Routledge
270 Madison Ave, New York NY 10016

Routledge is an imprint of the Taylor & Francis Group, an informa business

© 2001, 2004, 2008 Beverley Milton-Edwards and Peter Hinchcliffe

Typeset in Times New Roman
by Keystroke, 28 High Street, Tettenhall, Wolverhampton
Printed and bound in Great Britain
by TJ International Ltd, Padstow, Cornwall

British Library Cataloguing in Publication Data
A catalogue record for this book is available from the British Library

Library of Congress Cataloging in Publication Data
Milton-Edwards, Beverley.
 Conflicts in the Middle East since 1945 / Beverley Milton-Edwards
and Peter Hinchcliffe. – 3rd ed.
  p. cm. – (Making of the contemporary world)
 Includes bibliographical references and index.
 ISBN 978–0–415–44016–5 (hardback) – ISBN 978–0–415–44017–2 (pbk.)
 1. Middle East–Politics and government–1945– 2. Mediation, International.
I. Hinchcliffe, Peter. II. Title.
 DS63.1.M566 2007
 956.04–dc22   2007013317

ISBN10: 0–415–44016–5 (hbk)
ISBN10: 0–415–44017–3 (pbk)
ISBN10: 0–203–93443–1 (ebk)

ISBN13: 978–0–415–44016–5 (hbk)
ISBN13: 978–0–415–44017–2 (pbk)
ISBN13: 978–0–203–93443–2 (ebk)

To the children of conflict

Contents

viii *Contents*

Maps

Map A – Middle East and Gulf

Preface

The second edition of this book was written just after a series of momentous events that have coloured the first years of the twenty-first century. They placed new pressures on the forces for peace and conflict in the Middle East region and influenced the impact that the politics of this region has on the wider international order. Accordingly, that edition took account of such events as the '9/11' al-Qaeda attacks on America, the subsequent American declaration of global war on terrorism, the invasion of Iraq and the subsequent capture of Saddam Hussein, and the virtual collapse of the Middle East peace process within the Oslo framework. Events move on rapidly and it is now time for further important revisions for this third edition. We have again been able to take account of the useful criticism and helpful suggestions by earlier readers and users of this text. In particular we have brought the sad story of the ongoing Arab–Israeli conflict up to date by including the war in Lebanon during summer 2006, the emergence of Hamas as the dominant player in Palestine following the 2006 elections and the continued bitter conflict between Israeli security forces and Palestinian militants, particularly in Gaza since the withdrawal of Israeli settlements in the summer of 2005. All this in the context of continued paralysis and stalemate in the Middle East peace process, with the international community unwilling to deal with a Palestinian government led by a Hamas prime minister with a majority of his party in the National Assembly. Such stresses engendered Palestinian inter-factional fighting and led to the eventual formation of a national unity government in February 2007. Further developments in the Middle East have impacted negatively on stability and provoked conflict in Iraq and Lebanon, and between the USA and Iran.

We are generous with our definition of the Middle East and the territories and peoples who have been affected by conflicts since 1945. In the interests of brevity we have concentrated on the more important events, so some war zones, such as the Sudan, Eritrea and the western Sahara, are not featured. In this respect we are not entirely bound to territories or states but seek to explain conflict in terms of other actors, such as social or religious ones. We concentrate on territories, however, that have been badly scarred by conflicts of a very modern variety. All too often conflicts are about modern boundaries and barriers, but we choose to overcome them in presenting a different style of analysis in this book.

This text is aimed at a variety of readers. We aspire to open up what appear to be complex and intractable conflicts to readers who are motivated by a variety of reasons to know more about the region and its political dynamics. Our original concept was to produce a book for an undergraduate audience, but perhaps because of renewed interest in Middle Eastern affairs and Islam, triggered by 9/11 and the war in Iraq, the book has proved popular with the general reader, becoming something of a bestseller.

So much has been written about dispute and conflict, war and peace-making in the Middle East. The Arab–Israeli conflict, the dimensions of the Palestinian–Israeli battle, the two Gulf wars (Iraq/Iran and the Kuwait War), Lebanon, the Kurds and the 'rise' of political Islam have all demanded explanation, historical record and, often, competing perspectives in terms of explaining why collapse into violence has occurred in such contexts. The need for an accessible synthesis tying together all the complex and tangled skeins has been apparent for some time. It is our aspiration that this book goes some way towards meeting such a need.

Acknowledgements

The co-authors of this book would like to thank David Evans and Ruth Henig for their encouragement during this project. We hope it will offer some critical insight into a variety of conflicts associated with the region which might be unfamiliar to the first-time reader. This project in itself has encouraged us to remain eternal students of the region, making new discoveries and friendships along the way. We would like to extend our gratitude to all at Routledge who have encouraged us to embark on this third edition. Our thanks also to the many friends within the region and those we made during the writing of this book. We are also grateful to our colleagues in the School of Politics, International Studies and Philosophy at Queen's University, Belfast, the Institute for Arabic and Islamic Studies, Edinburgh University, and the Kenyon Institute in Jerusalem. To those of our students who have played a role in the dialogue about conflict in the Middle East we also extend our deep appreciation. Our final thanks to our lifelong partners Graham and Archie, and to our children who have happily supported us in our endeavours.

Beverley Milton-Edwards
Peter Hinchcliffe
Jerusalem and Edinburgh, February 2007

Chronology

1945   End of Second World War.

1947   (November) UN adopts Partition Plan for Palestine.

1948   (May) The outbreak of the first Arab–Israeli war and birth of the Palestinian refugee issue.

1950   Jordan annexes the West Bank.

1951   (July) King Abdullah of Jordan assassinated at the Temple Mount in Jerusalem.

1952   Free Officer Coup in Egypt. Gamal Abdel Nasser becomes President in 1954.

1956   (October) Suez Crisis following nationalization, brings Britain, France and Israel into military confrontation with Egypt.

1957   (January) Eisenhower Doctrine issued by US government.

1963   (March) Ba'ath Party comes to power in Syria following *coup d'état*.

1964   The Palestine Liberation Organization founded by Egypt.

1967   (June) Six-Day War. Arab armies defeated, Israel occupies Palestinian, Syrian and Egyptian territory.

1968   (January) Fatah, the Palestinian resistance movement led by Yasser Arafat, formed.

        (July) Ba'ath Party coup in Iraq.

1970   (September) President Nasser dies and Anwar Sadat becomes President of Egypt. Civil war in Jordan as Palestinian resistance forces and Jordanian armed forces clash.

        (November) Hafez al-Assad becomes President of Syria.

1973   (October) Yom Kippur War brings Egyptian and Syrian troops into confrontation with Israel. Israel defeats the Arab armies once more.

1974   (March) Autonomy foisted on Iraqi Kurds by Saddam Hussein.

1975   (April) Outbreak of the Lebanese civil war.

1976   (January) Syrian army enter Lebanese arena.

1977   (November) President Sadat of Egypt pays historic visit to Jerusalem.

1978 (March) Israeli forces invade Lebanon.
(September) Israel and Egypt sign Camp David Peace Accords. UN establishes multinational peacekeeping force (UNIFIL) for South Lebanon.

1979 (January) Revolution in Iran. Shah is toppled and Ayatollah Khomeini returns from exile.

1980 (September) Outbreak of the Iran–Iraq War.

1981 (October) President Sadat of Egypt assassinated by Islamic militants.

1982 (June) Israel invades Lebanon.
(September) Massacres in Palestinian refugee camps of Sabra and Shatila in Lebanon by Phalangist allies of Israel.

1983 (May) Israeli–Lebanese Accords signed.

1984 (March) Israeli–Lebanese Accords abrogated.

1985 (January) Israel withdraws some troops from Lebanon.

1986 (April) US raid on Libyan capital of Tripoli.

1987 (December) Outbreak of the Palestinian uprising (Intifada).

1988 (July) King Hussein abrogates annexation of West Bank.
(August) Ceasefire agreed between Iran and Iraq.

1989 (October) Ta'if Peace Agreement brings civil war in Lebanon to an end.

1990 (August) Saddam Hussein orders Iraqi troops to invade and occupy Kuwait.

1991 (February) Allied forces successfully end Iraq's occupation of Kuwait. Outbreak of Kurdish and Shi'a uprisings in Iraq.
(October) First multilateral peace conference on Arab–Israeli dispute held in Madrid.

1993 (September) Israel and the PLO sign the Oslo Accords establishing Palestinian autonomy and agenda for final status negotiations.

1994 (August) Yasser Arafat returns to Gaza.
(October) Israel and Jordan sign peace treaty ending conflict.

1995 (November) Prime Minister Yitzhak Rabin assassinated by Jewish right-wing fanatic at peace rally in Tel Aviv.

1996 (March) Palestinian Islamists embark on suicide-bomb campaign against Israel.
(June) Israelis elect right-wing Likud leader Binjamin 'Bibi' Netanyahu as Prime Minister.

1999 (February) King Hussein of Jordan dies. His son Abdullah is crowned.
(June) Former army general Ehud Barak elected in Israel as Prime Minister on pro-peace process platform.

2000 (May) Israeli troops withdraw from South Lebanon and its local proxy the South Lebanon Army collapses.

(June) Hafez al-Assad of Syria dies. His son Bashar elected presidential successor.

(September) Following the visit by Israeli Likud leader to Temple Mount and al-Aqsa mosque in Jerusalem, Palestinian protest and Israeli violence lead to a subsequent Israeli declaration of 'time out' from the peace process and the second Intifada is announced.

(October) Al-Qaeda attack on USS *Cole* moored in Yemeni waters.

2001 (September) Al-Qaeda, led by Usama Bin Laden, launch attacks on New York and Washington.

(October) Allied alliance begins military operations against Afghanistan.

(November) Kabul falls.

(December) New interim administration led by Hamid Karzai takes power.

2002 (April) Israel reoccupies West Bank and the government of Ariel Sharon declares Yasser Arafat an 'enemy of the state'.

(June) President George W. Bush recognizes that two states must form solution to Palestinian–Israeli conflict.

(November) UNSCR 1441 passed against Iraq and weapons of mass destruction.

2003 (March) War against Iraq launched by Allied forces led by the United States of America.

(April) Baghdad falls and the regime of Saddam Hussein collapses.

(June) Leader of Algeria's outlawed Islamic Salvation Front (FIS) Abassi Madani and his deputy Ali Belhadj are freed after serving twelve-year sentences.

(December) Saddam Hussein captured in Tikrit.

2004 (March) Suicide bomb kills 140 in Karbala and Baghdad

(April) Abdelaziz Bouteflika is elected to a second term as President of Algeria in a landslide poll victory.

(September) UN Security Council resolution – aimed at Syria – demands that foreign troops leave Lebanon. Syria dismisses the move. Parliament extends pro-Syrian President Lahoud's term by three years. Rafiq Hariri resigns as Prime Minister.

(November) Yasser Arafat dies.

2005 (January) Mahmoud Abbas elected President of the Palestinian National Authority. Elections in Iraq.

(February) Former Syrian Prime Minister Rafik Hariri assassinated in Beirut.

(March) Hundreds of thousands of Lebanese attend pro- and anti-Syrian rallies in Beirut.

(August) Israeli evacuation of the Gaza Strip.

2005   (September) In Algeria voters support reconciliation referendum including an amnesty for many of those involved in post-1992 killings.

(December) Elections in Iraq.

2006   (January) Hamas wins majority of seats in Palestinian Legislative Council and form government. Israeli Prime Minister Ariel Sharon collapses and falls into a coma. Ehud Olmert appointed to replace him.

(July) Israel attacks Lebanon following Hizballah raid on Israeli soldiers.

(November) Ministers from Hizballah and the Amal movement in Lebanon resign shortly before the cabinet approves draft UN plans for a tribunal to try suspects in the killing of former Prime Minister Hariri.

(December) Saddam Hussein executed in Iraq. Hundreds of thousands of opposition supporters demonstrate in Beirut to demand the resignation of the government led by Fouad Siniora.

2007   (January) US government announces new strategy for Iraq.

(February) Mecca Declaration ends inter-factional fighting and leads to formation of Palestinian government of national unity. Suicide bomb in Baghdad kills more than 130 people. Fighting between Hamas and Fatah in Ramallah and Gaza.

Introduction

One fundamental question should be asked of many contemporary accounts of the history and politics of the Middle East in the latter half of the twentieth century. Why does so much analysis of the region take as read that the Middle East, unlike most other regions of the globe, is characterized by a Hobbesian state of nature where war and conflicts are inevitable and endemic? This book sets out to address this perception through examining a series of examples by way of a variety of factors and conditions which have given rise to war and conflicts.

Rather than comparing the region with others with a similar history of conflict, such as Africa and Latin America, we have kept our focus on the Middle East. Suffice it to say that conflict-ridden though this area has been since the Second World War, its history of confrontation and instability is arguably little different from that of war-torn western and central Africa or the former Yugoslavia. It is also worth recalling that much of the genesis of conflicts in the region has arisen from the same factors, such as the legacy of colonialism and superpower rivalry, as in other parts of the globe. Nevertheless, the dominant perception in a West fed by prejudicial images of bloodthirsty Arabs pitted against their enemies or fighting among themselves demands an explanation. We have sought to find one in this book without, from the outset, accepting Hobbesian assumptions but seeking instead to find a less 'Orientalist' and more rational explanation for the presence of conflicts within the region.[1]

The Arab–Israeli dispute has been the most dominant and enduring feature of the post-war Middle East. But it is only one of a number of conflicts that this book will address. Conflict in the region is and has been multifaceted. As we shall explain, it is not just about state-to-state war, the traditional combat between sovereign nation-states in dispute, but also other kinds of tension. These have led to internal, inter-state and regional conflagration sometimes lasting many decades. Although such conflicts are said to characterize the region and be indicative of its war-mongering peoples, they have, in many cases, roots in the history of persistent intervention by outside powers pursuing strategic interests, including access to the area's economic riches – particularly oil.

Indeed, we would contend that since 1945 the peoples of the region have often been subjected to some of the most aggressive and predatory policies of outside powers. This is partly, but only partly, explained by superpower rivalry and compounded in the case of the United States by domestic pressures, which have seemingly prevented it exercising its power and influence in an even-handed manner in accordance with generally accepted international norms when dealing with much of the conflict bedevilling the region. On first reading, such an assertion may appear unduly hard, but in the following chapters we will present evidence to support our contention.

We will show how conflict in the Middle East is made manifest in many ways, including actual warfare, political violence, low-intensity conflict, perceived failure of diplomacy, virulent propaganda, political and economic boycotts, disputes over land and water, resistance to occupation and deeply ingrained cultures of antagonism. By the same token we believe the majority of these conflicts have taken three principal forms. First, long-standing regional disputes; second, short-lived military hostilities; finally, localized disputes. Inter-state conflict has included Arab against Iranian, Israeli against Arab, and Arab versus Arab. Regional conflict has been primarily in the context of the Arab–Israeli dispute, while conflict between regional players and outside actors is typified by the Suez crisis of 1956. In the same category, the Kuwait crisis uniquely brought together an alliance between local and outside powers confronting an Arab aggressor. Internal state conflict and sectarian violence is epitomized by our case study on the Lebanon, devastated by fifteen years of civil war from 1975 to 1990. We have also looked at the tragic case of the Kurds – a people scattered throughout several countries in the region who have failed to achieve any acceptable degree of self-determination and whose struggle for the recognition of their legitimate political rights seems almost hopeless.

Previous treatments of conflicts in the region have examined such factors as traditional state-to-state rivalries and competition for control of natural resources, such as oil and water. It was only in the 1990s, in the wake of the Cold War and following the end of superpower rivalry, that historical accounts of conflict in the region addressed new issues. These included ethno-national rivalry and the impact of continued foreign interference in the region in supporting a variety of corrupt and authoritarian regimes. In addition, debates in the 1990s began to focus increasingly on the issue of regime legitimacy and a linkage to continuing conflicts. In some cases, like that of Iraq, people questioned the morality of allowing authoritarian leaders like Saddam Hussein to 'engineer' national crises through provoking conflict in order to entrench their autocratic systems of rule. The validity of the arguments put forward by both the former Soviet Union and the United States in defence of their roles in the region has also been questioned in an era where the latter's foothold in much of the area has largely been the target of popular resentment; in contrast with the less critical attitude of those regimes dependent on Washington for support and protection.

This book does not include a chapter specifically about the military and its role in the Middle East. But the predominance of the armed forces in much of the politics of the region, their role in the nature and process of state formation and nation building, needs to be understood in the context of the wider debate about conflict. Since 1945 there have been major wars between Israel and the Arabs, as well as the Iran–Iraq war and the Gulf crisis of 1990 to 1991. In addition there have been civil conflicts in Iraq, Syria, Algeria, Jordan, Oman, Yemen and Lebanon in which the armed forces of these states have played a major role. Such wars have been described by Bromley as 'the main source of conflict in the Middle East', and are 'concerned with the internal pacification and repression of domestic populations'.[2]

A further reflection of the ill-defined nature of the state in the region has been the numerous border disputes which have erupted over the years. They have included conflicts between Egypt and Libya, Morocco and Mauritania, Jordan and Syria, Israel and Lebanon, Iraq and Kuwait, Iran and Iraq, Saudi Arabia and Yemen, and Bahrain and Qatar. Much of this conflict is the legacy of colonial-inspired or -crafted state formation from the turn of the twentieth century to the 1970s. The carve-up of much of the Middle East was determined by the strategic objectives of the former colonial powers – principally Britain and France – who created highly artificial states, many of whose borders remain subject to dispute. Such strategic objectives were largely pursued with no consideration for the interests or wishes of the indigenous peoples of the region; the same people who were obliged to live within the boundaries of new, highly artificial states which they themselves had taken no part in shaping. In many contemporary accounts of the origins of war in the region such factors are often forgotten. But the terrible (if unforeseen) consequences of colonial ambitions are not forgotten by many in the region who still perceive Arthur Balfour and the British as the architects of problems which continue to the present day.[3]

The arms race in the region has also played its part in perpetuating conflict. Arab states, Iran and Israel all spent decades building up significant arsenals, including conventional weaponry, chemical weapons and, certainly in Israel's case, nuclear capability – thus the real fear, particularly in the 1970s, of a nuclear Armageddon in the area. Iran's nuclear capacity has come to dominate US policy in the region under the Bush administration, reaching a tipping point not just of international censure but actual confrontation.

Western (and previously Soviet) support for the arms race has been ill disguised and used to further vital economic and/or strategic interests within the region. National spending on arms and the military in the region is higher than in other developing regions of the world: while in the Middle East spending on arms and the military is on average 15 per cent of national income, it is only 5 per cent in the rest of the developing world.[4] In Syria, for example, defence expenditure is as high as 18 per cent, and the army constitutes 3.9 per cent of the total workforce, compared to 0.8 per cent in the United States.[5]

In such an arena of conflict awash with arms, the role of the military in the political systems of the area can scarcely be exaggerated. Military coups and revolutions have been significant features of the Middle East and military-based regimes characteristic of states such as Iraq, Syria, Libya and Egypt. As part of this phenomenon, or because of it, the emergence of the soldier-politician linked to the militaristic nature of the state in the region has a direct cause-and-effect relationship on the political processes of countries like Syria, Turkey, Libya and Iraq. This is the case even in democratic Israel, where the military records of its soldier-politicians, including Prime Ministers Yitzhak Rabin and Ehud Barak, are promoted (and admired) as positive attributes of a national leader.

The domination of military rule over national political systems, however, is not of course unique to the Middle East and remains a feature of many Third World regimes all over the globe. Indeed, in the 1960s, the role of the military in the politics of the region was perceived as a positive development heralding progress, technological advancement, modernization, and the promotion and safeguarding of an appropriate nationalist agenda. A dramatic volte-face in popular attitudes occurred two decades later. The true nature of conflict and the military in society had convinced many that the negative effects of this feature of politics in the region was unacceptable:

> The pervasive nature of factionalism and internal strife within the officer class, the lack of economic development, economic crises, widespread corruption, coercion and lack of democracy convinced many that . . . whatever degree of order and discipline the military have been able to provide, it has been outweighed by the blocking of the assumption of responsibility on the part of ordinary citizens for their economic and political affairs.[6]

In addition, the closing decades of the twentieth century witnessed a steady transition from military to civil rule elsewhere in the world. But despite this sea change in popular sentiment, this did not happen in the Middle East, where, as Halliday comments, 'relations between states are dominated by suspicion, a stance reinforced by popular attitudes on all sides where memories of recent war remain strong'.[7] While the role of the military and conflict has been debated extensively in many texts on the subject, other explanations of conflict also need to be highlighted. Conflicting ideologies, ethnic and religious differences, superpower rivalry and the development of state nationalism are all factors that have been cited to one degree or another in explanation of conflict in the region. All these factors are examined in the case studies we have selected for treatment in this volume. There are obvious omissions, such as the troubles of Sudan and Morocco, hostilities in the Horn of Africa, Britain's withdrawal from South Yemen and subsequent confrontation with Marxist rebel forces in Oman, plus other bloody colonial disengagements such as by the French in North Africa. In such a short volume we have had to leave some of the regional conflicts to one side, but we hope that the themes we highlight in discussing some will go some way in shedding light on most of the others.

We have laid out the book as follows. In the first two chapters we examine two important dimensions of the Arab–Israeli conflict. We disentangle the narrower Palestinian–Israeli dimension from wider disputes between the state of Israel and the Arab states of the region. Some might argue that to treat the conflict in this way does a disservice to the much-vaunted principle of solidarity and unity sought by the Arab people in its confrontation with Israel. We, however, are not arguing that separate treatment necessitates a separation of the unifying principles at the heart of such struggles. Rather, we take a pragmatic approach to assist the first-time reader in understanding the roots of such conflicts while reflecting, as we do in both chapters, on the linkages within the dispute.

In Chapter 3 we examine the impact of the Soviet Union and the United States in the region, as well as superpower rivalry and its influence on the course of conflict and peacemaking from the 1950s onwards. No account of conflict in the region since 1945 can afford to dismiss the role played by such actors and the impact the Cold War had on both hindering the resolution of conflict and actively promoting it to satisfy superpower strategic objectives. In Chapter 4 we address the dominant perception in the West that in the latter decades of the twentieth century Islam has been a primary catalyst for conflict and a major threat emanating from the region. We aim to debunk much of the reductive rhetoric associated with this perception and put so-called 'Holy Terror' in its proper perspective.

In Chapter 5 we look at manifestations of the religious nature of conflict in the region through an examination of the causes of the civil war in Lebanon and how it fitted into the larger jigsaw puzzle of the Arab–Israeli dispute and superpower politics. Further ethnic dimensions of conflict are explored in the following chapter on the Kurds, where we chart the rise of ethno-nationalism in the context of uniting ideologies of nationalism and the challenges presented by minority groups agitating for their rights, including that of self-determination.

A clash of ideologies of sorts is explained in Chapter 7, where we discuss the nature of the war between Iran and Iraq, which dominated the Gulf throughout the 1980s. Described by one writer as a 'meaningless' conflict with uncountable costs, we examine the political motives that brought these neighbouring states into major confrontation and the destabilizing impact this had throughout the Gulf region. The battle for local hegemony and a desperate scramble for resources, also in the Gulf, are identified in Chapter 8 as the main factors in explaining Saddam Hussein's disastrous invasion of Kuwait in August 1990 and his subsequent defeat at the hands of the Desert Storm coalition.

In Chapter 9 we describe how the nature of conflict in the region was changed by a variety of concerted attempts in the 1990s to bring them to an end. In Lebanon, for example, where significant civil conflict had gripped the country since 1975, an Arab-sponsored deal brought the conflict to a halt and allowed the country to begin a return to parliamentary politics. While the root causes of the conflict in Lebanon remain unresolved, there is hope that appropriate scenarios can be designed to satisfy the more pressing demands of the various factions in this state. Elsewhere in the region, other Arab attempts at conflict resolution have been marginalized, and it has only been the influence of outside agencies, especially the United States, that has brought formerly intractable enemies to the negotiating table. These recent developments have the potential to alter the political landscape of the region significantly, but comprehensive peace remains elusive.

Our last chapter outlines the inexorable rise of new conflicts in the region as the fallout from 9/11 and the American-led war against Iraq continues to affect the whole Middle East. As described in the Preface, the earlier event cast a shadow on the then virtually stalled Middle East Peace Process (MEPP), led to regime change in Afghanistan and, as part of President Bush's wider war on terrorism, started the countdown to the invasion of Iraq in March 2003, Iraq having been categorized by Bush as the primary target within the 'axis of evil'. Its ramifications will clearly be with us for many years, as the quick coalition victory 'liberating' Iraq (or at least putting the Saddam regime to flight) seems to have been the easy bit. Nation rebuilding in this traumatized and divided country has proved to be a major headache for the international community and, more immediately, for the coalition partners cast as much in the role of occupiers as of liberators.

We also look at the Middle East Peace Process in the light of the launch of the 2003 'Roadmap' – a blueprint for a lasting and comprehensive solution to (nearly) sixty years of war. Even cautious optimism was premature, despite President Bush's apparent determination to emulate his predecessor's personal engagement, as the process got off to an uncertain start amid a new welter of bloodshed. As in Iraq, the international community faces an uphill task if it truly seeks to forge an end to conflicts in the Middle East.

1 The Arab–Israeli conflict
Ways of war

> It is not true that the Arabs hate the Jews for personal, religious, or racial reasons. They see us, rightly from their point of view, as Westerners, foreigners, even invaders who seized an Arab country to create a Jewish state . . . Since we are obliged to achieve our aims against the wishes of the Arabs, we must live in a permanent war.
>
> General Moshe Dayan[1]

For the best part of a century the Arab–Israeli conflict has been a complex problem with important ramifications for the international community. As other chapters in this book will highlight, this conflict has embroiled other actors, such as the USA and the former Soviet Union, into, on one occasion, near nuclear confrontation. It has had a major impact on the international and more specifically capital-based economies of the international order, and promoted extravagant, wasteful and profligate spending on arms to the point where Kalashnikovs are apparently more valued by many of the region's political leaders than a decent standard of living for its citizens. How then does one begin to make sense of this bitter feud between the Jews and the Arabs, the state of Israel and the Arab (and other) states of the region, between religious cousins and territorial neighbours? In our first two chapters we aim to analyse this problem by making a distinction on the one hand between the wider Arab–Israeli conflict – marked by the wars of 1948, 1967, 1973, 1982 and 2006 as well as the peace treaties of 1978 between Israel and Egypt, and 1994 between Jordan and Israel – and on the other the more narrowly focused Palestinian–Israeli dispute that resulted in the Arab revolt of 1936 to 1939, the wars cited above and the outbreak of the Palestinian uprising (Intifada) in 1987, as well as attempts at peacemaking between the two parties from 1993 onwards.

Some might argue that making such distinctions is unhelpful; after all, should we not liken the conflict to the chicken-and-egg conundrum, asking

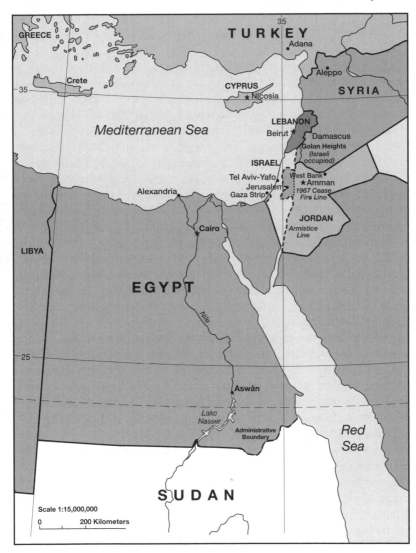

Map B – Israel and neighbouring states

which came first, the Arab–Israeli dispute or the Palestinian–Israeli? Such conundrums rarely have a simple answer, which is why we believe it is best to try to make distinctions between the two in order to assist understanding rather than obscure or confuse. It is true, of course, that the Palestinian issue lies at the heart of the wider conflict. We will argue, however, that the importance of the Palestinians as the primary focus has waxed and waned over the past century and that other factors, such as the competition between rival Arab states for regional leadership, need to be explained if this conflict is to be adequately understood. The conflict between those regularly referred to as the 'Jews' and the 'Arabs' has been well under way for nearly a century. The reignition of war between Israel and Hizballah forces in Lebanon in the summer of 2006 and the absence of meaningful peace between Israel and the Arab states of the region continue to augur badly for lasting peace. Within its confines the differences between these peoples, religions and attitudes have at times manifested themselves in conventional wars, and led to the militarization of the entire region, where even aspiring democrats have only recently begun to discard their military uniforms. Inevitably under such a climate, economic relations, culture, history, literature, mass media and communications, international organizations, regional associations and interest groups have all been enlisted and manipulated to demonize the enemy. Rival nationalisms, the superpower conflict, the right to self-determination, Islamism, anti-Semitism, control of oil, and the emergence of Third World radicalism and anti-Western sentiment have all played parts, making up the cocktail of conflict described by Sahliyeh as 'the most lethal and volatile . . . and the most difficult to resolve'.[2]

Although the essence of the conflict is the battle between two people over one land – the territory of the Holy Land, including Jerusalem – over time the Arab–Israeli dimension has developed characteristics often far removed from the original Palestinian issue and territorial focus. One example is the bitter dispute and battle that has raged from the late 1970s between Israel and the Lebanese Islamic resistance movements, and latterly the Shi'a Hizballah organization. While Israel's original motives in invading and subsequently occupying Lebanon in 1978 and 1982 were to rout the Palestine Liberation Organization (PLO), once the PLO had left the country the Israeli Defence Force (IDF) remained as an occupying force and made themselves the principal enemies of the Lebanese Shi'a population.[3] Hizballah was subsequently formed as a resistance movement to end Israel's illegal occupation of southern Lebanon and, until Israel's withdrawal in spring 2000, waged a major military campaign against its enemy and those perceived to be its supporters. The latest reignition of the Israeli–Hizballah battle occurred following the kidnap of Israeli soliders by Hizballah when Israel launched a major military offensive against the whole of Lebanon. While it may be true that there was little love lost between the PLO and Hizballah during the Lebanese civil war, they ended up sharing a common antipathy to Israel as an occupying force on Arab lands. Certainly, this is an instance where Israel's policies may have inadvertently created allies out of enemies, thus undermining its own security.

The roots of this conflict lay in the resistance mounted by the Arabs and their leaders in the region against the initial attempt by settler Zionists, most of whom were immigrants from Europe, to build a state in Palestine. But it was the subsequent dispossession of the Palestinian Arab population, the creation of a Palestinian national identity and the emergence of new Arab nationalisms united in opposition to Zionism and to the close association it was perceived as having with the forces of imperialism and colonialism that gave the conflict its wider dimension. The struggle to gain and retain Arab rights to self-determination over Palestine in the face of European dominance over the entire region had its roots in the First World War, when the British made contradictory commitments to the Arabs and to the Zionist Jews to enlist their support against Germany and its Ottoman (Turkish) allies. The Arab leadership was led to believe that Arabs would control much of the region following the defeat of the Ottomans, but at the same time the British and French were planning to replace Istanbul as the dominant power centre in the region. The situation was complicated further by a British promise to the Zionists to support the establishment of a Jewish national home in Arab Palestine: the Balfour Declaration (described in Chapter 2). The expediency of measures taken to further war aims was to be questioned in the decades that followed. It soon emerged that the British had promised more than they could deliver and had engaged in duplicitous behaviour described as a 'disgusting scramble for the Middle East'.[4]

When the Ottoman Empire was dissolved at the end of the First World War most of the Middle East became subject to colonial rule or influence. European powers, principally Britain and France, redrew the boundaries of the Middle East and many Arab areas came under their direct political control. This period of direct and indirect colonial control, short lived though it was, resulted in the invention and promotion of new Arab rulers and monarchs presiding over newly created states within artificial boundaries. It sowed the seeds of future conflicts – between Israel and the Arabs (involving the Iranians) and among the Arabs themselves – that for the most part remained unresolved throughout the last century.

As we describe in the next chapter, the incipient conflict between the Jews and Arabs in the region took shape during the first three decades of the twentieth century and culminated in the first direct war in 1948 as Britain ended its mandate in Palestine, which had lasted since 1919. During this period the British authorities were, according to the official remit of the mandate as agreed by the League of Nations, supposed to assist the mandated territory to self-government. But they were caught between conflicting pressures: Zionist attempts to establish their own state (something more than the 'national home' envisaged in the Balfour Declaration, as incorporated into the mandate's provisions) and Arab efforts to oppose this in the pursuit of their own national aspirations.[5] In these circumstances the British had little option but to pursue an often oppressive policy of control and public order.

The grievances of the Palestinian community in Palestine at the time (particularly over the large influx of Jewish immigrants) raised tension between the two communities and resulted in the 1929 riots when Jews in Jerusalem and Hebron were murdered. This event was followed by further conflict, including the 1936 General Strike and the Palestinian revolt from 1936 to 1939. The British authorities, also under attack from militant Jewish organizations, appeared to be unable to develop policies or strategies to resolve the conflict, and the outbreak of the Second World War in Europe in 1939, and the Nazi-perpetrated Holocaust against six million Jews, had unforeseen consequences for the future of Palestine. After the war Jewish immigration reached new heights, and pressure for a Jewish state in Palestine as a haven for the persecuted survivors of the Holocaust grew relentlessly. The British were increasingly unable to maintain law and order, and meanwhile the Palestinians and their national leadership demanded self-determination. Eventually the whole problem was turned over by the British to the newly established United Nations, which decided to resolve the competing claims for self-determination by promoting partition between the Jews and the Arabs, with Jerusalem falling under international authority. The Zionist movement accepted statehood as a much better deal than the national home they had been offered under the Balfour Declaration amid considerable hostility and nascent conflict from their Arab neighbours. There was a belief that securing statehood would promote a much-needed sense of security for the Jewish people and an end to their exile. The diaspora could be gathered in under the flag of Israel. However, the Palestinians and Arab states rejected the UN partition plan, arguing that it was inherently biased and ignored the legitimate rights of Palestinians, who complained that their land was being given away as a means of appeasing European guilt over the Holocaust. When the British withdrew in May 1948 the battle for the land of Palestine broke out in earnest between the Israelis and the Arabs.

The war started shortly after the Israeli Declaration of Independence on 15 May 1948, as units from the Arab armies of Egypt, Jordan and Syria (backed by forces from Lebanon and Iraq) attempted to win back the Palestinian soil that had been lost to the Israeli state. The Arab armies, poorly led and equipped, were ultimately unsuccessful and failed to defeat the small but well-motivated and highly trained Israeli Defence Force. Armistice negotiations did not occur until January 1949, by which time between 700,000 and 800,000 Palestinians had fled their homes or been forced to flee. In some cases Palestinians, encouraged by their Arab leaders, left the battle-zones in the belief that after a swift Arab victory they would be able to return. In other cases they fled their villages after hearing news of the massacre by Israeli forces in the village of Deir Yassin. As Rodinson notes, 'Many leading Jews were glad to see the departure of a population which by its very presence presented an obstacle to the realisation of the Jewish state projected by the Zionists.'[6] The Palestinians who arrived as refugees in Lebanon, Transjordan, Syria, Egypt and the Gaza Strip quickly realized that they had lost their homes and would not be allowed to return to them. The only comfort that the leaders of the Arab world could offer was the promise that this first encounter was just one war in a major conflict that would continue on their behalf. The Palestinian community refers to this period in their history as '*al-nakbah*' – the catastrophe.

In terms of territory the end of the war meant the effective partition of Palestine, as it was formerly known. The West Bank and East Jerusalem (including the old city) came under the control of Jordan and its monarch King Abdullah. The Egyptian government administered the Gaza Strip from Cairo. The rest of the country, which as a result of the armistice had enlarged from 14,000 to 21,000 square kilometres, came within the new Israeli state. The Arabs were thus left with one-fifth of the original territory of their land and their aspirations for an Arab Palestine battered and weakened by the war.

Thus, within days of its birth the new Israeli state had been compelled into war with its Arab neighbours. The war lasted until armistice agreements secured in January 1949. Aware of their poor chances, the intertwined political and military leadership of Israel had no option but to engage in the fight against the six Arab armies ranged against them. One advantage that the Israelis believed they had over their enemy was referred to by Israeli Chief of Operations Yigael Yadin in May 1948 when he remarked, 'the problem is to what extent our men will be able to overcome enemy forces by virtue of their fighting spirit, of our planning and our tactics'.[7] The new state, forged in war, emerged from that experience with a unique character and an emphasis on institutions, such as the military, which might not, under more peaceful circumstances of statehood, have been necessary.

The repercussions of the conflict were widespread and enduring. Among them was an initial period of instability in the Arab countries as they came to terms with their defeat, and a backlash against British and Western influence in the region. This was most noticeable in increasing popular opposition to the British-supported Hashemite monarchies in Iraq and in Jordan. In 1951 Jordan's King Abdullah was assassinated and the new King Hussein – bowing to popular pressure – dismissed General Glubb Pasha, the British commander of the Arab Legion. The upsurge of popular nationalism elsewhere across the region in response to the Arab defeat signalled the end of the corrupt royalist regime in Egypt, where, in 1952, the

Free Officer Movement led by Gamal Abdel Nasser mounted a coup, trumpeting the rhetoric of Arab nationalism and unity in the face of the Zionist enemy across the region. In the eyes of Arab nationalist radicals in Cairo, Beirut, Baghdad and Damascus, Israel was an enemy not just because of the injustice against their brethren in Palestine but because of its close association with what they perceived as Western imperialist aspirations towards the region and in particular its recently exploited massive oil reserves. Thus, radical Arab nationalism and pan-Arab pretensions created a new dimension in the conflict with Israel, as was strikingly demonstrated during the 1956 Suez War.

The Suez conflict, which erupted over the decision by Nasser to nationalize the Suez Canal Company in July 1956, was a major escalation of anti-colonialist and, by association, anti-Zionist sentiment in the Arab world. The Suez Canal was built in the 1860s and by the late 1880s came under British and other foreign control (via a number of shareholders), maintained by British occupation of Egypt. The British saw the canal as an essential element in their control of the main sea route to India. In the four-year period leading up to the nationalization of the canal, Nasser embarked on a programme of pan-Arab cohesion and made military pacts with Syria, Saudi Arabia and Yemen. His goal was the restoration of the Arab nation under Egyptian leadership and an end to foreign influence in the area. The nationalization of Suez was the first time that a Third World country had successfully regained one of its major foreign-owned assets.

Both the French and the British were outraged at Nasser's decision. A highly secret tripartite operation in collusion with the Israelis was organized which hatched a plot to regain control over the canal. On 29 October 1956 the Israeli army launched Operation Kadesh; their forces crossed the border and entered the Sinai Desert. Over a period of five days they routed the Egyptian army and approached the canal. In accordance with a prearranged plan – 'Operation Musketeer' – the British and French bombed Egyptian targets and sent their troops to occupy Port Said and Port Fouad on the pretext of protecting them from hostile action, whether from Israel or Egypt. The Israelis had accepted a ceasefire as part of the secret prearrangement with the British and French, but the Egyptians refused to pull their troops back from the canal, as had been anticipated by the three colluding powers. Despite the military successes, the British and French were forced to accept a ceasefire and withdraw their forces as a result of US economic pressure on Britain and international public opinion as expressed through the UN. Nasser had held on to the canal and Arab nationalist feelings and anti-imperialist sentiment reached an all-time high.

The dispute between the Arabs and Israelis was exacerbated by the Arab perception of the Israeli role in the conflict as nothing more than defender of Western interests in the region. As a result tensions remained high and the deep animosity between the nations worsened. By siding with France and Britain and continuing to occupy the Gaza Strip between 1956 and 1957, the Israelis managed not only to deepen the rift with Egypt further but to anger the USA, bringing a close relationship under severe pressure. Within Israel the involvement of their armed forces in the 1956 crisis was perceived quite differently. The Israeli political and military establishment were concerned by persistent Arab attacks on Israel mounted from Gaza and the Sinai and by the Egyptian blockade of the Red Sea; consequently, the Israeli port of Eilat took defensive steps against Egyptian belligerence. While it is true that the Israeli withdrawal from the Sinai in March 1957 was prompted by US and UN pressure, Israeli involvement in Suez, secret agreements apart, would have been considered part of the domestic security strategy and sold as such to the Israeli people. In many respects the legacy of 1956 would not be visited upon the Israelis for some ten years or more. There can be little doubt, however, that Nasser's motives in 1967 were, at least partially, rooted in the 1956 encounter and his memories of military humiliation.

The war of 1967 was inevitable; the disputes between the Arabs and the Israelis had remained unresolved and the era of fervent and self-confident Arab nationalism was at its peak. On the eve of the war the combined Arab troop numbers were more than double those of the Israelis. The Arabs also had three times as many tanks and aircraft. Yet within six days they were totally routed by the Israeli army. The build up to the war on the Arab side had been fraught with reckless rhetoric and strident propaganda about the military prowess of the 'Arab people' and their ability to defeat the Israelis, to sweep them into the sea and win back Palestine. Egypt was the most eager of the combatants and was in a sense a victim of its own propaganda, which grossly exaggerated its potential as a military power. The Syrians and Jordanians, with territory at stake, were somewhat less hawkish but came under pressure from Nasser and the weight of their own public opinion intoxicated by the prospect of victory.[8] Nasser, determined to earn his place in the history books as the undisputed leader of the Arab world, pursued the liberation of Palestine as if it were a Holy Grail. At the same time he oppressed the Egyptian-administered Palestinian population of the Gaza Strip and the refugee community in Egypt, imprisoning thousands of them throughout his presidency.

The war took place between 5 and 11 June. The Jordanian army was defeated and its air force destroyed; similar Israeli victories occurred over the Egyptians in the Gaza Strip and the Syrians in the Golan Heights. By Saturday 10 June the Israeli army occupied the Sinai Peninsula, the Gaza Strip, the West Bank (including East Jerusalem and the Old City) and the

Golan Heights. The acquisition of this territory increased Israel's size by six times (almost half that formerly administered by Jordan), which had massive logistical, military and political implications for the Israeli government. Once again Israel had prevailed militarily despite the odds stacked against it. Following the appointment of Moshe Dayan as Defence Minister just days before the war, the Israeli armed forces had meticulously planned their daring campaign against a belligerent Nasser and his Egyptian forces. By seizing the initiative, launching the war before the Arabs could, the Israelis were able to dominate the rest of the military campaign, first by air and then by land. By the end of the war, Israel, a 'country that had felt embattled and threatened only days before was now the decisive military power in the Middle East . . . Equally Israel had changed in the process, for she was now an occupying power.'[9] The role of the UN during the hostilities was minimal. However, on 22 November, after five months of bargaining, it passed Security Council Resolution 242, which required a withdrawal of Israeli forces from the occupied territories in exchange for the cessation of fighting, the recognition of all states in the region, freedom of navigation in the Suez Canal and the Gulf of Aqaba, and the creation of demilitarized zones.[10]

The fourth conflict between Israel and the Arabs six years later had a number of unique features. First, Egyptian and Syrian forces were able (albeit temporarily) to break through Israeli lines, an unprecedented military success for the Arabs. Second, although Israel was the ultimate victor, the perceived weakness of the army in the initial stages of the hostilities affected national morale and self-confidence and led political leaders to rethink their position vis-à-vis their Arab neighbours. Third, the war was an Egyptian and Syrian attempt to recover their own territory, with the Palestinian issue coming a poor second in terms of strategy and objectives. Finally, it was during this war that the Gulf states started to use oil prices and boycott as major weapons against the West. For the first time the West was made aware of the significant leverage the Arab states held over the oil-dependent economies of the capitalist world.

In 1973 Nasser's successor, President Anwar Sadat, announced that he was preparing to attack Israel in an attempt to recover territory lost in the war of 1967. Sadat had been making such statements for a number of years while conducting a low-key campaign of attrition across the canal, so his latest announcements were not treated seriously. Although both American and Israeli intelligence networks were to a great extent aware of the plans, little was done in preparation for an attack. Nevertheless, on 6 October, the Egyptians crossed Suez and the Syrians attacked the Golan Heights. The USA and the Soviet Union immediately commenced a diplomatic effort to halt the conflict. At this point, as we discuss further in Chapter 3, neither of the superpowers wanted to risk being drawn into the war. Within two weeks the situation had begun to turn in Israel's favour, reversing earlier Syrian and Egyptian gains. By 24 October Israeli tanks had reached the suburbs of Cairo. At the last minute the Americans began to pressurize the Israelis, and Sadat went to the UN for a ceasefire agreement. The UN passed Resolution 338, calling for the ceasefire. On 24 October the fighting stopped. The Israelis had ultimately been successful, but the war demonstrated that they now had to regard Arab forces – especially the Egyptians – as being a match for their own and that the conflict would inevitably continue.

While the superpowers had been able to impose the ceasefire agreement, arranging an enduring peace was shown to be a difficult and lengthy process. One outcome of the war was that the US administration was forced to make a serious effort to push for peace between Israel and the Arab states. The war had exacerbated the instability of an already unstable Middle East, had frustrated American ambitions in the region, and had hit the US economy through the oil embargo announced by Arab oil producers. An OPEC (Organization of Petroleum Exporting Countries) increase in oil prices of several hundred per cent, plus the total embargo against the USA announced by Saudi Arabia and other Arab oil producers on 19 October, was intended to achieve a number of goals, with the resolution of the Palestinian issue among them. As Gerner notes, 'analysts differ on whether the events of 1973 resulted in a fundamental restructuring of the relationship between the Arab oil-producing countries and the West'.[11] It seems likely that it did.

At Camp David – the summer residence of the US President – on 17 September 1978 President Carter succeeded in getting the leaders of Egypt and Israel to sign a peace treaty between their two countries and agree to a framework of negotiation for peace in the Middle East. This was a momentous event in the history of the Arab–Israeli dispute. After the 1973 war Sadat felt he had little to lose in 'throwing in his lot' with the USA. He knew that in terms of diplomatic settlement only the Americans could deliver Israel into a peace, for they alone had enough influence over the Israelis to prise concessions out of them. He was also hopeful that a programme of US economic assistance would benefit the Egyptian economy. For Sadat, initially, one important aspect of the treaty was the opportunity to link the Egyptian–Israeli peace to the issue of the Palestinians. However, the Egyptian domestic situation, especially economic pressures, made him desperate to reach an agreement even in the face of minimal Israeli concessions. The Palestinians were suspicious of Sadat's role and reluctant to be associated with an agreement negotiated in their absence. This resulted in the Palestinian issue becoming sidelined in the peace negotiations, it being seen as too difficult to resolve. Sadat paid a high price for his willingness to make peace with the government of Israel: it ultimately led to his assassination on 6 October 1981. The peace treaty also left Egypt isolated in the Arab world, declared a pariah and shunned by the other Arab states.

The Egyptian–Israeli peace treaty was the product of intense negotiations, accompanied by theatrical grandstanding, influenced by an array of economic inducements and domestic pressures, and achieved through the success of the American government in bringing the two parties together. It demonstrated that Washington had the ability to influence Israel when its interests demanded such a course. It has been argued that the treaty was purely the result of US pressure for settlement of the Arab–Israeli conflict (which among other things was destabilizing world oil prices). Certainly the American role at this stage of the peace process could accurately be described as dominating and exclusive. Attempts by Sadat in 1976 to get the UN to resolve to internationalize the peace conference were thwarted by the Americans, a policy that Washington has tended to follow ever since. Carter recognized the importance of the Palestinian issue as central to the resolution of the Arab–Israeli conflict: a separate peace would flounder if Palestine was not dealt with, and Camp David proved him right. To a certain degree US influence in the peace process meant that it was able to establish a new foothold in the Middle East while enhancing its special relationship with Israel. However, this was the limit of American achievement. It had been hoped that the peace process would encourage other Arab states – like Iraq, Lebanon, Jordan and Syria – to enter into a similar process. Instead these states joined the Soviet-sponsored radical 'Rejectionist' front, headed by Syria, which aimed the majority of its attacks at American 'imperialist and Zionist' policies.

The Israelis, for their part, viewed the treaty as a success. Although they had succumbed (to some extent) to US pressure in making peace with Egypt on terms Cairo could accept, overall they had gained much and conceded little (merely a return of the Sinai to Egypt). They had also effectively neutralized the one Arab power that presented a significant military threat to their security. The adage 'No war without Egypt' accurately applied here. In addition, by pursuing a bilateral peace treaty they adroitly avoided linkage to the Palestinian issue. Egypt may have regained the Sinai but it lost the respect of the rest of the Arab world and was regarded as an outcast. The Palestinians gained nothing from the peace treaty – not that they had sought anything. The Israelis promised unspecific long-term considerations for granting Palestinian autonomy, but in the meantime Israeli concerns focused on the Palestinian threat both within and outside their borders; more specifically the escalation of 'fedayeen' attacks from the southern area of Lebanon which was then termed 'Fatahland'. In this context it was no surprise that the Israeli Prime Minister, Menachem Begin, made no secret of the fact that as far as he was concerned a peace agreement with Egypt would ignore the Palestinian right to self-determination.

Begin's decision to invade Lebanon was in some senses an Israeli answer to the Palestinian issue but ultimately embroiled others further in the conflict and put the usually cordial US–Israeli relationship under severe pressure. Israeli logic behind the invasion was twofold: first, to protect its northern borders from Lebanon-based Palestinian guerrilla attacks; second, to expel the PLO from Lebanon. Aware that Sadat's only concern was not to compromise regaining the Sinai, and knowing that the Arab world was divided and the PLO relatively isolated, Israeli leaders felt they had a free hand to sort out Lebanon for themselves. In 1978 they had already briefly invaded the country, establishing what was referred to as a 'buffer zone' in its southern territory. But they had been forced to retreat as a result of US pressure.

Throughout 1981 there was a noticeable rise in tension: a missile crisis with Syria in spring was followed on 7 June by a raid against the Iraqi nuclear centre of Tammuz. By December Israel had formally annexed the Golan Heights, which had been captured from the Syrians in the war of 1967. But, crucially, in June 1981 the IDF and PLO troops based in south Lebanon had shelled each other until the United States negotiated a ceasefire with the two parties. Against this background, it was inevitable that certain elements of the Israeli military would use their influence within government to take action against the PLO in Lebanon. Although there were splits within the military over this issue, the 'hawks' prevailed and steered Begin into a further course of invasion.

'Peace for Galilee' was the name given to the Israeli invasion of Lebanon in June 1982. Officially the Israelis declared that their march across the border was only a question of affirming control of a forty-kilometre strip, from which terrorists would no longer be able to shell the north of the country. Yet, despite these apparently limited aims, the IDF soon found itself in Beirut. The city was soon under Israeli-imposed blockade. Thus began the siege of mainly Muslim and Palestinian West Beirut, where Palestinians and the Lebanese National Movement fought side by side, while the Christian Phalangists lent support to the IDF as it attempted to eradicate the PLO. There seemed no end to the phosphorus, napalm, cluster and imploding bombs that relentlessly poured down on the starving, parched west section of the city. Apart from 6,000 PLO guerrillas in the besieged city, there were some half a million Lebanese and Palestinian civilians, and every day of the bombardment about 200 or 300 of them were killed.

As the bombardment went on, day after day, the international community looked on impotently, seemingly mesmerized by the brutal nature of the Israeli action. The European Economic Community (EEC), the UN Security

Council and other bodies issued condemnations, while the United States remonstrated ineffectually with its protégé and was brusquely snubbed. Yet it is difficult to disagree with Gilmour's conclusion that

> the most feeble reaction came from the Arab world which seemed petrified into silence and inaction. Beirut, the ideological birthplace of Arab nationalism and for long the intellectual and commercial capital of the Arab world, was being pulverised by a brutal foreign army while the Arab states did nothing.[12]

In this respect Israel succeeded in its greatest victory in its conflict with the Arab world, and exposed the hollow posturing of the grand slogans of 'Arab unity' in the face of the Zionist threat. If the leaders of the Arab world could not rally to the defence of its brethren in Beirut as Israeli tanks rolled into its suburbs, what did 'unity' mean?

On 30 August 1982 the PLO admitted defeat and the leadership and guerrillas left Lebanon in shame. Its leader Yasser Arafat moved on to Tunis and the PLO network went with him. The departure of the PLO, however, was not the end of Israel's battle against the Palestinians of Lebanon. On 16 and 17 September Israeli troops moved into West Beirut, and their Phalangist allies massacred at least 2,000 children, women and elderly men in the refugee camps of Sabra and Shatila. Israeli collusion in the massacres appalled the world.

Such was the tragic end of the first phase of the Lebanon War. A second phase now began: that of Israel's occupation of southern Lebanon. For eighteen years Israel remained in Lebanon and promoted its presence through its local ally, the Christian-led South Lebanon Army (SLA). UN forces, mandated in 1978 to act as peacekeepers until Israel withdrew, found themselves embroiled in various battles between Lebanon's militias and the SLA and IDF. Israel's northern border remained vulnerable to attack and domestic pressure grew for an end to Israel's Lebanon experience. As Israeli casualty rates rose the country's political leaders responded. In 1999, following his election as Prime Minister, former Defence chief Ehud Barak announced that Israeli troops would finally be withdrawn from Lebanon. They finally did so in humiliation in May of the following year after Hizballah resistance fighters had inflicted heavy casualties on the Israelis and brought about the total collapse of the SLA.[13]

The Israel–Lebanon War of 2006, discussed in detail in Chapter 5, altered the balance of forces viz-à-viz the Arab–Israeli conflict more widely. First, the war demonstrated an unprecedented weakness in both the Israeli military establishment and the political leadership of the country. The fact that a well-armed militia so severely undermined Israel's defensive capacity has led to a major domestic fallout in Israel. The war also established a linkage between actors and events in Iraq, Iran, Syria, Lebanon, Israel and the USA that continues to hinder efforts at resuming a peace process that engages all the major parties in the Arab–Israeli conflict.

As this chapter has demonstrated, there are no outright winners and far too many losers in this brief balance sheet of the Arab–Israeli conflict. During the course of these hostilities national revenues have been squandered on the purchase of weapons. Some states have further impoverished themselves in seeking loans from Western arms manufacturers and governments to purchase a technology dedicated to regional domination rather than development. In as much as the Palestinian issue has closed Arab ranks in the quest for justice it has perhaps also done as much to divide the Arab world, ordinary citizens and leaders alike.

Progress towards resolving the dispute seems to have been achieved only under two significant conditions. The first is American pressure, influence and guarantees in winning concessions from Israel and rewarding the parties involved (mostly financially) for taking risks on peace. The second is the Israeli-preferred route of negotiation via bilateral rather than multilateral or international forums, such as the United Nations. Washington, generally speaking, has supported this tactic and facilitated such a process at Camp David in the negotiation of a separate peace between Israel and Egypt. For those who still believe that the only way a just and comprehensive peace can be forged in the Middle East is through the participation of the international community and specifically the UN, there can be little cause for comfort in achievements so far. But, however reached, a lasting and just peace depends not on treaties forged by outside parties able to cajole and pressure leaders but in the quality of that peace and its sustainability through popular acceptance over present and future generations in both Israel and the Arab world. Sadly, there is currently little evidence that this new dawn is anything but a distant prospect.

2 The Palestinian–Israeli conflict

Hostages to history

Some of the most enduring images of the twentieth century have been generated by the Palestinian–Israeli conflict. The historic handshake in September 1993 between Israeli leader Itzhak Rabin and Palestinian chief Yasser Arafat is but one of them. For the better part of a century the conflict of two peoples over one land has defined the politics of the region and has had a major impact on many aspects of international politics, including political economy, and international and state terrorism. In some respects, as we argue in this chapter, both the Palestinians and the Israelis have been hostages to their own histories as well as to each other. In addition, the nature of the contemporary world since 1945 can go some way in explaining the nature of this conflict and the major factors that have dominated it at various junctures.

The themes of the conflict, as we shall discuss in this chapter, embrace many of those tensions that characterize the modern world and its development. Thus it should be made clear that we do not subscribe to the argument that for centuries the Arabs and Jews have been in a fatal, atavistic embrace based on primordial hatred. Instead, we agree with Tessler, who asserts that 'both Israel's Jews and Palestinians have legitimate and inalienable rights. These rights are rooted in the historical experience of each people', rather than other factors.[1] Since the early roots of the conflict the battle between Palestinian and Israeli has been about territoriality, identity, ethnicity and religion, economics, competing nationalisms, colonialism and imperialism. Attempts to resolve the conflict, once described as one of the most intractable on earth, have in the past floundered on mutual suspicion and antagonism often exacerbated by the influence of other actors on the conflict. In this chapter we shall discuss these themes rather than present a chronology of events and hostilities.

The Palestinian–Israeli conflict reveals that the divisions that run between Palestinian Arabs and Israeli Jews are multifaceted. Some might argue that the conflict is a religious and sectarian issue and go some way in agreeing with the primordial argument that there is something inevitable about such a relationship. Others perceive the conflict as ethnic and point to the incompatibility, despite the same Semitic origins, of two such distinct groups as Arab and Jew. Some view the deep divisions between Palestinians and Israelis as the results of competing nationalist agendas, each with a unique political view. And still others explain the conflict as a classic class-based colonial paradigm under which only a united working class (Arab and Jewish) will bring about peace and political change. All of these interpretations, along with others, have had roles to play in explaining why Palestine and its territory became the most enduring battleground of the twentieth and early twenty-first centuries.

For our purposes the examination begins at the end of the nineteenth century. The roots of the conflict lie in ethno-political rather than purely religious differences. Indeed, under the rule of the Ottoman Turks the Jews, Christians and Muslims of Palestine coexisted peacefully. Like all peoples of the region, however, the inhabitants of Palestine were deeply affected by the intervention of the West, not just in terms of ideas and culture but by the consequences of colonial control and foreign penetration of Arab lands. In terms of European ideas and movements, one of the most influential was nationalism. Indeed, the settlement of land by Jews from Europe from the late 1890s onwards happened as a direct result of the influence of a new Jewish nationalism entitled 'Zionism'. The congruent origins of Zionism and the rival Palestinian nationalism need to be stressed, not just in the historical context but in terms of explaining the course of the conflict throughout the twentieth century. Indeed, it is both remarkable and unfortunate that at the same historical juncture both Jews and Arabs became motivated and conscious of the same themes of self-determination, nationhood and statehood in response to the motifs so strongly associated with nationalism.

'A country without a people for a people without a country' (Chaim Weizman, World Zionist Congress). The emergence of Zionism crystallized the desire within the Jewish diaspora for a Jewish homeland for the Jewish people. Its chief architects, such as Theodor Herzl, a European Jewish intellectual, who in 1896 published a book entitled *The Jewish State*, maintained that assimilation for Jews would never happen and that the Jews should found their own state, preferably in Palestine, the ancient home of the Jewish people. As Gresch and Vidal point out, the link to the former homeland was strong: 'The memory of the lost homeland and the desire to return there were long fostered by religion alone: "Next year in Jerusalem" believers prayed each year.'[2] The call of Zionism was the direct product of hundreds of years of European anti-Semitism and the persecution of Jewish communities, including the Russian pogroms. Zionism was an ideology of its time and place – a product of Western political thought and intellectual trends embracing the nationalist vision.

From 1897, when the first Zionist Congress was convened in Basle, Switzerland, to 1917 the Zionists promoted their vision and lobbied the 'great powers' of USA, Britain, France and Russia for political support. At the same time the first Zionist settlers set off for Palestine to join the members of the Jewish community who were already there. From 1897 to 1903 some 30,000 Jews emigrated and by 1914 there was a total of 80,000 Jews in Palestine. The Zionists in Europe found most sympathy among members of the British government (by this time involved in the First World War), who, through a mixture of hard-headed military strategy and romantic pro-Zionist sentiment, saw some value as part of their war strategy in the movement. The culmination of this support, as discussed in Chapter 1, was the Balfour Declaration. For the Zionist movement the declaration, although by no means everything they wanted, was a significant recognition of their cause and their claim to the historic home of the Jewish people in Palestine. In later years, during Britain's mandate of Palestine, however, many in the Zionist movement viewed such patronage with barely disguised frustration and hostility towards their former British friends, whom they felt were not wholeheartedly supporting the creation of a Jewish state – as opposed to merely a Jewish national home.

One major obstacle stood in the way of Zionist aspirations: Palestine's Arab population. Yet, as Gerner points out, for the Zionists, the fact 'that Palestine had an existing population . . . was no more relevant than was Kenyan history to the British or Algerian society to the French'.[3] However, as Jewish immigration to Palestine increased, new Zionist communities were established, economic methods were implemented and society changed, the Palestinians began to organize themselves, establishing their own new nationalist movements and parties in the belief that they had a legitimate right to self-determination alongside others of their Arab brethren across the region. Nevertheless, the Palestinian Arabs could only stand by in dismay as Britain laid claim to their land, as subsequently endorsed by a League of Nations mandate at the end of the First World War. Such decisions, along with continuing tensions with the Zionist settlers, further galvanized the Palestinians. So the roots of Palestinian nationalism lay in the same rights-based principles as Zionism.

With the establishment throughout the 1920s and early 1930s of nationalist organizations, the Palestinian political elite lobbied for change. By 1936 such frustrations had reached fever pitch as the Palestinian leadership called a major general strike and the country fell into a revolt that would last some three years. In 1939 the revolt collapsed as the Palestinians descended into bitter internecine struggle. In addition, the British authorities had deported or imprisoned the major leaders of the Palestinian nationalist movement. In one sense the outcome of this period of mandate was that the two principal communities of Palestine, in their commitment to competing nationalism, drew a growing set of boundaries between each other which created economic, religious, cultural and political cleavages that made the likelihood of integration and cooperation increasingly difficult. For example, while the Zionists deliberately pursued a policy of denying employment opportunities to the Arabs, the Arab leadership issued fatwas (religious sanctions) against anyone selling land to the Jews. The many, increasingly insurmountable, frontiers between these communities became a form of partition unanticipated by the country's rulers.

The British struggled for a political solution to the ever-deepening divisions between Jews and Arabs in Palestine under their rule. One commission after another was formed to address the issue. However, both the Zionist movement in Palestine and the Palestinian Arab factions were steadily undermining British rule. In 1937 the Peel Commission first proposed the partition of Palestine into three sectors: an Arab state, a Jewish state, and an area including Jerusalem. Two years later the British announced a limit on the number of Jewish immigrants who would be allowed into Palestine. But this measure would have only a temporary impact and would be turned on its head in the face of the massive tide of Jews fleeing Hitler. By the end of the Second World War the British had thrown in the towel. Clement Attlee admitted that Palestine was an 'economic and political liability' and called on the newly formed United Nations to resolve the problem of this 'twice promised land' which it then attempted to do by opting for partition, as the British had. But this two-state solution to the conflict between Palestinians and Zionists in Palestine was unacceptable to the Palestinians and triggered further embittered and embattled relations between the two communities for the next half a century.

'On this day that sees the end of the British mandate and in virtue of the natural and historic right of the Jewish people and in accordance with the UN resolution we proclaim the creation of a Jewish state in Palestine.' These were the words with which, on 14 May 1948, David Ben Gurion, leader of the Zionist movement, announced to the world the birth of the state of Israel. He affirmed the new state's claim to legitimacy: that of the Jewish people's right, according to biblical promises made by Jehovah to Abraham.

The new state, however, although recognized by the UN, immediately found itself in confrontation with its Palestinian population and their Arab supporters. Further conflict seemed to be the only item on the agenda. The war of 1948 proved a victory for Israel and a national disaster for the Palestinians, hundreds of thousands of whom found themselves dispossessed of their homes, land and historic heritage, and crammed into squalid refugee camps dispersed across the Arab world. The precise events of the war are widely disputed by historians, and both official Zionist and Arab versions are often misleading. On one side historians such as Karsh assert that 'the Palestinian tragedy was not the inevitable outcome of the Zionist dream but primarily a self-inflicted disaster'.[4] However, 'revisionist' Israeli historians – among them Benny Morris and Ilan Pappe – have started to challenge the official version of events, arguing, among other things, that the newly founded state of Israel was guilty of the deliberate 'ethnic cleansing' of Palestinian communities in the war.[5]

Not in doubt is that by the end of the war, the new state of Israel controlled over three-quarters of Palestine, twice as much as originally proposed by the UN. Immigrants settled into many previously Palestinian homes and villages in the new Israeli state. Other former Palestinian settlements were destroyed and deliberately erased from the map. Jerusalem, which the British and UN had declared should be internationalized, became a divided city, the two halves under the respective control of the Israelis and the Jordanians.

There is certainly enough 'evidence' on all sides to generate the important founding myths that are needed to galvanize nations, build new states and sustain liberation movements for many decades. For the Zionists, the founding myths of the state and its conflict with the Palestinians have played a part in helping to create a nation from a settler and immigrant community gathered from many parts of the globe. On the other side, the folklore that surrounds the events of the dispossession has played an important part in sustaining a dispossessed and stateless community that is now scattered across the globe. In both cases competing nationalisms and ideological impulses have encouraged many to sustain those myths as important national motifs setting one community apart, once again, from the other.

Those Palestinians finding themselves within the frontier of the new Israeli state became unequal citizens. In more than half a century there has been no sign of integration between the Jews and the Arabs of Israel. Separation of these groupings has been officially encouraged; intermarriage is rare and not permitted under religious law in Israel. Schooling, housing and other services are largely confined to one ethnic group or another. This official policy promotes division within Israeli society because it does not embrace the separate but equal philosophy in practice. Arabs and Jews remain unequal parties in many aspects of life.

Within the new state of Israel a number of ethnic and religious groups vied with each other for power. Palestinian refugees in the Arab world organized themselves politically, embracing and developing a nationalist programme based on the right of self-determination. Their claims and rights were recognized by the UN but were largely ignored in practice by the international community. Under the limitations imposed by the vagaries of

Arab authoritarian rule the refugee populations in exile planned their liberation. From this point it appeared that intractable lines of conflict were drawn between the Israelis and the Palestinians. Political solutions to the conflict were in short supply and focused on the tried yet largely unsuccessful formula of partition that, given its ineffectiveness in promoting the resolution of other ethnic disputes (namely Ireland), was questionable in the first place. Throughout the 1950s and 1960s, as Israel embarked on a major process of state consolidation, there emerged sharp divisions over the proposed frontier of the state. On the right wing, the Zionist goal of establishing a Jewish state in the whole of Eretz Israel (biblical Israel) was developed and publicly debated. Such expansionist plans were not shared by all of Israel's political leaders, though, as many felt they would condemn Israel and the Palestinians to further conflict. The majority of Israelis clung tenaciously to their new state, enshrined its Jewish identity through the law of the 'right of return', founded in the aftermath of the Holocaust, and were dedicated in safeguarding themselves and future generations. The maintenance of the security of the state and its people, surrounded as they were by so many neighbours who were enemies, became a major preoccupation of the political establishment, with the military gobbling up a consistently large share of the country's gross domestic product. Many Israeli leaders claimed that they were not courting further conflict but rather seeking to establish the security of the state for present and future generations.

If, as we noted in Chapter 1, the Israeli victory in 1967 meant that Israel got more than it bargained for in terms of the newly acquired territories and the Palestinian Arab populations of the West Bank, Arab East Jerusalem (including the Old City) and the Gaza Strip, there was also evidence of splits within the political establishment over what strategy to adopt next. While it is true that the Israelis have remained in continuous occupation of these lands ever since, there have always been opposing arguments against the maintenance of Israeli control (or sovereignty) over them. From a strategic point of view, by holding on to the West Bank, for example, Israel could better defend its borders and major centres of population. On the other hand, there were some who believed that if land were traded for peace with Israel's Arab neighbours, then relinquishing the West Bank or elsewhere would be worth the strategic cost. By and large, however, the strategic arguments have prevailed and remain an important aspect of the present-day peace negotiations between Israel and the Palestinians.

While the Israeli occupation has been a military one, the strategic foothold established in the West Bank, the Gaza Strip and the Golan Heights has been facilitated by the settlement of Israeli Jews on large parts of Palestinian land in direct contravention of UN resolutions on the issue. Many types of settlement activity, some ideologically motivated, others religiously, and yet more 'paramilitary-security' based, emerged over the ensuing decades and were tacitly supported by the state. The settlement of Palestinian land started in earnest in the early 1970s and by the late 1990s hundreds of thousands of Israeli Jews were living in illegally constructed settlements in the West Bank and Gaza Strip, and were proving to be a major and growing obstacle to the resolution of the Palestinian–Israeli conflict. Even American threats in the 1990s to halt 'soft loans' to Israel failed to stop the support offered by successive Israeli governments to the right-wing-led settler movement, many of whom were financed by members of the Jewish Zionist diaspora, especially in the United States.[6] Settlement activity has created new demographic realities to which Israel is committed. Nevertheless, the future of the settlements remains a key item on the agenda for the final status negotiations.

Since 1967 the Palestinians, through the extension of their commitment to nationalism, have established formidable political movements for national liberation and self-determination. The best known of these groups is the Palestine Liberation Organization (PLO), officially established in 1964, an umbrella organization representing four major nationalist factions: Fatah, the Communists, the Democratic Front for the Liberation of Palestine (DFLP) and the Popular Front for the Liberation of Palestine (PFLP). In 1968 the PLO fell under the control of Yasser Arafat and his comrades. Although the organization is large, bureaucratic and extremely factional, it has attempted to provide for and serve the Palestinian refugee community, conducted an armed struggle, and represents to the rest of the world the legitimate rights of the Palestinian people to self-determination and independence. Regarded as the 'legitimate' representative of the Palestinian people, including the refugee population, this movement, and its often dissident offshoots, has engaged in a struggle for national liberation. Over its forty-odd years of 'armed struggle', the PLO and other Palestinian dissidents have been involved in acts of political violence – such as hijackings, bomb attacks and assassinations – against Israel and its representatives abroad, including American Jews. It has also confronted two major Arab states – Jordan in 1970 and Lebanon between 1975 and 1982, where it became engaged in civil conflict with state authorities and was accused of running a 'state within a state' for major Palestinian refugee communities resident in both countries.[7] Indeed, until the late 1980s the Palestinians were regarded as synonymous with terrorism the world over. Supporters of Palestinian rights to self-determination argued that the terrorist strategy was part of a cycle of desperation at a time when they were denied political rights or statehood. Many others, however, particularly in policy-making circles in Tel Aviv, Washington and other Western capitals, were not prepared to tolerate the pursuit of politics through the barrel of a gun.

The Palestinian nationalist call to arms was finally set aside in 1988 when Yasser Arafat literally delivered an olive branch at a specially convened meeting of the UN General Assembly in Geneva. At this event Arafat declared, 'we totally and absolutely renounce all forms of terrorism, including individual, group and state terrorism'.[8] The statement was considered a clear indication that the PLO sought full admission into the international fold. It would take five more years before the announcement of Israel's decision to recognize the PLO as the legitimate representatives of the Palestinians and the initiation of the peace process that in early 1993 culminated in an agreement for limited Palestinian autonomy and an agenda for final status negotiations between the two sides. Until that time the Palestinians and Israelis had appeared to live in two separate worlds, each denying the right of existence to the other. But the path to resolving the conflict would still be a long and tough one.

The two communities, however separate in terms of political coexistence, have never lived in total isolation from each other. Hostility and mutual antagonism, however, often characterize their relations. Within Israeli society the state functions very much like that of any other liberal democracy: regular and free elections are held, the citizens are enfranchised and the electoral system is one of proportional representation based on a single constituency. Yet, in the occupied territories, the Israeli state, obsessed with security, has often acted in an authoritarian and repressive fashion. Until 1993 the Palestinian population was governed by myriad military orders requiring permits for every aspect of their lives and eschewing any attempt by the Palestinian community to take power for itself and determine its own affairs. Israelis, on the other hand, believed they lived under the constant threat of Palestinian attacks from all quarters. Such fears were compounded by the very real threats posed by an organization dedicated to armed struggle in the realization of its goals. While hundreds of thousands of Palestinians worked in Israel as day labourers, they were compelled by Israeli law to return to their homes over the 'Green Line' by nightfall. While some friendships managed to grow, they were largely exceptions to a rule on both sides that kept the two communities apart. Although economically tied together, there were very few political, religious or cultural motifs that were common or shared between the two groups. Even in Jerusalem, Israel's so-called 'united capital', Israelis and Palestinians lived very different lives from each other and few urban spaces were available for all to access equally.

In addition, it has to be noted that the economic relationship between Israel and the Palestinians has been undeniably exploitative on Israel's part. The occupied territories became Israel's largest export market and source of cheap labour, and the Palestinian economy was crippled and penalized in return.[9] Until the outbreak of the Palestinian uprising, or Intifada, in 1987 there was also evidence of growing support on the Israeli right wing for the annexation of the West Bank. (Annexation would provide a direct economic benefit to Israel). The only problem facing the annexationist lobby was the issue of what to do with the Palestinian population of the area. By this point a number of political groupings and parties had emerged advocating the 'transfer' or 'mass deportation' of Palestinians to Arab states like Jordan. Indeed, in 1987 the mainstream Israeli press were willing to air debates entitled 'Jordan is Palestine' that openly promoted 'transfer' as a solution to the growing demographic threat within the occupied West Bank.

Within the Palestinian community there was increasing resentment and frustration at the restrictions they faced in everyday life. Any form of political activity was criminalized by the military authorities: the PLO was outlawed, people were banned from free assembly, public meetings were forbidden; membership of political organizations was punishable by long prison sentences, often without trial. By the late 1980s, with the PLO expelled from Lebanon, Jewish settlement continuing apace and the 'iron fist' of occupation perpetrating an almost perpetual stranglehold, a sense of desperation began to permeate Palestinian ranks. In the West Bank and Gaza the Palestinian refugees felt increasingly abandoned by their Arab brethren, who appeared preoccupied with other regional matters. The international community held little sympathy for Palestinian 'terrorists'; and Israel, bolstered by a 'special relationship' with the USA, despite its illegal acts of settlement in the West Bank and Gaza Strip, seemed untouchable.

The outbreak of the Intifada in December 1987 marked the culmination of growing political awareness among young Palestinians and starkly exposed the fault line in this conflict between Palestinian and Israeli. The long-term goals of the uprising were articulated as a desire to bring an end to the Israeli occupation of the West Bank and Gaza Strip, and the establishment of a Palestinian state. In the short term, though, the plan was to disengage from the structure of the Israeli occupation as much as possible and achieve a greater level of Palestinian self-reliance and unity of purpose. The local economy, for example, was boosted through consumers boycotting Israeli products.

The Intifada was a major turning point in the Palestinian–Israeli conflict. The Palestinians, through the quickly established framework of the uprising, indicated that they were rejecting anything that represented Israeli rule over their lives. They were sending a message that said 'no' to Israeli control. This mass rebellion also communicated an important message to the PLO leadership in Tunis, and, as Khalidi asserts, 'betokened a realisation by the PLO leadership that the future of the movement lay in Palestine, rather than outside it'.[10] It is widely acknowledged that this popular-based uprising took the PLO and other Palestinian leaders as much as Israel by surprise.

But the question we must now ask is: did the Intifada galvanize the Israelis and Palestinians into seeking a solution to the deep breach between them? The Intifada shook Israel because of its spontaneous and widespread nature. This was portrayed positively in the international media, which flocked to Israel and the occupied territories to film poignant scenes such as small boys having their bones deliberately broken by Israeli soldiers acting under the express orders of Defence Minister Itzhak Rabin. Initially the Intifada was not a planned event but rather a very powerful and spontaneous Palestinian protest against the everyday indignities inflicted by Israeli control. The first months of the uprising were characterized by mass demonstrations involving every sector of society. The international media's portrayal of women and children, the young and the old demonstrating with such passion went some considerable way in rehabilitating or altering the perception of Palestinians, presenting them not as terrorists but as victims of a military occupation that had lasted some twenty years. The uprising was quickly harnessed by locally based committees, which were formed to help people at every level. The establishment of the United National Leadership of the Uprising (UNLU) – representing all factions of the PLO as well as the Islamic movements Hamas and Islamic Jihad – to provide direction to the uprising also represented a major development in Palestinian politics. It demonstrated the maturity of the local political leadership when pursuing a national agenda.

The Israelis had no immediately successful answer to the campaign of mass civil disobedience. Their army, trained and prepared for combat on the battlefield, was often faced with an enemy made up of unarmed women, children and young people whose major weapons against Israel's hi-tech armoury were rocks and Molotov cocktails. The Palestinians had from the outset decided to refrain from the use of firearms against the Israeli army and settlers – a highly successful ploy that played well internationally. But, of course, there were several disturbing aspects to the Intifada, too.

First, the uprising was only serving to deepen divisions between Israelis and Palestinians. However objectionable the policies of the occupation, it had at least forced some level of daily contact between the two groups. The uprising ruptured this tentative relationship that had built up over twenty years. Each side retreated into the laager of their own society, and cross-community contacts were frowned upon and treated with mistrust as dangerously disloyal. Second, the atmosphere of war-like, low-intensity combat meant that informal channels for conflict resolution were eroded or eliminated. Almost as soon as the first attacks on Israelis were launched by such groups as Hamas and Islamic Jihad, moderate organizations in Israeli society like Peace Now were ridiculed and marginalized. Accordingly, the Israeli right wing gained increased support because of their resolutely anti-Palestinian stance. Indeed, in the 1988 Israeli election, the right wing won a victory at the polls and headed the national unity government. Moreover, extremism and religious radicalism found support within the communities of both Israel and Palestine. Third, the uprising challenged overnight the status quo in the occupied territories. Attempts to quell it by the Israeli army proved ineffective, which in turn affected army morale and led to public debate in Israel about the role of the military. The Israelis realized that they had to do something about the Palestinian issue immediately and had to accept that previous talk of annexation or even maintaining the status quo ante was now completely out of the question. In addition, international pressure was making itself felt to an unprecedented extent within the Israeli political establishment. The international mass media had transmitted film for prime-time viewing of Israel's soldiers taking on unarmed women and children. Commentators criticized Israel's treatment of the Palestinians, and human rights abuses came to light. Both at home and abroad many Jews began to question, for the first time, the efficacy of the occupation of the West Bank and Gaza Strip. This exposed fissures and tensions within the Jewish community, undermining the previous solidarity of public opinion. For once, the Arabs were ahead in the PR battle for international opinion.

It was also clear that the fissure between the Palestinians and the Israelis had become so deep rooted that the only solution was to offer some glimmer of a negotiated peace process. As it happened, however, it was another event, well away from the West Bank and Gaza Strip, that would create the conditions for decisive change, encouraging all the parties involved, crucially including the Americans, to make a concerted effort to kick-start the peace process.

The Iraqi invasion of Kuwait on 2 August 1990 and the ensuing Gulf crisis (see Chapter 8) had important implications for the Palestinian–Israeli conflict. Most importantly, it stimulated an American-led initiative to secure some kind of Arab–Israeli peace process in the Middle East. In the wake of the crisis the USA sought to re-establish stability in the region, and once again recognized that the Palestinian issue was at the heart of any settlement between Israel and the Arab states. This had to be addressed. With the eclipse of the Soviet Union and the emergence of a 'new world order', a historic opportunity to go for peace was now at hand. The moment also provided the Americans, the one remaining superpower, with a chance to dictate the peace they envisioned rather than rely on one promoted by actual parties to the conflict.

The right-wing Likud government in Israel, led by Prime Minister Yitzhak Shamir, refused, however, to enter into any direct discussion with the Palestinian leadership. Shamir's government still did not recognize the PLO and made it clear that the most they were prepared to concede to the Palestinians was a limited form of autonomy (similar to that discussed with Sadat at Camp David) in which Israel would retain ultimate control over the West Bank and Gaza Strip. It was under these unpromising preconditions, with the Jordanians providing a cover for the Palestinian negotiators, that the historic first round of Arab–Israeli peace talks were convened under the auspices of the USA and the former USSR in November 1991 in Madrid. Thus a spontaneous mass rebellion in coincidental conjunction with a war elsewhere in the region temporarily and unprecedentedly united East and West. For a variety of reasons, which in one way or another had a linkage back to the dynamics of the Israeli–Palestinian conflict, this proved to be the catalyst in promoting a new attempt at a negotiated settlement of that conflict.

Within Israel the election of a Labour government in June 1992 on a pro-peace platform reflected Intifada fatigue within the electorate. This was recognized both at home and abroad as a brave step within the larger national framework of debate about security versus peace. The Intifada had directly affected many sectors of Israeli society – through the increased deployment of Israeli conscript and reserve troops to the West Bank and Gaza Strip, and the issue of Palestinian labour in Israel. Ordinary Israelis no longer felt free to travel without fear in the West Bank and Gaza Strip, and increasingly by the early 1990s a new form of fatal attack was affecting Israeli cities like Tel Aviv: car- and suicide-bomb attacks carried out by Hamas and Islamic Jihad. In this new political climate secret negotiations were subsequently proposed and approved in left-leaning Israeli circles and met with the cautious approval of Prime Minister Rabin himself. In public, however, the formal Madrid process floundered as one obstacle to negotiation after another stymied the ineffectual attempts on all sides to get to grips with the main issues.

As we now know, while the official peace process was seen to stagnate throughout 1993, Israel and the PLO were conducting a highly secret channel of negotiations in Norway. These culminated – to universal surprise – in the official White House ceremony and signing of the 'Declaration of Principles' (DoP). The DoP, or Oslo Accords as they are now called, permitted limited and phased autonomy in the West Bank and Gaza Strip. They also provided a future framework for the peaceful resolution of the most important issues pertaining to the Israeli–Palestinian conflict: land, Jerusalem, refugees, settlements, security and borders. This was the event that produced the stage-managed handshake between Rabin and Arafat with which we started this chapter. Stage-management, however, would not be enough to establish a meaningful process of trust-building between Israel and the Palestinians and the conclusion of final status peace talks outlined under the Oslo framework. The peace process continued to be stymied and bedevilled at almost every turn. The reality and pressures of transition and peace-building shattered dreams on both sides of the divide. In Israel Itzhak Rabin was assassinated, the right-wing Likud gained new ascendancy on an anti-negotiation platform, troops were not ordered to redeploy according to agreed timetables and remained on territory they were supposed to evacuate. The newly established Palestinian Authority, headed by PLO-leader Yasser Arafat, failed to deliver security, economic or political dividends for the Palestinians. Escalating Islamist violence against Israel, manifest in the continuing use of suicide bombs, added new dimensions to the conflict and attempts to establish security and peace at one and the same time.

Nevertheless, the election of a new Labour government led by former army general Ehud Barak again on a pro-peace platform in 1999 promoted an illusion that peace might be found. Yet the bitter fallout and absence of genuine compromise on final status issues dogged the talks process throughout 1999 and 2000. Palestinian frustration at perceived Israeli arrogance crystallized around the deliberately provocative visit of former Likud minister Ariel Sharon to Jerusalem's Islamic holy site the Dome of the Rock in September 2000, and a new Intifada broke out. With that, death and violence superseded peace and reconciliation, and the shallow foundations of the Oslo Peace were exposed. Both sides believed, once again, that they were engaged in a war of independence in which there could be only one victor and the enemy must be vanquished. Peace through negotiation fell into abeyance and in the absence of sustained American pressure the two sides fell back into deep suspicion of each other.

However, in 2003 a 'roadmap' sponsored by the UN, USA, Russia and the European Union (known as the Quartet) was formally tabled as a kick-start to a new MEPP, with peace to be concluded as early as 2005. This formula began with US acceptance of a two-state solution to the Palestinian–Israeli conflict. But the process demanded that mutual suspicions needed to be banished, and both sides had to negotiate with flexibility and good faith. How easy that sounded! How often had we been here before! The 'roadmap' was particularily difficult for the hard men of the Palestinian Authority and of the state of Israel, and American pressure would be needed to convince the extreme right-wing government of Ariel Sharon. This presented a major challenge to George W. Bush that, given his increasing problems in Iraq, he was not willing or able to address. The President, moreover, faced fresh elections in 2004 and could not risk alienating traditionally pro-Israeli Republican voters by launching a confrontation with Sharon. Even with a win under his belt in that election, it was clear in 2005 and 2006 that the Bush administration would not take Israel to task. Indeed, bilateral Israeli steps, such as the withdrawal from Gaza in the summer of

2005 and the war in Lebanon in 2006, were strongly supported by the Bush administration.

For the Palestinians, the death of their leader Yasser Arafat, a man whom the USA, Israel and others had considered an impediment to peace, and the presidential election of the moderate Mahmoud Abbas (Abu Mazen) did not lead to the anticipated accelerated resumption of the peace process. In January 2006 legislative elections led to the victory of the Palestinian Islamist movement Hamas, partly as a protest vote against perceived corruption within the outgoing government. Almost immediately the Quartet announced that the incoming government would face sanctions if it did not recognize the state of Israel and renounce violence, and respect previous agreements signed between the Palestinians and Israelis. Implicitly, this signalled the Quartet's rejection of the result of a democratic election that had been deemed free and fair by most official observers. Financial sanctions were swiftly imposed upon the new government, creating a state of siege in the West Bank and Gaza Strip. Denied money for government coffers, Hamas was compelled to seek other donors, such as Iran, to replace lost revenues. This led to further pressure and intervention of the USA in support of President Abbas, with a worrying consequent development of parallel government. This support also raised the spectre of the USA (and possibly other Western powers) allying themselves with one faction against another, especially as, by the autumn of 2006, inter-factional Palestinian fighting had broken out. This reached disturbing new heights in January 2007, having the appearance of an all-out civil war. The following month, negotiations in Mecca led to the formation of a national unity government, with so-called 'independents' holding important ministerial portfolios such as Finance and Interior. But in Israel and elsewhere the new government was not warmly welcomed and it was still widely perceived as an impediment to peace. Meanwhile, Palestinians continued to complain that Israeli actions – such as building what the Palestinians, supported by a wide body of international opinion, regarded as an illegal wall in the West Bank, continuing with settlement measures, the arrest and detention of Palestinian legislators, human rights violations, and the erection of barriers and checkpoints that were killing the internal Palestinian economy of the West Bank – were also significant impediments to peace that the international community nevertheless seemed reluctant to censure. The notion that the conditions were ripe for peace and justice seemed as elusive on all sides as ever.

3 Superpower conflict in the Middle East

War by proxy

The rivalry between the United States and the former Soviet Union has made a major contribution to the dynamics of politics and conflicts in the Middle East. From the end of the Second World War to the present day the influence of American interests and, until 1990, Soviet interests and ambitions in the Middle East was easily discernible. The turning point in this superpower competition was the Gulf crisis in 1990, when an economically debilitated and politically weakened Soviet Union bowed out of the race with the United States and Soviet President Gorbachev gave US President George Bush his backing in the Allies' effort to end the Iraqi occupation of Kuwait. Until that point both had competed for influence in the region in an attempt to safeguard oil interests and strategic routes. Throughout this period neither side was willing to let the other steal an ideological march in a part of the world that was regarded as so vital to both superpowers and, in particular, to the oil-dependent industrialized nations of the West.

The Middle East was an extension of the Cold War theatre between the USSR and the USA for four decades. The impact of the Cold War in contributing both to the rise in tension and the growth of conflict made its mark in the area, particularly throughout the 1950s, 1960s and 1970s. In seeking to extend their influence over the region, both the United States and the Soviet Union engaged in attempts to create 'client' states that would act as local proxies and allies. In pursuing this strategy policy-makers in Moscow and Washington exploited new fissures and tensions, severely exacerbating pre-existing ones, such as the Arab–Israeli conflict.

This extension of superpower rivalry to the Middle East did not occur overnight. The growth of Soviet and American power and influence gradually filled a vacuum created by the post-war decline of former colonial powers, notably Britain and France. Keen to step into the breach, the USA in particular made an early start and tried to remain a step ahead of the Russians in a bid to protect strategic interests in the region. In the wake of the Second World War newly exploited oil and pressure from American commercial interests were the major motives for Washington's involvement in the area.

But, as Chomsky notes, 'At the rhetorical level, the threat from which the Middle East must be "defended" is generally pictured to be the USSR.'[1] Thus, from the first days of the 'Truman Doctrine' in 1947 (see below) to the turbulent months of 1990, when the USA led the Allied forces into conflict in the 'Mother of all Battles' with Iraq, the impact of the superpowers on regional issues was immense.

The outcome of the superpower conflict, as this chapter will illustrate, was a confrontation in which the USA, despite its emergence as the dominant power in a 'new world order', failed to achieve a clear victory. The arena in which the two sides engaged in a battle of proxies is littered with the legacy of major arms races, client–patron relationships and uneasy alliances that run counter to the national interest of many of the states in the region. While it is true that there were many other 'battlefields' in the Cold War, the Middle East, due to its oil and its strategic position, seems to have suffered most.

According to Rodinson, in its attempts to limit Soviet influence, the American 'effort to enrol the Arabs in the coalition encircling the Communist world had in fact driven the Arab peoples, profoundly uninterested in the struggle for world mastery, into a sympathetic attitude towards the hated power'.[2] This was a Cold War in which, when the Berlin Wall came down in 1989, pundits and policy-makers alike found there was little of value to commemorate in the posturing and ideological battles that had been waged in the previous decades. In their post-Cold War questioning they increasingly doubted whether the former Soviet Union had posed the 'real' threat they had widely believed it had possessed.

In March 1947, as Europe embarked on the reconstruction of nations rent asunder by war, US President Harry Truman announced a new doctrine for the Middle East that would have a major impact on emerging conflicts and future tensions for decades to come. Fearful of a Soviet expansion of power through Eastern Europe and on to the shores of the Mediterranean and the Arab world, the US government announced its intention of containing the Soviet threat. Each administration from Truman onwards reiterated similar commitments to resist the spread of Soviet influence, thereby safeguarding the Western world's access to oil and other strategic interests. Yet one factor which was to complicate Washington's attempt to influence the Arab and other Muslim states was America's burgeoning 'special relationship' with Israel. (Even though this relationship was initially slow to develop. Intensive support for Israel did not become a major US policy plank until the late 1950s. Up to the Suez crisis, for example, France was the major arms supplier (and military partner) of Israel.) Thus, as Lesch has pointed out, while the 'value of the Middle East became contemporaneously linked to the emerging cold war between the United States and the Soviet Union', the special link with the state of Israel 'also complicated Washington's relations with and objectives towards the Arab world as Arabs increasingly perceived US and Israeli interests as being one and the same'.[3] Over the decades the legislators in the American Congress have remained largely sympathetic to Israel, passing bills that have provided massive financial and military support. The pro-Israel lobby in the United States may have had to weather some significant spats with successive political administrations, yet it has still been recognized as a significant pressure on the American government, policy-makers and opinion-formers across the country. While it is easy to be cynical about such statements as former President Jimmy Carter's that 'It's absolutely crucial that no one in our country or around the world ever doubt that our number one commitment in the Middle East is to protect the right of Israel to exist', it is only the depth of sincerity that should be questioned when held up against the whole gamut of American national interests.[4] What Carter and other US presidents were really saying was that, given the powerful influence of the Zionist (pro-Israel) lobby in US domestic politics, it would be a bold or rash administration that took any action that might arouse its ire. Especially at election time! And so experience has proved. As Sir Christopher Meyer, recently the British Ambassador in Washington, pointed out in 2006, the 'special relationship' most valued by the US government is not the much discussed one with the UK, but the one with Israel.[5]

There are a number of objectives that the USA has consistently pursued over the years in determining its policies towards the Middle East and bilateral relations with the Arab and other states of that region. These broad objectives are as follows:

- *Economic and commercial*: to maintain the steady flow of Iranian and Arab oil to the Western states of the capitalist world. Arab oil was, and remains, vital to Western interests; without it, GNP in the USA would be cut by 13 per cent. In addition an objective within this sphere is to promote the interests of US companies throughout the region, especially in the wealthy markets of the Gulf states, including Saudi Arabia.
- *Containment*: to prevent perceived Soviet expansionism. The United States saw it as its objective (especially following the Soviet invasion of Afghanistan in 1979 and the collapse of the pro-American regime in Iran) to 'protect' the independence of the Arab states and to defend their free choice to continue to supply oil to the West unhindered by the Soviet Union or any of its allies in the area.
- *Commitment*: to maintain not only the security but the prosperity of Israel. This is the essence of the 'special relationship'. The United States perceived Israel as a strategic ally and its regional partner. The drawback

is that this policy has threatened and continues to undermine Arab–American relations and endangers US commercial interests in the wider region.

- *Aid*: to use aid as a strategic tool. As an instrument of American foreign policy aid has secured the dependency and often grudging fealty of the region's largest state, Egypt, and by the mid-1990s had succeeded in bringing Jordan firmly into the aid-dependent American orbit. In addition Israel has traditionally enjoyed a privileged position in its receipt of US government subsidy, receiving more per capita assistance than any other country in the world. In 1997 alone Israel received some $240 million of non-military assistance from the USA.

- *Arms*: to maintain the arms balance in the Middle East. The United States has been involved in supplying a number of states with weaponry. In so doing it has sought to ensure that the balance tips in the favour of its clients, thus brokering a multi-billion-dollar industry that has armed and even trained such disparate clients as the pre-revolutionary Iran, Afghan anti-Soviet guerrillas, the Israelis and the Saudis. Israel, for example, has been gifted billions of dollars' worth of arms by the USA. In addition, between 1982 and 1986 Egypt was in receipt of a $2.4 billion grant from the US government for the purchase of American arms and military supplies.[6]

These objectives, which underpin American policy in the Middle East, also determine its basic features. The first feature is the desire of the USA to disadvantage Western competitors. Under cover of the 'open-door' policy, the United States has assured itself an indisputable supremacy both in political influence and in commercial matters – as Chomsky has observed in the case of Iran in 1953 where 'one consequence of the CIA-backed coup that restored the Shah . . . was to transfer 40 per cent of Iranian oil from British to American hands'.[7] This policy was pursued with growing success: first after the Second World War with the promulgation of the Truman Doctrine, then following Suez with the 'Eisenhower Doctrine'. By the 1970s, with the waning of British influence in the Gulf, the USA stepped into the breach, and more recently in the same area it has extracted commercial contracts as a quid pro quo for its support of the Gulf monarchies in the aftermath of the Kuwait crisis. The same policy was quickly pursued in 'liberated' Iraq, too, where the downfall of the regime in April 2003 was immediately followed by the American-controlled interim administration granting contracts for reconstruction projects exclusively to US companies.

The second feature was the attempt to form a massive regional alliance directed against the Soviet Union and its local allies. This quickly paid dividends in the north (Greece, Turkey, monarchist Iran), but failed in the south, where any prospect of cooperation between Israel and the Arab countries inevitably ran up against the obstacle of the Palestinian issue.

The third and final feature was the determination to resort to any means, including military, to pursue these aims – as illustrated in Lebanon in 1958 and during the Gulf crisis of 1990 to 1991. As Alin argues, the motives for America's involvement in the civil crisis in Lebanon in 1958 were clear: 'By sending US troops to Lebanon, the Eisenhower administration sought to uphold Western interests in the Middle East against the perceived challenge of Arab nationalism and, to a lesser extent, communism.'[8] There were also sound commercial reasons. Lebanon was a valuable market for American business, especially as a banking centre, and it was important for would-be US investors that stability be restored.[9]

At various stages of US involvement in the region policy has been affected to a greater or lesser degree by these objectives, and some have assumed more importance than others at different times. Nevertheless, successive US administrations have expressed a clear commitment to achieve these goals in furtherance of the American national interest. Sometimes the convenient ideological cloak of democracy, freedom and the virtues of capitalism has been used in support of apparently contradictory military and other actions but few have ever been truly convinced that US interest in the region stems purely from the ideological pledge to promote and protect democracy. Indeed, American policy-makers have often been prepared to prop up and assist authoritarian and anti-democratic regimes in the Middle East if such actions furthered the protection of US strategic and commercial interests. Support for Saddam Hussein's Iraq against Ayatollah Khomeini's Iran is a case in point, as is the US relationship with Saudi Arabia. The role of the CIA in training the anti-Soviet Afghan mujahideen in the 1980s is another example.

Following US diplomatic intervention in the Suez crisis (against Britain and France) and the brief interlude in Lebanon in 1958, a reorientation of American activity in terms of implementation became apparent. During the 1960s and early 1970s US policy in the region was restructured. As Soviet influence and Arab nationalist hostility grew, Washington's reluctance to supply advanced weaponry abated. The Arab–Israeli War of 1967 transformed the military and political balance in the region, and Israel's relationship with the USA strengthened as Washington increasingly affirmed the Jewish state as a reliable partner. Soviet influence over Syria and Egypt in the wake of the war and the intensification of ideological and other forms of support to the Palestinian guerrilla movement were also increasingly apparent. This policy was pursued throughout the Nixon administration (1969–74) and the furtherance of this relationship was seen in terms of an economic–military strategy.

American policy shifted again after the 1973 Arab–Israeli War and the use of oil as a weapon by the Arab states to support Egypt and Syria. There was a discernible move towards recognizing the significance for US interests of the conservative Arab regimes, although Israel and the Shah's Iran were still supported by the increasingly influential pro-Israel lobby in America. Hoping to win friends and influence the right people, American foreign policy-makers used arms sales, for example, as a lever in improving US–Saudi relations. In overcoming opposition, both at home and abroad, to the policy of encouraging a closer relationship with the Gulf monarchies, the USA used the sale of arms as a general panacea. Such a strategy not only boosted the American arms industry but accelerated both the arms race between Arab and other states and competition with the Soviet Union, who also played the 'arms card' on a regular basis with its regional clients.

In 1979 the Iranian revolution was a severe setback for US ambitions and its influence in the area. The fall of the pro-American Shah left the Gulf without an influential, reliable client for the United States. Israel remained the only credible ally in the Middle East, with no worthwhile back-up from either the Iranians or the Arabs. Indeed, the new regime in Iran was bitterly anti-American, characterizing Washington as the 'Big Satan'. Aware of the undue influence this might give Israel and the lack of a reliable and influential ally in the Arab camp, US policy-makers, according to Stork *et al.*, 'were suddenly desperate for a short-term resolution to Arab–Israeli differences in a manner that could embrace Egypt as a sort of strategic apprentice and avoid debilitating tensions with Israel'.[10] In addition the revolutionary leadership in Tehran capitalized on American vulnerability in the area to engage the USA on another ideological battlefront, this time between the forces of Islam and imperialist, 'satanic' America.

In an attempt to contain Soviet ambitions in Afghanistan, on the doorstep of both Iran and Pakistan, and seeking to block Ayatollah Khomeini's efforts to 'export' Islamic revolution, successive US administrations led by Presidents Carter and Reagan became increasingly embroiled in the major conflicts in the region, including support for the mujahideen in Afghanistan, and assistance to Saddam Hussein's Iraq during its war with Iran throughout the 1980s. American troops were also sent back to Lebanon in an abortive attempt to restore stability, and there was the 'Irangate' scandal (see Chapter 7). There was barely any encounter in the region that in some way was not openly or covertly influenced by US machinations or involvement. In the twenty-first century the evidence of American interference in the region continues: American intervention in Iraq ended the regime of Saddam Hussein, but since 2003 the country has endured a downward spiral of civil war and the continued presence of thousands of American troops; in Lebanon the USA was accused of assisting and propping up the government of Fouad

Siniora throughout 2006 in an attempt to wage a proxy war against the Syrian- and Iranian-influenced Hizballah; in the Palestinian territories the USA has assisted in the process of arming Palestinian forces loyal to President Abbas in a showdown with the Hamas government.

Returning to the 1980s, that decade was marked by an increasing tension between US intentions and strategic goals vis-à-vis the region and local resistance to these objectives. Old relationships were put under strain, such as that between Israel and the United States, when the former sought to pursue its own interests even at the expense of its patrons in Washington. Efforts by US administrators in 1982 to revitalize the Arab–Israeli peace process through the so-called Reagan Plan were an ill-disguised attempt to appease Israel and bring it back under American direction.[11] It was remarkable that some forty years after the end of the Second World War and the fall of the Iron Curtain dividing Europe the superpower conflict and the perceived Soviet threat were still major features of US interest in the Middle East. Nevertheless, the Reagan administration and that of his successor George Bush did achieve some small successes: the PLO was largely neutralized; Egypt was firmly held within the American camp; Iraq was used to prevent Iran (for the large part) from threatening oil interests in the Gulf area; shipping lanes were kept open; and the mujahideen in Afghanistan, trained and armed by the CIA, successfully battled against the Soviet army and its local proxies, while Iran and other pro-Soviet states such as Syria were successfully characterized as international pariahs and quarantined accordingly.

The conflict against the Soviet Union, which over more than forty years had brought other disputes and tensions into its orbit and absorbed them, looked set to continue well into the new millennium until those fateful days in the late 1980s and early 1990s when the communist regimes in the Soviet Union and Eastern Europe unravelled. From that point on, the former Soviet Union – consisting of many states, from Russia, Estonia and Latvia to Kazakhstan, Armenia and Azerbaijan – would not possess the influence and strength to challenge American hegemony in the Middle East. But the previous four decades had been very different.

Quite simply the history of the Soviet Union and its role in the Middle East can be addressed by looking at one question: was Soviet policy designed to support the worldwide advance of communism and socialism or was it more definitely cast to support the USSR's own national security interests? Studying this question in the context of forty-odd years of Cold War throws up some conflicting evidence.

During the 1940s Moscow tried to take advantage of post-war confusion in order to buttress its existing, and create new, zones of influence on its south-western as well as Eastern European borders. Although the Soviets emphasized ideological objectives, their commitment to aid was small due to their own war-ravaged economy. The way chosen, therefore (in accordance with the 'spread revolution' concept), was to support leftist opposition groups without too much concern for relations with individual governments. In the 1950s, under Khrushchev, this policy changed, and the period has come to be known as the 'courtship phase'. Under the threat of encirclement from the West through the Baghdad Pact (essentially an anti-Soviet alliance in the region spearheaded by the USA), the USSR again gained access to the Middle Eastern theatre. It accepted non-alignment as a potentially positive attitude, even supported it, perceiving it as essentially 'anti-Western', and exploited the benefits of that policy through a Czech arms deal with Egypt in 1955. However, its involvement in the region remained limited, and cordial relations with Arab states were largely a result of anti-Western feeling rather than pro-Soviet sentiments.

Only in the 1960s does hard evidence of Soviet attempts to consolidate its political role in the Middle East emerge. In 1963, for example, it requested a base in Egypt. The USA continued to be perceived as a threat, hence the Soviet Union's renewed emphasis on military expansion and consolidation in the area, embodied in the establishment of the Mediterranean Squadron. Consolidation of power and the establishment of condominium with the USA based on a relationship of parity became the main aims of Soviet policy.

Following the wars of 1967 and 1973 the two superpowers realized the wisdom and necessity of détente, having come very close to direct nuclear confrontation via their local protégés during the 1973 hostilities. Yet the Soviet Union was still willing to maintain its influence with its allies – taking Egypt's side during the conflict in Yemen. During this period the Soviets enjoyed a fairly strong relationship with the 'progressive' or 'radical' Arab states (Egypt, Syria and Iraq), but it was already clear that they were mainly reacting to developments that they did not really control – this was no pro-active embrace of revolutionary socialism, nor were the ideologues in the Kremlin so idealistic as to believe that pragmatism had no role to play in these relationships. Thus, for every copy of *The Communist Manifesto* shipped from Moscow to the Arab capitals, there were many other more practical 'gifts': boxes of ammunition, shipments of tanks, MiG warplanes and scholarships for doctors and engineers. Other forms of practical assistance were also forthcoming as indications of Soviet support, although many items, especially military hardware, were not free, nor were they always representative of the cutting edge of Soviet technology.

From 1973 Soviet influence in the region began to wane. Even such friendly regimes as Syria and Iraq did much as they liked when their aims were criticized for conflicting with those of the USSR. On the whole the USSR had little real influence in the Middle East, and no success in bringing about changes in leadership. They even had very little hold over the local Arab communist parties: the regional backlash against a communist plot in Sudan in 1971, which the Soviets had advised against, probably meant the beginning of the end for Soviet ideological appeal in the area as a whole. Any improvement of Soviet standing that did occur was really only success by default, caused by playing off one superpower against the other.

In any case, it was clear that Soviet policy in the Middle East had undergone a shift – particularly since the 1960s when, as McLaurin notes, 'a noticeable status quo element made itself felt in Soviet foreign policy', and this was indeed reflected in the conduct of Soviet policy in the Middle East.[12] Some non-communist regimes were supported, the Arab–Israeli conflict was 'managed' carefully and restraint was shown in arms sales to local allies (qualitatively rather than quantitatively). All this seems to confirm the view that détente and state interests were, at least after the 1960s, all-important for the USSR. Ideology and support for the 'progressive' tendencies were of minor concern, and were often used merely as justification in selling such policies to the domestic Soviet audience. However, this view does not give the full picture.

The Soviets perceived their own aims in a different light. Dawisha and Dawisha note that there was a clear strategy based on the concept of the 'correlation of forces', which is 'as much a definition of power as it is a formula for the application of power based on the notion of not maintaining the status quo but transforming it'.[13] There were four elements to this policy:

1   Manipulation of class consciousness.
2   Short-term aims should further long-term goals.
3   Regional policy must be determined with reference to global strategy.
4   The wider interests of Soviet socialism should always take priority over the parochial interests of national liberation movements. Accordingly, the maintenance of the security of the borders of the Soviet Union must take precedence over national liberation movements.

This in itself forms a basic principle of Soviet strategy. In addition, one difficulty in pursuing such a policy related to the dissonance between Soviet objectives and local factors, which effectively acted as a constraint on Soviet ambition.

Most of the Soviet Union's policies can be explained with reference to the above framework, which appears to be designed to avoid risk of conflict, particularly through confrontation with the USA. Soviet support for 'progressive regimes' remained desirable since they opposed imperialism; however, the USSR's strategic interests were more important and in certain circumstances led to the withdrawal of such support. Even support for individual parties could be abandoned in favour of bourgeois national liberation movements if this became necessary for wider strategic reasons.

A tentative conclusion would therefore be that ideology in Soviet foreign policy thinking remained ultimately important, if only as a defining principle. Pragmatism and subordination of the ideological dimension (support for 'progressive against less progressive' tendencies) in the circumstances occurred partly as a consequence of *realpolitik* beyond the Soviets' control, and partly because of the flawed nature of the planning of their overall strategy, which, as designed by Kremlin officials, was often unrealistically ideological and dogmatic in its approach. But this pragmatism had its place in the long-term strategy, which continued to aim at the establishment of a Soviet-allied bloc of Marxist-led states. Although by the early 1970s there was some evidence of an emerging pro-Soviet bloc, including Syria, Iraq and the People's Democratic Republic of Yemen, ultimately this strategy was unsuccessful in the Arab world, where arms sales were not enough to win support in perpetuity.

Soviet justification for their actions was subject to the criticism (not least from the Chinese) that such an interpretation of communist ideology was merely a screen to justify a foreign policy that was in reality solely based on state interests. In other words, the USSR was acting like a normal superpower: defending its own security interests and striving to maintain parity with the USA. We believe that this purely 'positivist' approach – considering Soviet actions as determined solely by its interests as a superpower – does indeed offer an adequate interpretation of Soviet policies in the Middle East.

Soviet policy towards the USSR's supporters in the region changed in the mid-1980s in the context of the domestic revolution sparked by the coming to power of Mikhail Gorbachev and his programmes of glasnost and perestroika. Changes on the domestic front also affected the conduct of foreign policy, including Soviet relations with the Middle East. The Kuwait crisis is a case in point, as Mirsky highlights: 'things began to move with the advent of the "new political thinking", particularly when "de-ideologicalisation" of foreign policy was announced. This entailed a decline of ideological priorities and "socialist" commitments abroad.'[14] It also implied a retreat from the confrontation, on all levels, with the USA in the Middle East arena. This transition in Soviet thinking was well managed on all sides, particularly during 1990 and 1991, when the Gulf crisis could have threatened the new relationship that was being carved out between Moscow and Washington. US sensitivity to changes in the Soviet approach to international relations played an important part in maintaining a policy of constructive cooperation with the Kremlin.

Did the Soviet Union's new absence from the Middle East signal a decline in conflict? In many respects one might be tempted to argue for a correlation between the end of the Cold War and extension of superpower rivalry in the Middle East and the American-proclaimed decade of peacemaking that characterized the 1990s. Indeed, American sponsorship of peace negotiations throughout the 1990s resulted in historic peace conferences bringing together Israel and its Arab enemies, the conclusion of a peace treaty between Jordan and Israel, and a timetable for peace negotiations and limited autonomy for the Palestinians. This picture of peacemaking, however, does not tell the full story, and American efforts must also be scrutinized in other areas of the region, such as Iran, Iraq and the Maghreb. As one recent critic of US policy has noted:

> today more than half the Middle Eastern landmass is without US diplomatic representation. Yet incredibly, we are asked to admire the United States' political 'success' in the Middle East – and to have faith that the grotesque imbalance built into the Arab–Israeli negotiations represents a just peace.[15]

But even that comment cannot conceal the fact that after forty years of antagonism between two superpowers, at the beginning of the twenty-first century US influence in the Middle East faced no serious external competition. In many respects, however, such superiority over the region cut both ways. In the absence of external competition successive US administrations have been constrained only by internal political dynamics and the ways in which they have also been experienced as forms of terrorism against US targets within the region, as well as outside it. This concern was reflected, for example, in the policy of 'dual containment' that characterized the Clinton administration's (1993–2001) attitude to the Middle East. Dual containment was a strategy of isolating Iran and Iraq as threats to Western and specifically American interests in the Middle East. It was also apparent in the personal and sustained commitment by President Clinton to achieving a peace settlement between Israel and the Palestinians. However, at the end of his tenure it seemed that such strategies had not been completely successful, especially with regard to the by-then-faltering MEPP, and would not be pursued by his Republican successor, George W. Bush.

For the Bush administration, there was little intent to involve itself overly in Middle Eastern affairs, with the exception perhaps of Iraq. Here there were a variety of voices at the US table that proposed seeking some kind of resolution to business left unfinished in 1991, addressing the erosion of international support for maintenance of the UN sanctions against the regime and tackling the threat posed by Saddam Hussein to US interests in the Gulf region. The events of 11 September 2001, however, changed the thinking and policy of the Bush administration almost overnight. The issue of American strategic, economic and political interests throughout the Middle East suddenly rose to the top of the administration's agenda. In this respect George W. Bush had no option but to confront the Middle East as a major feature of policy-making in his government. The attacks perpetrated by al-Qaeda on 9/11 were not the first against US targets but they were the first on American sovereign territory. They underscored the consequences of hostile perceptions of US policy and its effects in the Middle East as experienced by the citizens of the region on a daily basis.

In many respects the change in US policy towards the Middle East, and the means by which it addressed issues such as the Palestinian Israeli conflict, was inevitable and has only been accelerated by a new analysis of events and their import to the region as a whole in the wake of the 9/11 attacks. The stamp of the Bush administration was always going to be apparent in a shift away from a self-defined mediator function – characterized by Clinton, who sought to create a momentum in conflict resolution which he hoped would start with Ireland and end with Israel and Palestine. In this respect Bush was never going to pick up from where Clinton left off in either theatre, and this has been demonstrated in both contexts. He has consistently demonstrated a disinclination to become 'fully involved' in progressing the conflict out of violence and into resolution/negotiation mode. In an address to the American people in Janaury 2002, following the fall of Kabul in Afghanistan and the ousting of the Taliban regime and most al-Qaeda elements, Bush identified two states in the Middle East, Iraq and Iran (along with North Korea), as elements in an 'Axis of Evil', declaring, 'states like these, and their terrorist allies [are] arming to threaten the peace of the world . . . Our war on terrorism has begun.'[16] This was a clear indication that the administration in Washington would now pursue a series of strategies, including a military one, against such regimes. This had enormous consequences for public opinion within the region towards the American government, and a sense of disquiet was prevalent among the leaderships of ruling regimes across the region. If Bush was to be taken seriously, then the 'war on terrorism' was sure to target the Middle East in the not-too-distant future. By March 2003, despite lack of support in the UN, the USA, and its coalition partners, launched Operation Iraqi Freedom and Bush announced:

> the US and our allies pledged to act if the dictator did not disarm. The regime in Iraq is now learning that we keep our word. By our actions, we serve a great and just cause . . . Free nations will not sit and wait, leaving enemies free to plot another September 11th . . . And

by defending our own security, we are freeing the people of Iraq from one of the cruelest regimes on Earth.[17]

In 'winning' the military campaign in Iraq (i.e., defeating Saddam's armies and achieving regime change), however, a positive outcome in terms of the objectives of American interests in the Middle East became more difficult to achieve. Iraq has become a quagmire instead of a model for democracy that the rest of the Middle East would follow. US credibility has been damaged by its policies there and the balance of power in the rest of the region has been affected. In terms of the war on terrorism, there is a widespread belief within the region that US policy has engendered more not less violence. By 2007, the Bush administration was pleading with a Democrat majority in Congress to allow the military presence in Iraq more time to succeed, but there was little optimism that this would win the war on terrorism in a way that would end conflict in the Middle East.

4 Generation jihad
Conflict in the name of Islam?

Hostages kidnapped and murdered in Beirut . . . Tourists murdered in Luxor, Egypt . . . The destruction of the Twin Towers in New York . . . Simultaneous suicide attack on the Pentagon in Washington . . . Shoppers killed in a suicide bomb in a Baghdad market . . . A tour party murdered in Yemen . . . The American Embassy bombed in Nairobi . . . Algerian schoolgirls stabbed to death . . . Israelis bombed in street-side cafés. The litany of Islamic violence from and in the Middle East appears limitless. The rise of the so-called 'Green Peril' of Islamic-inspired violence and conflict dominates newspaper headlines, television images and radio reports on an almost daily basis. With the end of the Cold War, the fall of the Berlin Wall and the collapse of the Soviet Union and communism, many were ready to declare Islam the new menace to global peace and stability.

Writing in 1993, an influential American academic declared that 'Islam and the West are on a collision course. Islam is a triple threat: political, civilisational and demographic.'[1] For this writer, and many others like him, the relationship between the West and Islamic civilization has always been and will always be based on military conflict. Muslims are perceived and portrayed as an aggressive civilization, Islam has 'bloody borders', violence is repeatedly cited as an indiscriminate way of life against Serb, Jew, Hindu, Buddhist and Catholic. The locus of this threat was the Middle East and it was argued that Muslim fanatics would ensure that the region became synonymous with conflict in a battle with the West for global command.

Indeed, much contemporary debate about the resurgence of political Islam in the Middle East has been based on the facile assumption that Islam itself is inherently violent and militant. Accordingly, the presence of a majority Muslim population in the countries of the region will always lead to violence, terrorism and protracted conflict-engaging jihad-minded mujahideen. But is this the sole explanation behind the headlines so many in the West view, hear and read? Is Islam the most formidable threat to the stability and security of the entire region and even the entire globe? This is the fundamental question that this chapter seeks to answer.

At present a perception of permanent conflict and violence is the primary image of Islam, which influences a number of policy-makers and the media, and colours common perceptions of many people in the West. Since the success of the revolution in Iran in 1979 and the establishment of the world's first Islamic republic based on rule by a Shi'a clergy, there has been a growing fear of Islam in the West. The roots of this fear of the 'other' lay in Orientalist traditions that have characterized European (and later American) relations with the Middle East since the nineteenth century. Such traditions have always cast the Arab East in a negative light and have been politically motivated by the inherent desire in the West to dominate the region.[2] In terms of events since 1979, and the concurrent emergence of political Islam, the West has been guilty of choosing to interpret and represent those events and processes in a limited dimension. Edward Said puts it succinctly when he declares that in the West,

> knowledge of Islam and of Islamic peoples has generally proceeded not only from dominance and confrontation but also from cultural antipathy. Today Islam is defined negatively as that [with] which the West is radically at odds, and this tension establishes a framework radically limiting knowledge of Islam.[3]

That cultural antipathy is reflected throughout the Western media and results in Islamophobia through the hostile stereotyping of Muslims as terrorists and enemies (see such films as *Rules of Engagement, Executive Decision, The Siege* and *True Lies*). Newspaper and television headlines and images regularly associate Muslims with violent depictions – holding guns, masked and engaged in wars, intent on oppressing their own as much as outsiders, and hostile to the West. Such depictions help biased and bigoted policy-makers draw a Manichaean distinction between the Christian West and Muslim East that becomes a virtual reality through the support of such simplistic divisions in the modern media. We will argue that the construction of this view of Islam is diametrically at odds with the real relationship between faith and struggle (jihad) which continues to be important to the majority of Muslims across the globe.

On 13 March 1996 in the Egyptian resort of Sharm al-Sheikh the leaders of some thirty countries met for a half-day under the auspices of the American-convened and pretentiously titled 'Summit of the Peacemakers'. The meetings, speeches, photo opportunities and declarations that resulted were designed to communicate an important message to the Palestinian Islamists of Hamas and Islamic Jihad who had detonated a series of suicide bombs in Israel that had killed sixty-one people in the previous month alone. In an attempt to save the beleaguered Middle East peace process, which such attacks were undermining, the 'peacemakers' declared that they were ready to wage war against the Islamists. While it can be assumed that no one seriously believed that a hastily convened day trip to Sharm al-Sheikh would win the so-called war against the Islamists, the Summit of the Peacemakers left a strange impression within the international community that terrorism, particularly of the religious type, was a real threat not only to the Middle East but to the entire international order.

The attention paid to the issue of so-called Muslim or Islamic terrorism in the Middle East was highlighted by the summit. Indeed, throughout the late 1990s many writers emerged to condemn Islam as a religion of violence, identifying a new generation of activists across the region dedicated to jihad, or what they called 'Holy War'. As one such writer asserted, 'in Islam's war against the West and the struggle to build Islamic states at home, the end justifies the means . . . radical political Islam placed atop these societies in the Middle East has created a combustible mixture'.[4]

Does this categorization of a religion representing millions of Muslims in the Middle East adequately explain patterns of conflict across the region? Lewis believes it does, declaring that 'the Muslim world [not just the Middle East] is again seized by an intense and violent resentment of the West'.[5] Yet such sentiments stand in stark contrast to the measured tones of Egyptian President Hosni Mubarak (himself a Muslim), who remarked at the summit that 'Islam, like any other religion, is against violence, against any act of violence under any title.'[6]

Nevertheless, the political perspective that Islam was established through the sword, and that the founder of the faith, the Prophet Mohammed, was a radical military and political leader, has sunk deep into the collective consciousness of Westerners. From this foundation further fear was fuelled, particularly in America, in response to such acts of terrorism as the events of 9/11. The American media, policy-makers and public have been alarmed at this phenomenon of terror in their own country, and more specifically they have struggled to make sense of such violence in a post-Cold War era when peace and security were supposed to be guaranteed. The current fixation with the 'Green Peril' has been manifested in a variety of ways, and from this a fear of Islam per se has been generated.

In the Middle East itself, however, Islam and the role of Muslim populations in the conflicts of the region are perceived from a variety of standpoints, rather than just one. Conflict involving Islamists – those Muslims who are politically active – is not always manifested through violence. Opponents of Islamist activism, such as the secular Ba'athist state in Syria, have often been responsible for perpetrating the violence, the conflict and the worst atrocities. In 1982, for example, the Syrian authorities massacred 10,000 members of the Muslim Brotherhood – a Sunni Muslim reformist organization that engaged in welfare and education activities – in the town of Hama following a civil protest against the Ba'athist authorities. In Lebanon, subject to fifteen years of civil war, occupation by Israel and a military presence by Syria, the breadth and diversity of Islamist views of conflict are wide. There are followers of Islamist preachers and activists, both Sunni and Shi'a, who believe that change within the system is the best way to achieve their goals. In Iraq under the regime of Saddam Hussein, thousands of Shi'a Muslims were persecuted and murdered by the Ba'athist leader of this secular state. In post-war Iraq, countless Islamist militias are engaged in a jihad that has turned into a civil war as well as an anti-occupation insurgency. Yet, for the majority of Muslims, there is no role for violence as a dominant motif of Islamic resistance, as interpreted according to religious law, to foreign occupation or oppression. In reality, and very much contrary to the popular perception current in the West, Islamism in the Middle East has largely played its part in *opposing* despotic and authoritarian rule through legitimate means, promoting civil society and a regeneration of grassroots politics. Where the state has failed to provide even the most basic of services to its people, Islamist organizations have stepped into the breach to ensure that the poorest citizens are in receipt of basic welfare support.

A resurgence of Islam and the revival of the religion in the social, economic and political life of the Middle East has been identified since the late 1960s. However, this has been viewed much more negatively than a parallel revival of Christianity, whose evangelical movements are not perceived as a threat to any regional or international order. Single events, such as the revolution in Iran in 1979, when Shi'a clergy led by Ayatollah Khomeini emerged dominant from the revolutionary coalition that over-threw the Shah, are represented as defining and universal moments for the entire Muslim population of the Middle East. Despite the religious, cultural and ethnic differences in a region dominated in number by Sunni Muslims, fundamentalist, anti-Western Islam as perceived in the Iranian context throughout the 1980s has been held up as typical of Islam throughout the region.

In Egypt, Jordan, Lebanon, Saudi Arabia, Algeria, Tunisia, Syria, Kuwait and even Israel, however, Islamism could be identified in each context in many guises. While it is true that conflict and associated violence often came to dominate relations between Islamists and the state, there have been only a handful of occasions when Islamists formed organizations or movements for specifically violent purposes. In Egypt, for example, we may find in the variety of Islamist groups – the majority of which have never engaged in acts of violence – a few whose acts of terror have grabbed the headlines and resulted in a full-scale onslaught by the state against Muslims from across the political spectrum. In the past the institutions of Islam supported (rather than came into conflict with) the Egyptian state, but the later decades of the twentieth century witnessed the emergence of a dichotomy in this respect. While Islamist groups have been active in the country since the late 1920s and tension between such groups and the state rose under the secular leadership of President Nasser (1952–70), violent conflict only truly emerged from the late 1970s onwards. The establishment of radical Islamist cells whose members were influenced by thinkers such as the Egyptian Sayyid Qutb led to violent conflict and confrontation with authority. In 1981 one such group, Jamaat al-Jihad, assassinated Nasser's successor, Anwar Sadat. These groups condemned the hostile attitude of the state to Islam, decried the government and its leadership as apostate and atheist, thus declaring that they were compelled by the laws of Islam to declare a 'defensive war' (*jihad bis saif*). From that time these radical groups have been responsible for attacks on government institutions and more assassinations of politicians, as well as of poets, authors, journalists and foreign visitors to the country. Yet, as Esposito observes, by the end of the 1990s, 'despite sporadic eruptions of violence and continued confrontation between the government and Islamist militants, in general a quiet rather than violent revolution had occurred in Egypt'.[7]

So Islamist conflict with the Egyptian state has been an important element in domestic politics since 1945. But in terms of a historical overview we would argue that the conflict was as often as not generated by the state in its attempts to quell the emergence of a mainstream opposition movement that engaged in legitimate protest against state corruption, anti-democratic practices and political authoritarianism against *all* its opponents, whether Islamist or secular. It would therefore be misguided to declare that Egypt's Islamist movement has been engaged in violent jihad directed at the overthrow of the state and the establishment of a theocracy. Conflict has been very much a two-sided affair. In 1992, for example, in response to extremist violence directed at state officials, Egypt's rulers ordered a security crackdown in the poverty-stricken neighbourhood of Imbaba in northern Cairo which was home to approximately 250,000 people. In early December some 15,000 police, army and intelligence officers descended on Imbaba, declared the area a no-go zone and imposed a curfew. During the curfew more than 800 people were arrested on suspicion of involvement in Islamist opposition and terrorism. This campaign proved deeply unpopular with the majority of ordinary Egyptians and was seen as further evidence of the degree to which the state and its leaders were out of touch with their own citizens. Nevertheless, in 2006–7 the Egyptian state sought to exclude Islamists such as the Muslim Brotherhood from the political mainstream by again making mass arrests, freezing finances and raiding businesses owned by Brotherhood supporters. This policy of suppression was inaugurated by the ruling regime after the Brotherhood had made significant gains by fielding candidates as independents in parliamentary elections.

In the Israeli–Palestinian context, by the mid-1990s jihad (as formal resistance waged by Palestinian Islamists) against Israel had become yet another new but depressing facet of this particular conflict. Two Palestinian Islamist groups, Hamas and Islamic Jihad, were responsible for bombings and suicide missions against Israeli civilians. In 1996 alone hundreds of Israelis, including non-combatant women and innocent children, were killed in such attacks, launched by a political leadership that called for an end to Israel's occupation of Palestine. Hamas leaders contended that conflict with Israel through other means (national, armed, secular-based struggle) had failed the Palestinian people in the quest for liberation from Israeli rule.

The emergence of an actively Islamist–nationalist dimension to the conflict with Israel, particularly during the Intifada in the late 1980s, succeeded, in some quarters, in adding a potent religious dimension to the conflict. Thus, for many young Palestinians of the refugee camps Islamist rhetoric and a return to the mosque became the primary lens through which they now viewed their enemy and interpreted the long conflict that had engulfed them. On the Israeli side the increasing manifestation of the Islamist phenomenon (which they had been partly responsible for encouraging), and the ensuing violence, had a major impact, not only on the peace process but on internal security concerns and the whole gamut of national politics. Israel's own religious radicals upped the ante, declaring they would confront the Islamist threat to Judaism.

Yet the issue of conflict through a religious campaign of violence by elements within the Palestinian camp turns on whether groups like Hamas and Islamic Jihad are innately predicated on violence and terror or whether such actions are simply component parts of a wider campaign for liberation from foreign occupation for which much of the international community has also censured Israel. As such it touches upon the more philosophical debates about religion and violence, as well as armed struggle, as parts of liberation movements. Hamas leaders claim they are legitimately waging a jihad against foreign occupation. Their campaign of bombs and suicide missions, however, has been called into question in an era of peacemaking when the use of violence is viewed with suspicion as much within the Palestinian community as outside it.

Hamas, like its predecessor the Palestinian Muslim Brotherhood, was initially established as a reform movement that did not specifically advocate violence as a means of achieving its goals. In some respects conflict with

Israel was initially to be avoided while members of the movement concentrated on winning support through a combination of preaching and education. Coercing people back to the active practice of their faith in all spheres of life was not actively encouraged. By the end of the 1990s, though, the organization's position had shifted. With the PLO and Israel having signed up to a peace process and interim autonomy, Hamas (specifically its armed wing the al-Qassam Brigades) was actively pursuing jihad not just against Israel's soldiers but against all of its civilians. To what extent such actions can be morally justified in Islamic teaching is highly questionable. There is no convincing doctrine advocating, for example, that the lives of women and children should ever be taken, even in a war in defence of Islam on Muslim territory occupied and ruled by a foreign power. By 2006 Hamas had eschewed suicide bombing as a major strategy and had proposed several ceasefires, which were repeatedly refused by Israel. The organization's arrival in the political mainstream of the Palestinian polity presented it with a major challenge with respect to the notion of resistance and the demand of the international community that it must renounce violence and recognize Israel.

In Algeria, where serious civil conflict gripped the country from the early 1990s, Islamist violence had a major impact on the descent into chaos and the loss of many thousands of lives. Here an authoritarian secular regime engaged in a battle against a broad Islamist opposition movement. In addition, the conflict in Algeria was about the impact of political liberalization or democratization on developing societies where the majority chose a path that was at odds with the economic and political reforms advocated by the international community, and where the level of assistance offered by international financial institutions (such as the World Bank) and major bilateral donors (such as the United States) was conditional on the progress of liberalization. Indeed, it should be remembered that the Algerian situation was precipitated by a decision to halt elections – in effect putting a stop to democratic process and change – as a result of foreign (US and French) desire to limit the success of Islamists at the polls. As such Algeria, while it reflects bitter decline into internal conflict involving Islamists, is also an example of the impact of Western perceptions of the threat posed by Islam to an international order dominated by Western mores and values. Fearful of the emergence of a modern Algerian state based on the Iranian revolutionary model, the US and France used their influence to pressure the Algerian leadership into pulling the country back under military rule.[8] The crux of the conflict is a war in which 'on the one hand the state is characterized by illegitimacy and divided by "hawks" and "doves". On the other hand, Islamists with a goal of total hegemony – and who themselves are torn between "radicals" and "moderates" – are fighting to replace the existing regime.'[9]

The contest for power in Algeria was precipitated by an economic crisis that hit hard the population at large, though a corrupt and increasingly elderly national political leadership that had rested on the tarnished laurels of independence delivered from the French in the 1960s was cushioned against its impact. The vanguard of opposition against the government in the 1980s, like elsewhere in the Middle East, was increasingly Islamist in orientation. The main organization, the Fronte Islamique du Salut (FIS), quickly generated popular support in elections (local as well as first-round national) on an anti-establishment platform calling for the overthrow of the nationalist-dominated state and the establishment of an Islamic polity in its place. Fearing further popular gains in national elections scheduled for January 1992, the government sought to contain the Islamist 'threat' by suspending the elections, declaring a state of emergency and allowing the military effectively to seize control of the state.

It has been estimated that as many as 100,000 Algerians were killed during the course of this horrific conflict. A plethora of Islamist groups took up arms after the state of emergency was declared and brought war to the government. The majority killed in the massacres, bomb attacks, executions and stabbings that followed were ordinary civilians rather than the national army or various branches of the police force. The military defended itself but also took up the offensive against the Islamists: thousands of mujahideen were imprisoned, tortured and killed. A litany of human rights abuses were committed by both sides in this bloody civil war.

The religious nature of the war in Algeria has been called into question on many occasions. Amirouche, for example, argues that 'present-day Islamist insurgents, like their nationalist predecessors [who wrenched independence from the French] seek to achieve essentially secular goals irrespective of the utterances of orators or their avowed objectives'.[10] Religion, nevertheless, was a potent symbol in this conflict, motivating not just a handful of discontented and megalomaniac clerics but many thousands from all walks of life in Algeria to engage in a guerrilla struggle against the state.

War-weariness was certainly a factor in the election in spring 1999 of a new President, Abdel Aziz Boutefika, who pledged to promote national reconciliation and an end to conflict. His peace plan, backed by Algeria's generals, included an amnesty for Islamist rebels, which resulted in early 2000 in the announcement that the 8,000-strong Islamic Salvation Army, the primary guerrilla movement in the civil war, would be disbanded. Those failing to sign up to the peace deal were targeted in further military offensives on rebel hideouts and camps. In 2002 the Armed Islamic Group (GIA) were all but defeated and the war finally appeared to be over. Four years later a presidential decree announced an amnesty for both guerrillas and national armed forces, as well as compensation for victims of the conflict. Politics has now gained precedence over violence, but Algeria still remains vulnerable to the wounds of the not-too-distant past.

In Iran the popular revolution which overthrew the Shah in 1979 was commonly described as 'Islamic', thus altering the political landscape of the entire region. Even in the twenty-first century the political changes in Iran are still regarded as a signal of change in the rest of the region. The establishment of an Islamic state led by Shi'a clerics, notably the Ayatollah Khomeini, put a different face on many aspects of conflict within the whole region, not just in Iran.

A striking example is the Arab–Israeli conflict, in which Iran under the Shah was never perceived as a threat to Israel. All that changed with the establishment of the Islamic republic. Anti-Israeli and anti-American rhetoric was broadcast by the state-controlled media. In addition, as part of Khomeini's vision of exporting the Iranian revolutionary model, considerable support and funding were extended to those Arabs willing to subscribe to the Iranian agenda. Today the Hamas movement in the Palestinian territories is regularly accused of being a benefactor of Iranian support, arms and money in a conflict against not just Israel but secularist Palestinians in the Fatah movement. In Lebanon another radical Shi'a movement, Hizballah (Party of God), received millions of dollars from Iran in support of its guerrilla campaign against Israel, which, following its invasion of 1982 to oust the PLO, remained in partial occupation of the Shi'a-dominated south of the country. In Iraq, since the fall of Saddam Hussein, Iran is suspected of playing a major role in fomenting the Shi'a ascendancy in government and drafting proposals for a breakaway Shi'a republic in the south of the country, as well as inciting sectarian revenge against the minority Sunnis and plotting against American and other Allied troops that have been occupying the country since 2003. Once again, the whole region is becoming gripped by Sunni–Shi'a tension.

It might be argued that Shi'a characteristics of opposition, martyrdom and sacrifice have changed the emphasis and dynamics of several conflicts across the region. But it should also be remembered that the Iranian revolution and subsequent Islamic republic did not, as so many predicted, usher in an era of conflict and chaos leading to the downfall of an array of Arab regimes across the region. Well over two decades later, Iran is one of the few states in the region where fair elections are now a feature of the political system. In addition, the rise of reformists and their domestic victory over the country's more hard-line clerics proves that the winds of change are capable of influencing Islamism, directing it away from conflict, even if success is not always complete; nor, in some cases, long lasting, as hard-liners fight back (as has happened recently in Iran). It seems that constant struggle between conservatives and reformers will continue to be the *leitmotif* of the polities of such countries as Iran, Algeria and even Egypt.

To portray Islam as we have described – through the headlines and not the stories behind the headlines – is to give a false impression, both of the political spectrum that Islam in the Middle East represents and of the types of conflict which have drawn Islamist movements. Empirically, so-called Muslim terrorists remain a small and disparate group that has emerged out of a variety of political backgrounds whose power and impact among the masses have been exaggerated. Within the broad spectrum of Islam, groups like Islamic Jihad are marginal players. In our view they do not, as Rapoport claims, represent 'the gospel for the youth', inaugurating a 'new era in Islamic thought'.[11] Instead these Islamists, who are motivated as much by spiritual impulse as by more temporal concerns in the arena of conflict, and who embrace political violence, are a tiny minority. As we mentioned earlier, the extent to which Islamist organizations choose to counter the Western construction of negative stereotypes of them is questionable. In the majority of cases any dissemination of an alternative message in Western policy-making circles is greeted with hostility. Even those Western academics writing alternative accounts of Islamist movements are labelled 'apologists for terrorism'. In the USA, in particular, Muslim groups which seek to counter the stereotyping have faced a major uphill struggle, in particular when lobbying Congress, which is widely acknowledged as being historically sympathetic to the pro-Israel lobby. In the late 1990s attempts to promote warmer relations between the USA and Iran and to break down anti-Western and Islamophobic barriers met with only mixed success, not least because of insensitivity on the part of the Americans. For instance, one group of high-ranking Iranian officials visiting the USA found themselves subjected to stringent searches by immigration officials upon their arrival. By 2007, Iranian–US relations were again completely soured over issues such as the war on terrorism and Iran's nuclear programme.

The purpose of this chapter is not to deny that acts of political violence and terrorism have been perpetrated by individuals who employ the symbols of religion, whether Muslim, Jewish or Christian. Rather, it is to question whether specific religions themselves, Islam in particular, are by nature violent and conflict-driven. As Taheri asks, 'Is Islam a religion of terror?'[12]

In our opinion Islam as a faith system, as represented by its holy books and its preachers, is no more or less conflict-driven than elements of contemporary Hinduism, Judaism or Christianity. In modern times the importance of faith is not that it is the cause of conflicts but rather that conflicts have assumed religious dimensions among adherents of various faiths. This is a major challenge in respect of conflict resolution, as well as an inherent challenge to political orders or ideological viewpoints that are secular in foundation. In the twenty-first century Islamism is perceived as emerging in a political form that has less to do with protest politics and more to do with terrorism. Images of destruction arising from suicide bombers and especially the carnage of 9/11 bolster this perception. Within that framework of understanding, the concept of jihad and the generation of young Muslims commonly associated with it are labelled and understood as solely fixated with violence and terror. Acts of terrorism perpetrated by those understood as Muslim, who even claim to act 'in the name of Islam', acquire new meanings, new understandings and a sense of existential threat to everyone standing outside the Muslim circle. The fact that jihad within Islamic (rather than contemporary Islamist) discourse is understood in many dimensions and layers, including as a highly prescriptive, defensive act, and contains such harmless elements as encouraging Muslims to pursue a good education, is almost entirely obscured. Religious adherents may use their religion to promote a variety of routes through life, but in this context Islam is far from being the sole reason why the Middle East tends to be a byword for conflict in the modern world. The influence of some Islamists and their radical revolutionary messages may have led to innocent lives being lost and countries like Algeria being engulfed in internally generated conflict. But even in Algeria Islam or Islamism is not the sole reason for the predilection for violence. The state, as well as other political forces, is just as guilty of inflicting terror. Nevertheless, there is a real threat inherent to certain discourses of Islamism which have gripped particular constituencies in the Middle East that feeds on a culture (often created and perpetrated by the state) of brutality, totalitarianism and authoritarianism. In such contexts dimensions of Islamism become nothing more than a competitor in environments where other forms of politics are and have been absent for decades. Faced with repression and frustrated by the inability to create change peacefully, violence becomes the only expression of political power. The perceived complicity of Western states in supporting the perpetuation of such regimes undermines the philosophies of liberal democracy, open and plural governance. Thus, other, broader explanations have to be forthcoming; explanations that include these issues alongside the politics of authoritarianism, economic and social factors, and other problems that currently beset the region.

5   Sectarian conflict

Lebanon, state without a nation

The Lebanese state, which formally gained independence from the French in 1946, has been weak and precarious to say the least. The denominational system of politics and government in Lebanon has institutionalized sectarian differences between Christians and Muslims, who are further divided into a variety of denominations frequently at odds with each other. The sectarianism of politics has been the major factor propelling the Lebanese into conflict with each other. The savage civil war of 1975 to 1990, which left 100,000 dead, was complicated and exacerbated by the introduction of a Palestinian dimension and the consequent intrusion of two external powers, Israel and Syria, fighting their battles by proxy using allies among Lebanese society. With the enforced withdrawal of Israel and its surrogate militia from southern Lebanon in May 2000, against the background of some progress towards a comprehensive Middle East peace settlement, the prospects for the future stability of the country should have improved, but the domestic political system remains corrupt and flawed. Making sense out of the Lebanese tragedy and learning the lessons from this conflict is an ongoing project.

For many years Lebanon has been a classic example of a deeply divided society. There are obvious parallels with several other countries, including South Africa under apartheid, Northern Ireland and the former Yugoslavia. During the civil war Lebanese frequently killed each other for purely religious reasons, as white killed black (and vice versa) in the old South Africa and as Protestant killed Catholic (and vice versa) at times of seemingly mindless sectarian violence in Northern Ireland. In all three countries wider political contexts and external influences have distorted and aggravated religious, ethnic and racial divisions. Yet, as many writers have pointed out, Lebanon in the 1960s was held up as an example of a country that was an oasis of calm in a troubled region. To quote Albert Hourani, it was 'a country which had achieved an almost miraculous balance between different communities and interests, and which was enjoying political stability and

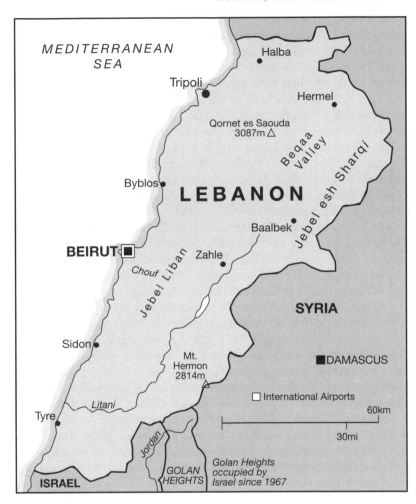

Map C – Lebanon

peace, a comparative neutrality in the conflicts of the region, and a prosperity which seemed to be self-perpetuating'.[1] So what went wrong?

Some of the answer lies in geography and much in history. The country is mainly mountainous behind a narrow coastal strip with a society made up of communities of ancient origin.[2] For most of the nineteenth century Ottoman imperial appointees sought to impose order on the various ethnic and religious minorities who had traditionally sought refuge from central authority on the 'Mountain', and who jockeyed for influence elsewhere in the more accessible areas. These officials, as part of the attempts by

Constantinople to centralize imperial authority, tried to extend their influence by undermining the long-standing system of feudal chiefly rule, which had held sway in the mountain fastnesses.

A significant development in the mid-nineteenth century was increasing interest and involvement in the Levant – the area that is now Israel, Lebanon and Syria – by the European powers, in particular France, whose self-imposed 'civilizing' mission in the region (exporting French culture and influence) involved offering protection to the Christian communities in Lebanon. France's first intervention in 1860 followed the destruction of a large number of Maronite (Christian) villages by their Druze (Muslim) rivals, allied to the Ottoman authorities. Subsequently an autonomous 'Little Lebanon' was established in the central mountains, with a Maronite majority and a Christian governor ruling with a multi-denominational council formed on a proportional basis: four Maronite, three Druze, two Greek Orthodox, one Greek Catholic, a Shi'ite Muslim and a Sunni Muslim. The Turkish authorities appointed the governor with the agreement of France and Britain, which was also seeking a role in the area in support of its commercial interests.[3] This religiously defined balance foreshadowed the political structure of a larger modern Lebanon, and European rivalry was finally settled in favour of France during the First World War: the Anglo-French Sykes–Picot Agreement of 1916[4] was endorsed by the award of a mandate for Lebanon (and Syria) to France at San Remo in 1920, following the post-war dissolution of the Ottoman Empire.

Thus 'modern' Lebanon emerged as a distinct geopolitical entity. It was constructed from part of the former Ottoman Greater Syria (referred to as 'Geographical Syria' in the Sykes–Picot Agreement). This new country was in effect a 'Greater Lebanon', twice as large as its 'Little' predecessor and with a more complicated sectarian diversity in which the combined Christian majority had been reduced from 79 per cent to 53 per cent of a population of just over 600,000.[5] Other new Middle Eastern countries created (or foreshadowed) by the colonial powers within artificial, unnatural frontiers at the same time as Lebanon also had inbuilt fault lines – both ethnic and religious. Israel, Turkey, Iraq and Syria are cases in point. But they could not match Lebanon's confessional jigsaw puzzle encompassing three significant Christian denominational divisions and three Muslim ones, plus a number of smaller Christian splinter groups.[6] A further potentially destabilizing factor was that there was no numerically dominant group forming an overwhelming majority of the population. The difference in numbers between the three major groups – Maronite, Sunni and Shi'a – is relatively small, with no single community accounting for even half the population. This is in stark contrast to some other countries with deep ethnic or religious divisions, such as Cyprus, Malaysia, South Africa, India (post-partition) and the Sudan.[7] A society deeply divided into even two factions is not a recipe for harmony; so how much more problematic is the situation in Lebanon, where there is great fragmentation within already complicated divides? Until 1943, when they lost their influence, the French dominated the Lebanese scene as a neo-imperial power. Communal differences were deliberately reinforced by a familiar colonial ploy of divide and rule. Under the guise of a fairly structured inter-sect political system, the French in effect reproduced the former confessional arrangements of the 'Little' Lebanon in the 'Greater', as if the Christians were still in a large majority. Accordingly, the Francophile Christians predominated with the connivance of the mandatory authorities, and their share of the important offices of state – including the presidency – was out of proportion to their ever-shrinking numerical superiority. (The census of 1932 estimated that the Christians constituted 51.3 per cent of the population.[8]) In consequence, almost half the population of the new Lebanon felt disempowered and many refused to work within the system. The Sunnis, a community dominated by notables educated under the former Ottoman Empire, opposed the very existence of the state. They yearned for a pan-Syrian identity, with many of them agitating for union of Muslim-dominated areas with Syria when in 1936 the French mandatory authority recognized the principle of Syrian independence with the establishment of the Syrian republic. Shi'ite notables tended to cooperate with the French, but ordinary Shi'as were suspicious of Christian domination. The other significant sect with Muslim origins, the Druze, also controlled by traditional chiefly families, was divided in its attitude to the government. Although disliking the Maronites, the powerful Jumblatt family, at least, was prepared to work with the French. Nor were the Christians united, with the Greek Orthodox – although concerned about Muslim rule – jealous of Catholic (Maronite) domination.

Stoten argues that Lebanon, although a recognized state, had not, even by the end of the civil war in 1990, developed the attributes of nationhood.[9] Imported European notions of statehood, of government independent of religious affiliation, made little impact in a country composed of a heterogeneous kaleidoscope of religious groups, all of whom were determined to protect parochial political interests. As we have just discussed, this was certainly true of Lebanon under the French mandate, where much of the population felt excluded from a share in power yet trapped within a state whose boundaries seemed to ensure perpetual control by one community supported by an external power. (This was not too far removed from the situation in Northern Ireland as perceived by the Catholic nationalist minority.) In the modern era most Europeans have become used to associating themselves with nation-states rather than an exclusive religious affiliation, but in the 1990s we have witnessed a new phenomenon with the breakdown of the politics of national identity. Now many European states (among them Belgium, Spain, the UK, former Yugoslavia and former Soviet Union) are experiencing the emergence of parochial nationalist and separatist tendencies and resisting supra-identity packaging within a wider European identity.

Another weakness of the Lebanese system (particularly during the mandate, but it has continued to inhibit normal political development in more recent times) has been the domination by notables, or small conservative elites. This was as true of the Christian factions, such as the modern Maronite descendants of the neo-feudal 'Lords of the Valley', as it was of the Muslims, whether under the sway of leading Druze families or their Sunni counterparts, among whom a handful of families tended to fill any ministerial posts that came their way. The Shi'a leadership similarly came mostly from large landowning families, and all of these notables, whatever their confessional background, protected their privileged positions by discouraging popular participation in the political arena. Up to 1957, 40 per cent of the parliamentary seats were held by landowners. Such political parties as did emerge and were represented within parliament were factional groupings or coalitions.[10] Ideologically motivated parties were active, but mostly outside the legislature, and even these tended to have a religiously doctrinal basis. Some of the Christian parties were also influenced by the European fascist movements of the 1930s.

Full formal independence for Lebanon in 1946 did not mark a new beginning, although it finally removed the French as players in its internal affairs. The 'National Pact' of three years previously was actually a more important milestone in the development of modern Lebanon. In essence this was an (unwritten) constitutional arrangement accommodating sectarian differences prevalent at that time, and it marked the culmination of a growing rapprochement between Maronite and Sunni elites. However, although an important reference point in the short history of Lebanon, in practice, as far as domestic politics were concerned, it represented little more than a fine-tuning of previous sectarian power-sharing formulas between the two principal participants, with provision for participation by other religious groups.[11] It entrenched a rigid system of sharing out the three top jobs: a Christian President, a Sunni Prime Minister and a Shi'a Speaker of Parliament. The Druze, further down the pecking order, were to provide the Foreign Minister. This system of government by triumvirate was still in place at the end of the twentieth century. The Pact, despite attempts by the French to retain some say in Lebanese affairs, paved the way for an independent Lebanon – this being the goal for Christians and Sunnis alike. It also represented a compromise between the Christian leaders who were shrugging off French tutelage and protection, and Muslim leaders turning away from pan-Arabism in accepting Lebanon as a separate entity – a country with an 'Arab appearance', as it was described at the time.[12] Thus Lebanon entered the post-Second World War era with the same flawed sectarian and elite-dominated system, with power shared mainly between the Maronites and the Sunnis, that it had experienced under the mandate. Yet from 1943 until 1975, with one hiccup in 1958, the Lebanese political system seemed successful in providing a basis for considerable political freedom and prosperity. Of all the Middle East governments, that in Beirut was the least intrusive. It practised *laissez-faire* at its most strikingly liberal, even largely absenting itself from the educational sector: only 40 per cent of children were at government schools in 1959, with most pupils at private religious institutions, which of course did nothing to help bring diverse communities together. Lebanon, with its liberalized market economy, free trade and the absence of exchange controls, became the banking centre of the Middle East and one of its main commercial hubs. This apparent prosperity, however, concealed a growing division between the Christian and Sunni elites (who benefited most from this commercial and financial activity) and the urban and rural poor. Among the underclass were an increasing number of Shi'as who swelled the ranks of the urban working class as the rural economy declined. The predominantly Christian leadership also sought to isolate the country from the tensions of the region, turning its back on crises in the Arab world brought about by the Arab–Israeli conflict, although Lebanon still became reluctant host to some 150,000 Palestinian refugees after the 1948 war. The events of 1958, however, demonstrated that it was impossible to keep the world at bay indefinitely.

The crisis of that year was at one level just another indication of the struggle for influence between Lebanese elitist factions, and it was eventually solved in the same way as earlier inter-confessional confrontations – by means of an adjustment of ministerial posts to include groups that had previously been excluded. But, significantly, it reflected growing popular opposition to Maronite ascendancy from mostly Muslim factions which were united in demonstrating the disenchantment of the urban poor at their exclusion from the country's apparent prosperity. The international dimension was also important, as this widespread popular opposition was partly a protest against the government's perceived empathy with Western policies in the region. The Maronite leadership's embrace of the American Eisenhower Doctrine (see Chapter 3) and its opposition to any manifestation of pan-Arabism (as demonstrated by its refusal to join inter-Arab unions, whether with Egypt and Syria or Jordan and Iraq) were interpreted as sympathy for the West. President Nasser's calls for Arab unity struck a popular chord throughout Lebanon, chiefly among the urban masses who resented and were ashamed of their Christian politicians' attempts to hold Lebanon aloof from the mainstream of Arab politics. Additional popular ferment was engendered by the overthrow of the Hashemite monarchy in Iraq, perceived to be Western-leaning and opposed to Nasser's strident pan-Arabism. The Lebanese army refused or felt unable to put down the disturbances, so it took the despatch of US marines to Beirut at President Sham'un's request to restore order. The crisis was contained, but two new elements in Lebanese politics – the activities of the urban poor and the influence and involvement of external actors actively being enlisted by rival internal factions – would come to threaten the Lebanese political system and eventually lead to its disruption and the destruction of much of Lebanon itself.

With the benefit of hindsight, we can see that the seeds of the Lebanese civil war, which erupted in 1975, were sown in the disturbances of 1958, which had graphically illustrated the depth of the fault lines in Lebanese society. Superficially, Lebanon continued on a path of comparative political freedom and vigorous commercial activity based on the same principles that had guided its development in the immediate post-war years: power sharing between the main religious communities, the deliberate restriction of state control and, as Yapp puts it, 'a tacit concern to set on one side the unresolved conflict about the nature of Lebanon – how much was it Arab and how much distinctively Lebanese'.[13]

Much has been written about the causes of Lebanon's tragic and bloody civil war. Was it mostly an internal phenomenon, another challenge to Maronite dominance by other factions within the Lebanese body politic? Or was it caused primarily by external factors brought about by the presence of Palestinians on Lebanese soil, which sucked Lebanon into the wider Arab–Israeli conflict? Most commentators agree that the fifteen-year confrontation was ignited by the clashes in April 1975 between Christian Phalangist forces and Palestinian fighters in which the mainly Muslim and pan-Arab Lebanese National Movement's supporters weighed in on the side of the Palestinians. This led remorselessly to a general free-for-all, with the collapse of the government, the disintegration of the army and widespread conflict, which had the character of a monolithically (if only superficially accurate) Christian versus Muslim confrontation.

There is no doubt that the presence of the Palestinians in the Lebanon since the 1948 war had been perceived internally as largely disruptive to the stability of the country. The refugee population swelled to some 400,000 and became thoroughly politicized, especially following the arrival in 1971 of the PLO leadership and a large number of fighters after their expulsion from Jordan. But even before that the Lebanese government had been drawn into a confrontation with Israel that it had wished to avoid, as it had been unable to prevent Palestinian commandos using southern Lebanon as a launch pad for raids into Israel. Indeed, as early as 1969 the Lebanese government had lost control of much of the south of the country to the Palestinian guerrillas. By this time the area was known as 'Fatah Land', where the Palestinians, with the support of much of the Arab world, had set up virtually a state within a state (just as they had tried to do in Jordan). All this invited Israeli retaliation as much against Lebanese as Palestinian targets in a vain attempt to pressurize the Lebanese into controlling the guerrillas' activities, a tactic the Israelis were still using up to the time of their withdrawal from Lebanon twenty-two years later.

The Palestinian dimension, and by extension the dynamics of the Arab–Israel dispute, cast a long shadow within Lebanon and became a major ingredient in exacerbating and prolonging internal conflict, feeding on the inherent instability of Lebanese society with its sectarian fault lines and dysfunctional government. A 'normal' and more 'natural' state could have coped with the Palestinian presence and its external ramifications, but the Lebanese regime, a major section of whose leadership was emotionally divorced from the region and its problems and probably yearned for a return to the cocooned security of a Maronite-dominated 'Little Lebanon', had no answer to forces unleashed by years of sectarian-based misrule and rampant Arab nationalism. Under pressure the Sunni–Maronite consensual partnership fell apart. Indeed, it fell at the first fence, fatally split on the issue of how to deal with the Palestinians, with the Christians looking for a military solution which they could not convince any significant Sunni leader to endorse. This was perhaps unsurprising, given the difficulty of deploying an army with mostly Christian officers and a mainly Muslim rank and file against a movement enjoying considerable popular Muslim support inside and outside the country. All this against the background of probable Syrian military intervention on behalf of Palestinian and local radical pan-Arab and Muslim factions. Predictably, the Lebanese government found itself paralysed by indecision and inhibited by gloomy forebodings of likely obstacles, most of which turned out to be self-fulfilling prophecies as the country disintegrated.

The main features of the civil war make horrific reading.[14] From 1975 onwards, with a few periods of remission and respite, Lebanon was engulfed in an expanding maelstrom of bloodletting and destruction. Inexorably, outside powers – the Syrians, the Israelis, Iran, the West and the UN – were sucked into a quagmire of Lebanese inter-factional turmoil compounded by external intervention. Lebanon became a major battleground within the wider issue of Arab–Israel confrontation. Syria, either through direct military involvement with stationing of troops in the country or via proxy groups such as the Shi'a Amal and various Palestinian militias, pursued its quarrel with Israel. At the same time the presence of several thousand Syrian regular soldiers increasingly limited the freedom of action of the Lebanese government itself.

The Israelis – via a policy of aggressive retaliation against Palestinian attacks, then partial occupation and eventually, in 1982, full invasion – sought to destroy or neutralize the Palestinians and their radical Arab supporters in southern Lebanon. They were also concerned to neutralize the threat presented by the stationing of Syrian missile batteries and other heavy weapons in the country. This was part of a broader strategy of carrying the fight to their Arab opponents, which included the formal annexation of the Golan Heights, captured from Syria in the 1967 war. With the support of their Christian Phalangist allies, they besieged and bombarded Beirut and forced 140,000 Palestinian refugees to flee from southern Lebanon for the security of the Syrian-controlled Beqaa Valley. One of the most horrific incidents of this time was the massacre in 1982 of about 2,000 non-combatant Palestinians, including women and children, in the refugee camps of Shatila and Sabra by Phalangist militia, unrestrained by their Israeli allies, who had surrounded the camps as part of an anti-'terrorist' search-and-destroy operation.

Eventually, under international pressure, the Israelis partially withdrew from the country, although they maintained their occupation south of the Litani River, which they also tried to protect with their local surrogates – most notably the South Lebanon Army (SLA), a Christian militia which they had trained and armed. (The Israelis were not averse to arming other groups, irrespective of confessional allegiance, as local circumstances permitted, but sometimes they found their arms subsequently used against them.) The SLA were then bogged down in a fierce local war with Druze fighters, which led to southern Lebanon being effectively partitioned between the warring factions. The Palestinians, battered by the Israelis, were themselves factionally divided, and the struggle for control led to more heavy fighting and to the expulsion of the PLO leader Yasser Arafat and 4,000 fighters from Lebanon. Attempts to re-establish a PLO presence in Lebanon were strongly opposed by the Syrians, who used their local allies in Amal against Palestinian supporters of Arafat, adding yet another dimension to the internecine conflict.

With constant inter-factional battling – Christians against Muslims, Sunnis versus Shi'as – the emergence of such ruthless organizations as Islamic Jihad, and the excesses of bloodthirsty militia from all quarters, Lebanon became synonymous with mindless violence, senseless sectarian killing and widespread destruction. The kidnapping of a number of Westerners by radical Islamic groups reinforced the negative image the civil war created in the world media and international opinion. The city and countryside were cantonized. At the height of the civil war Lebanon split into seven separate areas, each under the local control of one of the militias. In Beirut the 'Green Line' divided the Christians from the Muslims. On both sides of it the capital lay in ruins. The Lebanese army had long ceased to function; commerce was at a standstill; the banking community had fled; and inward investment had dried up. Ceasefires and fine-tuning the confessional balance within the government proved to be short-term and ineffectual palliatives. One episode of multinational military intervention in 1983 by a 6,000-strong US/French/Italian force to try to stabilize the situation following the Israeli withdrawal ended in failure, with heavy American and French casualties. This multinational deployment was perceived by the radical Muslim groups to be one-sided in its support for the Christian-led government. After this bloody rebuff for international peacekeeping it seemed to many in the international community that Lebanon was terminally dysfunctional and probably beyond help.

But by late 1990 the Ta'if peace agreement had led to the end of the internal conflict after the failure of a Pax Syriana to restore order, following fierce fighting between Amal and the Iranian-influenced and -financed Hizballah. Exhaustion and successful Arab mediation were the major factors. Indeed, this was a notable achievement for persistent and imaginative Arab diplomacy, in striking contrast to previous and subsequent attempts to find 'Arab solutions' to other conflicts (the Gulf crisis of 1990 to 1991 was to be a case in point). The contentious continued presence of Syrian forces in Lebanon was taken out of the hands of the Lebanese politicians during these negotiations and put to one side, awaiting agreement between the two governments – but not before several hundred more people had been killed in fighting between the rump of the Lebanese army, led by a Christian general, and Syrian forces stationed in the country. Attempts to replace the Syrians with a multinational Arab force failed because of Syrian opposition. Inter-sectarian face was saved via a Charter of National Conciliation, part of which involved the enlargement of the National Assembly, with seats, for the first time, equally divided between Christians and Muslims. Implementation of the charter proved troublesome and met with principally Christian opposition to what they saw as the further erosion of their privileged positions, but at last the civil war was effectively at an end.

The last decade of the twentieth century was an era of some hope for Lebanon, if not one of unbounded optimism. Stability of a sort was restored and large-scale reconstruction of central Beirut began. By 1992 all the Western hostages had been released, an indication of a return to something like normality in the domestic political scene. The Lebanese–Syrian security treaty of 1991 formalized the position of Syrian troops in Lebanon, and Damascus continued to call important shots in the formulation of Lebanese policy. Lebanon thus enjoyed the security benefits of a Pax Syriana but at the expense of significant restrictions on its room for manoeuvre. At the start of the new millennium, the success of Hizballah in forcing an Israeli total withdrawal from its self-styled 'security zone', and the rout of its proxy South Lebanon Army, brought temporary peace to the south. And until the Israel assault of 2006 (described below), Lebanon was largely freed from the fear of massive Israeli retaliation for attacks launched by Hizballah, on the pattern of the 1996 Israeli assault on Kana. So for all too short a period there was a prospect of government control being reasserted in an area which had for so long been ruled by militias. The death of President Assad and his son's succession to the Syrian presidency also brought hope of a less one-sided relationship with Damascus. Ordinary Lebanese Muslims, as well as Christians, were increasingly resenting the obtrusive heavy hand of their neighbour, although some of the more radical elements still saw the Syrians as their protectors of last resort. While in the first few years of the new millennium there was no significant decrease in Syrian involvement in Lebanon – some troops were simply redeployed out of the capital and into rural bases – there was a feeling that as the country recovered some of its past economic and political stability it might be able to find a productive *modus vivendi* with its powerful neighbour.

Unfortunately, this optimism was shattered by the assassination of the former Prime Minister Rafik Hariri in February 2005. Hariri had resigned the premiership in October 2004, almost certainly (although this was not publicly stated) because of differences with Lebanese President Lahoud over the extent of Syrian influence. This had become major issue in domestic politics since the beginning of the century, with the USA urging the Lebanese to form a new government that was truly representative of the people, composed of strong individuals who had credibility and integrity (in other words, one which would stand up to Damascus). This idea backfired, though, as Hariri's replacement as Prime Minister, Omar Karami, a strong supporter of Damascus, chose a strongly pro-Syrian cabinet, and in November 2004 President Lahoud publicly proclaimed a policy of maintaining close relations with Syria as one of the cornerstones of Lebanese foreign policy. This led to much activity by opposition, anti-Syrian forces, with popular demonstrations both for and against the Syrian connection. In December 2004 a widely based coalition formed the first united platform since the end of the civil war. They called for the resignation of Karami and demanded that Syrian troops redeploy to the border and cease meddling in Lebanese internal affairs. Previously, in September, the international community had once again got involved, with the UN Security Council adopting a US/France-sponsored resolution (No. 1559) calling for the withdrawal of Syrian forces, strict respect for Lebanon's territorial integrity, unity, political independence and free and fair elections without political interference.

Hariri and his supporters were high-profile members of the opposition coalition. His assassination by a car bomb was inevitably blamed on Syria or pro-Syrian Lebanese agents. Several hundred thousand people attended his funeral and popular pressure for a Syrian troop withdrawal grew. However, this was matched by counter-demonstrations urging them to stay. Prime Minister Karami eventually bowed to opposition pressure and suddenly resigned; and, despite mainly Shi'a, Hizballah-backed massive pro-Syrian demonstrations, President Al Assad announced a full Syrian military withdrawal, which was completed in May 2005. UN observers were not able to determine whether Syria had also dismantled its intelligence apparatus within the Lebanon. Subsequently, December 2005, a UN Commission of Inquiry into Hariri's assassination reported that Syrian and Lebanese security and intelligence agencies had been involved in the killing and criticized the Syrian government's slowness in cooperating with the inquiry team. In Lebanon itself a number of further assassinations and attacks were committed, mostly on anti-Syrian personalities (notably Pierre Gemayel, a prominent Christian politician). At mostly US and French instigation, the UN Security Council continued to involve itself in the Syrian–Lebanese question, seeking a normalization of relations leading to recognition by Syria of Lebanon's status as a sovereign, independent state. This would include, for example, the establishment of Syrian and Lebanese embassies in each other's capitals.

The most recent major disaster for a fragile Lebanon was the July 2006 Israeli offensive against Lebanese targets in retaliation for a Hizballah raid into Israel which killed a number of soldiers and kidnapped two. As usual, the Israelis held the Lebanese government responsible for the activities of an organization launching attacks from its territory. The southern border had continued to be tense ever since the Israeli withdrawal from Lebanon, and over the years there had been a number of incidents, including rocket and artillery exchanges. But nobody expected the scale of the July campaign by the Israeli airforce against Lebanon's infrastructure (including the airport, power stations and bridges) and civilian areas in south Beirut and southern Lebanon (Tyre and Sidon especially), where Hizballah had its main strongholds. By the end of the month about 1,000 Lebanese civilians had died and nearly a million were displaced. There were significant Israeli civilian casualties, too, inflicted by Hizballah's long-range rockets. Two thousand three hundred were fired, some well into Israel, in just two weeks, making this the most sustained assault on its territory since the 1948 war. After a series of ground clashes, it was clear that the Israelis would not be able to eliminate their opponents in the difficult terrain of southern Lebanon; nor could they silence the rockets. With neither side able to secure a decisive advantage, the fighting ceased in early August and the UN Security Council authorized the establishment of a French-led international peacekeeping force, although there remains some uncertainty about its exact mandate, which needs to be agreed between the Israeli and Lebanese governments. Lebanon is still living with this latest trauma. Despite much talk of reforms, the Lebanese political system is still fundamentally sectarian. Rule by triumvirate reflects a discredited and outmoded formula based on a deliberately fudged assessment of the country's demographic realities. Any new census would undoubtedly show the extent of the numerical superiority of non-Christians. It still endorses and systematizes sectarian division. Cracks are papered over but the basic fault lines remain. Elections, because of gerrymandering and manipulation, are an inaccurate test of public opinion, and not just because of the inflexibility imposed by sectarian straitjackets. The old familiar power-brokers continue to flex their financial muscles, just as they did in the elections of August/September 2000, demonstrating the ability of big business to purchase electoral support. And even if the institutions are made genuinely sound, as Luciani and Salamé have pointed out, 'it must be recognised that the formal existence of democratic institutions in no way guarantees per se that a segmented society will be able to achieve political unity and evolve towards integration'.[15] The fundamental question of whether Lebanon is a legitimate Arab state with a regional role or something different has yet to be settled to the satisfaction of many of its people, especially the Christian minority. The wounds of the savage civil war remain unhealed for many, and by 2007 there were profound fears that a new one might erupt.

The Palestinian refugees are still there, dispossessed, wretchedly poor and unwanted.[16] There has never been an attempt to integrate them into Lebanese society, nor does it seem likely that there will be a serious effort to do so. Their future largely depends on events beyond Lebanese control and the progress of the Middle East peace process. Recent developments can hardly be encouraging. How they and their supporters behave will continue to influence the Israeli attitude to Lebanon. Another connected issue is the future of Hizballah and Amal. Will they be content to act purely as Lebanese political parties? Hizballah, in particular, is riding a tide of popular support due to its successes against the Israelis in the war of 2006. And no wonder: we have seen the effectiveness of its militia. Prolonged stalemate or events elsewhere in the region might induce them to return to a more provocative anti-Israeli policy, using southern Lebanon as their launch pad with or without the consent of the Lebanese authorities.

The long-term Lebanon–Syria relationship is also a hostage to the fortunes of peacemaking. The Syrians are unlikely to have surrendered their ambitions to be a major power-broker in Lebanon and to trust the country to manage its affairs in a way that is not detrimental to Syrian interests: most importantly to the stability of the Western Levant. This is especially so following the removal of Saddam's regime because Washington has now turned its sights on Damascus and branded Syria a 'sponsor of terrorism'. And while Syria is not officially within the 'axis of evil', the Bush administration has remained stubbornly reluctant either to elicit Damascus's help to extricate itself from the Iraqi morass or to address it as an important player in the Middle East peace process. Syria's alleged continued support for Hizballah remains a bone of contention, just as Iran's does. Any major Iranian/US confrontation, which is ever more possible as a result of Iran's nuclear ambitions, could spill over into further attempts by surrogate parties once again to stir the Lebanese pot. By the spring of 2007 Hizballah and the rest of the predominantly (but not exclusively) Shi'a groups looking to over-throw Prime Minister Fouad Siniora's Western-leaning coalition government had become embroiled in a further round of sectarian tension, with a risk of all-out clashes reigniting civil war. In these circumstances even the very generous sums of aid and massive debt relief pledged by the donor community in January 2007 were no guarantee that war would not break out again in Lebanon.

6 Ethnic conflict

The forgotten Kurds

Under the banner of Arab nationalism and other unitary ideologies, ethnic-based claims to political and other rights in the Middle East have been suppressed. As a result, as the Kurdish question illustrates, ethnic conflict is a very real issue in the Modern world. The arbitrary nature of state creation following the collapse of the Ottoman Empire and the emergence of regimes striving to consolidate and maintain their authority within highly artificial borders has forced issues of ethnic identity underground without eradicating them. The responses by states to the pressures imposed by a growing ethnic and national consciousness among the Kurdish people has brought about sustained conflict within three countries in the region.

The Kurds, who number at least twenty-six million,[1] are, after the Arabs, the largest ethnic group in the Near and Middle East. About 90 per cent of the total Kurdish population worldwide live within the boundaries of one Arab country (Iraq) and two non-Arab states (Turkey and Iran). The remainder are found in Syria (about one million), the former Soviet Union (half a million), with 700,000 living in a wider diaspora, many within the European Union. Despite their numbers, the Kurds have consistently been denied the right to statehood and have been a persecuted minority in the region.[2] Kurdish demands for self-determination have for nearly a century led to conflict, particularly in Iraq, Iran and Turkey. The conflict has been both horizontal and vertical – within the Kurdish communities and between the Kurds and the state. Additionally, individual states have exploited Kurdish ambitions in order to promote tension or conflict with their neighbours. With little hope of establishing statehood or achieving secession from any of the states within the region, they have encountered armed repression in response to their attempts to obtain formal recognition of their claims for political and civil rights. The states' response to such demands, particularly in Turkey and Iraq, has been policies of enforced population transfer at one end of the scale of state-organized oppression to ethnic cleansing and wholesale massacre at the other. In this chapter we will examine why this is

Map D – Distribution of the Kurds across Turkey, Syria, Iran and Iraq so and look at the prospects for the Kurds in the opening decades of the third millennium.

The Kurds are descendants of Indo-European tribes (including Turkic, Armenian and Assyrian) who settled in the Zagros Mountains at various intervals, most numerously during the second millennium BC. This mountain range, which is still the heartland of their main population concentration, is where Iran, Iraq and Turkey meet. The region is not exclusively Kurdish, but Kurds form a significant majority in most of it. The name 'Kurdistan' was applied to this area as early as the thirteenth century AD. Later, in the sixteenth century, after the Kurds, via a number of tribal migrations, had moved north and west on to the Anatolian plateau, 'Kurdistan' became a common way of denoting a system of Kurdish chiefdoms or minor principalities. It appeared on a few maps, its boundaries were imprecise, but, as McDowell has pointed out, it is more than a geographical term as it also refers to a human culture that exists in the region: 'To this extent Kurdistan is a social and political concept.'³

Divisions among the Kurds themselves have, over the past century, frustrated attempts to achieve unity or indeed work towards any form of effective political mobilization. They lack a single systematized language, either spoken or written. Some dialects are incomprehensible to other Kurds, although many Kurds can understand one of the two major dialects. Nor are Kurds religiously homogeneous: the great majority are Sunnis but at least three million living in Anatolian Kurdistan are Alevis, an unorthodox form of Shi'ism; some other Kurds in Iran are also Shi'a. The Kurdish 'nation' also includes smaller sects, such as the Yazidis, and Christian minorities like the Assyrians and Syrian Orthodox. In some countries Kurds appear to suffer from something of an identity crisis.⁴ Tribal differences, the remoteness of many of their communities and the ambitions and influence of the traditional local leaders (the *aghas*) have also been obstacles to Kurdish unity.

The first stirrings of Kurdish nationalism, in a modern sense, probably began in the early twentieth century at the time of the revolution in Constantinople in 1908 led by the Young Turks. Their ideals of constitutional reform and representative government struck a chord with educated people within the Ottoman Empire, the Kurds being no exception. But Kurdish nationalists in their newly formed urban clubs and societies were not united and failed to attract the support of the rurally based *aghas*, who saw such movements as a threat to their position as the traditional community leaders. At any rate the whole process was undermined by the Ottoman declaration of war on the Allies in October 1914. In the ensuing hostilities the Kurds were used by the Ottomans to play an ignoble part through their involvement in comprehensive ethnic cleansing, amounting to genocide, of Armenians in Anatolia.

The defeat of the Ottomans by the Allies in 1918 ushered a new order into the region by the victorious European colonial powers. The old empire was dismembered and artificial new states within frontiers that took little account of pre-existing tribal and ethnic boundaries were created in the former Arab regions of the empire at the instigation of the British and French. Their ambitions were only partly tempered by the American President Woodrow Wilson, with his idealistic and unrealistic Fourteen Point Programme for World Peace. Point twelve affirmed that non-Turkish minorities of the former Ottoman Empire should be 'assured of an absolute unmolested opportunity of autonomous development'. This came too late to help the massacred Armenians but presented the Kurds with a brief and transient possibility of embryonic statehood.

However, it was not to be. This ethnic group was not at a stage of development that would equip it to rise to the challenge of post-war nationalism and seize the fleeting opportunity of benefiting from the precipitous creation of nation-states. In fact, the benefits of change seemed unclear to most Kurds. National consciousness hardly existed outside the confines of urban intellectual circles. Traditional tribal loyalties, rather than national ambitions, influenced village or pastoral Kurds in their mountain retreats. Here the *aghas* held sway, wary of any attempt by urban 'progressives' to undermine their positions, suspicious of neighbouring tribal leaders and unwilling to contemplate making common cause with old rivals for the nebulous and uncertain goal of a Kurdish ethnic entity. The status quo and its familiar security probably appealed to such conservative people who would anyhow feel remote and insulated from the dramatic changes taking place in the outside world.

For these reasons the provisions of the Treaty of Sèvres in August 1920 proved historically inopportune to the Kurdish people. At a later stage they would surely have welcomed the autonomy it envisaged for the predominantly Kurdish areas of Turkey and British-controlled Mosul (now in Iraq), with a view to eventual full independence. Many Kurds now regard the treaty as a sadly missed opportunity, but even if there had been an effective nationalistic Kurdish leadership at that time to pursue statehood, such an effort would almost certainly have been nullified by the revolt of the Turkish revolutionary leader Kemal Atatürk. In the name of a new unified Turkish state he repudiated the Ottoman government's signature of the Treaty of Sèvres. Most Kurdish leaders, influenced by religious rather than nationalistic sentiments, willingly supported Atatürk's revolt, which they saw as protecting their Muslim identity against threats from the Greek Christian forces that had invaded Turkey from the west and the Armenians (and Soviets) from the east.[5]

The Treaty of Lausanne in July 1923 tidied up issues left unfinished by the failure to implement Sèvres. Turkey's sovereignty over territory seized by Atatürk – including all of Anatolia – was accepted and Britain's suggestion that Turkey should recognize the Kurds as a 'national minority' was rejected. Although apparently Atatürk considered autonomy for the Kurds that same year,[6] it was never mentioned or discussed publicly. At any rate nothing came of it, and thus the ground was prepared for confrontation between the Turkish government and Kurdish nationalists.

We shall look further at the Kurds and the growth of Kurdish nationalism in modern Turkey later in this chapter, but first we will briefly examine their experiences in the other two countries where they comprise a significant minority: Iran and Iraq.

Iran: elusive independence

Over six million Kurds make up about 10 per cent of the population of Iran, which has several other significant ethnic minorities: Arab, Turkic and Baluchi. Kurds probably have more affinity culturally and linguistically with Iranians than with either Arabs or Turks. Nevertheless, their relationship with the government in Tehran has been an unhappy one, even though they have not suffered the same degree of consistent oppression and brutality as has been their experience in Turkey. Iranian Kurds have, generally speaking, been allowed to propagate their culture and speak their language, but any attempt to advocate separatism has been dealt with severely.

Reza Shah, who came to power in Iran after the First World War, was the first of the 'Persian' monarchs for many years to attempt a policy of firm centralization. His immediate predecessors had exercised varying degrees of control over their territory, but as with the Ottoman Empire, the hand of governmental authority often lay very lightly on the more remote regions. In these circumstances the Kurdish tribal chieftains enjoyed considerable local autonomy, often acting on behalf of the central government as the regional authority. Reza Shah changed all that as he sought to subjugate the tribes, including forcibly resettling nomads, which he managed to do by the 1930s. Tribal chiefs in most cases made the transition to landowners – stripped of civic position but retaining influence with their traditional tribal followers.

At the end of the Second World War about a third of Iran's Kurds experienced a fleeting moment of independence. Britain had occupied western Iran in 1941 to counter Reza Shah's perceived pro-German tendencies. At the same time the Soviet Union also intervened in an area of strategic interest to it. With the USSR's prompting, the Kurds living in north-west Iran, under the nationalist leadership of the Kurdistan Democratic Party of Iran (KDPI), declared an independent republic, as, separately, did the Azerbaijanis within the same region. The Kurdish entity called itself the

Republic of Mahabad. Due to its small size, it failed to attract many Kurds from other areas, either to join with it or to offer any support against government forces that re-established control following the Soviet withdrawal. Nor was there any support from Moscow, who dumped the Kurds, having cynically used them as a lever with the Iranian government. As with the Turkish Kurds at the time of Sèvres, the majority of the Iranian Kurdish tribal community was not motivated by nationalism, and the infant republic lacked enough popular inter-tribal and international backing to secure its survival. Indeed, some of the government troops who reoccupied the abortive republic were themselves Kurds from elsewhere in Iran, thus demonstrating the narrow appeal of Kurdish nationalism at that time.

The Kurdish experience under the last Shah of Iran and the successor regime of the Islamic republic continued to be unhappy. A small number of militant nationalists went underground following the dismantling of their republic and remained so for most of the Shah's reign. The majority of Kurdish areas stayed under martial law as the government was determined to suppress any movement that might threaten the unity and cohesion of the state. The new factor was growing Iraq–Iran inter-state confrontation and conflict (as described in Chapter 7). In the late 1960s, having taken refuge in Iraq, KDPI activists launched armed resistance against their government from Iraqi territory. Ironically, their activities were largely frustrated by Iraqi Kurds led by Mustafa Barzani, at the behest of the Tehran regime, which was at that time actively supporting an Iraqi Kurdish rebellion against Baghdad. This anti-KDPI activity by Barzani was doubly ironic as he and 3,000 of his Iraqi Kurdish followers had fought for the short-lived Mahabad Republic *against* the Shah barely twenty years previously! This was a striking example of something that was continually to bedevil pan-Kurdish ambitions: the inability of the separate Kurdish leaderships in Iraq and Iran to agree on a common cross-frontier policy. For both leaderships the overriding imperative was to seek autonomy within the state structure rather than to seek common cause with their tribal neighbours. As the Shah's land reforms had destroyed the economic power of the *agha* large landowners, 'Kurdistan' itself remained underdeveloped and impoverished in comparison with the rest of Iran, at the very periphery of the Shah's economic revolution.

Another opportunity for achieving a measure of autonomy for Kurds in Iran was not seized in the early, chaotic days of the Islamic republic. A movement led by some of the tribal chiefs to break away from state control was not supported by the KDPI, which, as a sophisticated urban party, opposed tribalism and regarded the rural Kurds as reactionaries. Moreover, a significant Shi'a minority among the Kurds supported the Ayatollah Khomeini's regime as being a Shi'a revolution and therefore objected to the policies of separatism espoused by the majority Sunni Kurds. In addition, the new regime strongly opposed any move towards autonomy by the ethnic minorities for fear of national disintegration at a time of great upheaval. Some Kurds living near the Iraqi border took advantage of the 1980s war with Iraq to achieve very short-lived local independence following Iraqi successes in the land war. But after the ceasefire the central government was quickly able to restore its authority throughout the Kurdish areas.

Since then the position of Iranian Kurds has greatly improved in terms of enjoying civil rights. They are, for instance, fairly represented in the Islamic republic's largely democratic institutions. But any dream of a separate, politically autonomous entity seems as remote as ever. Furthermore, the desire for secession seems relatively weak among Iranian Kurds. Such radicals as there are comprise the PJAK (or Kurdish Free Life Party), a close ally of the Turkish PKK, but they have been the target of recent combined military operations by Iranian and Turkish government forces. Jon Lee Anderson alleges that there has been covert US support for this group, and suggests that in the event of confrontation between the USA and the Islamic republic over nuclear issues, the 'Kurdish card' is one that Washington might play.[7] Moreover should the Iraqi Kurds ever achieve their own state, this could have a knock-on effect in Iran and stimulate pro-independence groups within it.

Iraq: brutality and ethnic cleansing

Modern Iraq was a British creation. Its establishment followed the capture of Mesopotamia from the Ottoman Turks in 1918. In determining the extent of the territory of the new state the British were uncertain what to do with the mostly mountainous Kurdistani regions lying to the north and east, but also including the major, ethnically mixed town of Kirkuk, which lay within a Kurdish hinterland. Post-war the immediate goal of the British was, at minimum cost and involvement, a desire to pacify the population living in the mountains of Kurdistan so as to remove the threat that their inhabitants posed to the strategically vital Mesopotamian plain. As in Turkey and Iran, the Kurds were divided and unable to agree upon a common strategy. Some looked for incorporation into the new Iraq, soon to be ruled by the British-appointed Hashemite King Feisal. Others, led by Sheikh Mahmud Barzinji, strove for some kind of independent entity free of foreign control, although they were initially happy to accept British protection. There were many who preferred to unite with those Kurds now in Turkey with whom they had close cultural and linguistic ties. And probably a majority of the *aghas* would have been content to further their local ambitions under the kind of *de facto* autonomy their ancestors had enjoyed in the old Ottoman Empire.

In the end the British yielded to pressure from Turkey and their client king in Baghdad. The Turks resisted any autonomous arrangement for Iraqi Kurds, which they feared would have dangerous implications for the status of 'their' Kurdish community, whose separate ethnic and cultural identity they were seeking to deny. King Feisal, meanwhile, needed to incorporate the Kurds of southern Kurdistan into his kingdom so as to ensure a Sunni majority in what otherwise would be a largely Shi'a state. From the beginning he had relied upon the support of the Sunnis, who made up the majority of people in central Iraq, including the major landowners around Baghdad. In return, he used Sunnis to fill senior positions in his administration and in the military. By contrast, southern Iraq was overwhelmingly Shi'a and potentially hostile to a Sunni-led regime. Control of all the Kurdish areas was also important to the economic viability of this new country, with the prospect of the Kirkuk region producing large amounts of oil. Accordingly, the British arranged for the former Ottoman province of Mosul to became part of Iraq. Subsequently, the Anglo-Iraqi treaty of 1930 conferred full independence on the kingdom and omitted any of the specific safeguards related to the preservation of a minimal Kurdish separate identity as a 'recognized minority' in their areas as the British had previously undertaken in negotiations with the League of Nations.[8]

Newly independent Iraq never achieved a good working relationship with its Kurdish community. Baghdad's aggressive and insensitive handling of what were primarily inter-tribal disorders provoked the growth of a more nationalist form of opposition to the regime by Kurds led by Mullah Mustafa Barzani. His nationalist fervour was also fired by the creation of the short-lived Republic of Mahabad in neighbouring Iran, which he had (vainly) helped to defend. But, as elsewhere, the Kurdish leaders could not agree on a common strategy. Many of the *aghas* preferred to cooperate with the regime rather than confront it, and Barzani split his own party by making a deal with the government in 1964, condemned as a sell-out by his main critic, Jalal Talabani. This split remained the basis for the continuing bitter rivalry between the two principal Kurdish political parties, the Barzani-led Kurdish Democratic Party (KDP) and the Talabani-controlled Patriotic Union of Kurdistan (PUK). As happened in Iran, the Iraqi Kurdish leadership exploited Iraq–Iran hostility in an attempt to further its aims, cooperating actively with Tehran during periods of conflict between the two regimes.

After Saddam Hussein came to power in Baghdad the Kurds of Iraq paid a dreadful price for their opposition to his regime, and especially for their opportunist alliances with the Iranians. Armed conflict with the regime in 1974–5 ended in defeat for Barzani's *peshmergas*[9] after Saddam had struck a deal with Iran over the Shatt al-Arab (see Chapter 7). With Iranian support now withdrawn, Barzani was powerless to prevent 500 Kurdish villages being razed and 600,000 villagers forcibly resettled by the Baghdad regime. This 'pacification' was followed by an offer of limited autonomy, rejected by the Kurdish leadership as being too restrictive. But the Iraqi leader's real savagery was reserved for the closing stages of his war against Iran in 1988, when he took his revenge for the Kurdish military alliance with his enemies. The well-documented chemical attack on Halabja in 1988 and similar assaults during the 'Anfal' operation may have cost as many as 200,000 Kurdish lives, with whole areas being 'cleansed'. Thus Saddam resorted to ethnic cleansing well before this phenomenon, as practised by other ruthless leaders, became all too familiar in the Balkans.[10] Following his defeat in Desert Storm, and with his forces routed in Kuwait, Saddam faced a spontaneous Kurdish revolt in the north, while the Shi'a rose in the south (see Chapter 8). This he partially suppressed with great difficulty, but continued Iraqi attacks on the Kurds led three Western members of the Allied coalition – the USA, Britain and France – to impose a safe haven in northern Iraq (north of the Thirty-sixth Parallel). This enclave, protected by allied air power – including an air-exclusion zone – and with some UN personnel on the ground, was still in existence at the start of the new millennium. Thus the Iraqi Kurdish problem was 'internationalized', which allowed a considerable number of Kurds to enjoy a large measure of *de facto* autonomy. They even had their own National Assembly. But, unfortunately, the two main parties, who share most of the Assembly seats, have not entirely abandoned old rivalries, and have intermittently engaged in fierce internecine conflict.

In the late 1990s the two main parties, partly due to US mediation, started to work more closely together, and this greater unity of purpose served the Kurds well when coalition forces invaded Iraq in March 2003. It was mainly Kurdish fighters (with US air support) who were instrumental in capturing both Kirkuk and Mosul in April. Under US pressure the Kurdish troops subsequently withdrew into their *de facto* autonomous areas. This followed threats from Turkey to intervene if the Kurds were permitted to hold on to these towns and the nearby oilfields.

Since the overthrow of Saddam's regime the Kurds are perhaps the only section of the Iraqi people who have benefited from the establishment of the 'new' Iraq. They are largely autonomous, have generally escaped the breakdown of law and order that has blighted the rest of the country, and their wide measure of self-governance has even been enshrined in the new Iraqi constitution. However, the Turkish government remains unhappy about increased Kurdish autonomy, now represented by the Kurdish Regional Government (KRG), and about the possibility that a viable, independent entity might emerge out of the chaos of a disintegrating Iraq. In such a

Kurdish entity the likelihood is that the Kurds would have control over Kirkuk and its oilfields. Elements of the radical Turkish-Kurd pro-independence party the PKK have bases within Iraqi Kurdistan, and it is probably only US influence which has prevented attacks on them by the Turkish military. Nevertheless, in November 2006 the Turkish Foreign Minister Abdullah Gül warned the KRG of dire consequences of further moves towards greater self-determination, insisting that the Kurds must abandon their designs on Kirkuk and stop sheltering PKK guerrillas.[11] He also said the Kurds could not rely on America's continued presence in the area, and they 'should not forget that Turkey will remain in the region for ever'.[12]

The Kurds in Turkey: the almost invisible people

As in Iraq, the story of the Kurds in Turkey is one of conflict and oppression. But in Iraq, even in Saddam Hussein's time, there were offers of autonomy and official recognition of a separate Kurdish identity (albeit grudging and tactical). By contrast, in Turkey as recently as 1987 a senior Turkish minister could ask, 'Is there such a thing as a Kurd?'[13] And that is in spite of the fact that the thirteen million or so Kurds in Turkey form over 20 per cent of the population. Kemal Atatürk's aggressive policy of Turkish nationalism shut out any hope of Kurdish autonomy or even recognition of a separate non-Turkish cultural identity. His modernizing secularism challenged the ideological basis of Kurdish belief in a Muslim state for which Kurds had fought alongside the Turks against the Greek and Armenian threat. From the beginning of their modern statehood the Turkish authorities were desperate to promote a new, homogenized identity for a new 'Turkish' nation. Hence a policy of ethnic cleansing by denial of any claim by the Kurds for a separate ethnic or political existence. In consequence all public vestiges of Kurdish identity were banned, including schools, associations and publications. Not surprisingly, there were spontaneous Kurdish revolts in 1925 and 1928. These were ruthlessly crushed, with many thousands of noncombatants killed. Subsequently, large-scale deportations from Kurdish areas were enforced in an attempt to assimilate the Kurds into the majority Turkish population. The Kurdish language was made illegal and the Kurds were officially referred to as 'mountain Turks', thus denying their ethnic identity; simultaneously, though, as non-Turks ethnically, they were classified as second-class citizens.[14]

Although such brutal repression kept Kurdish nationalism under control for many years, a powerful revival begin in the 1960s. As in Iraq, repression failed to quell the spirit of the Kurds; rather, it had the opposite effect, encouraging a rise in militant nationalism, as all other paths of self-expression seemed blocked by an obdurate state. Denied their own political parties, the Kurds united with Turkish leftist groups and gained, albeit indirectly, a political presence in the body politic. But it was a surge in radical extremism that was to hold centre stage. Right-wing reaction throughout the 1960s and 1970s led to further massacres and prepared the way for the appearance in 1984 of the previously unknown extremist Partiya Karkari Kurdistan (Kurdistan Workers Party – PKK), under the leadership of Abdullah Ocalan. The PKK's goal has been an independent, Marxist-style Kurdish state entirely divorced from Turkey and incorporating other ethnic Kurds, especially from Syria and Iraq. In the single-minded pursuit of its ambitions an organization quite as ruthless as its Turkish government opponent has evolved. Deploying a skilful guerrilla force, it has also been as savage in dealing with fellow Kurds perceived as supporters of the regime (such as landowners) as with the armed forces of the state. Like the Iraqi Kurdish nationalists, it has gone outside the state in search of support and refuge. Its ties with Syria have been close, and alleged Syrian support for the PKK has brought Turkey and Syria close to armed conflict.

After a decade of bloody conflict, with the Turkish state implementing measures of population transfer not far removed from ethnic cleansing, there was one crucial success for the government. The capture and trial in 1999 of the charismatic Abdullah Ocalan blunted the armed struggle, as the organization agreed a ceasefire, which was declared publicly by Ocalan himself from the dock. But, as we discuss below, Turkish Kurds were encouraged by the success of their kinsmen in neighbouring Iraq as the Saddam regime crumbled in April 2003.

One positive development in the last decade has been a softening of the attitude of inflexible non-recognition of a specifically 'Kurdish' issue by the Turkish government. Under pressure from the obvious popular support for the aims (if not the methods) of the PKK, senior Turkish figures have been more willing than hitherto to consider a political solution, at least as far as recognizing, somewhat tentatively, a separate Kurdish culture. Kurdish may now be used in many circumstances, including in publications – but still not for formal education or broadcasting. However, the Turkish constitution still does not permit a Kurd to be called anything other than a Turk, and persecution and harassment continues. The Kurds are effectively prevented (by administrative devices) from organizing political activities and the Kurdish community at large has remained highly politicized and anti-government. The Kurdish areas are underdeveloped, much poorer than the rest of the country, with high rates of unemployment. They are seemingly deliberately neglected, if not actively oppressed, by a central government which is doing nothing to diminish popular support for an independent Kurdish state as demanded by the PKK. Moreover, thanks to the activities of the PKK, strong anti-Kurdish sentiments run high among ordinary Turks:

the capture of Ocalan was hailed as a major victory and calls for his execution were widespread. These were rejected, but he remains in prison.

In 2003 the ceasefire Ocalan had proclaimed from the dock was abandoned as the movement hoped to take advantage of instability in northern Iraq to increase its influence. The scale of operations has been much less than before 1999, but the use of northern Iraq as a safe haven by up to 5,000 PKK militants has soured Turkish, Iraqi and US relations, as well as those with the Kurdish Regional Government in Iraqi Kurdistan. Attacks on the PKK within Iraq by the Turkish army remain a real possibility.

Nevertheless, a significant number of Turks have called for a political solution. European governments looking at Turkey's candidature to join the European Union may yet be able to moderate the regime's behaviour, making demands for a marked improvement in its human rights record. But these negotiations have dragged on, deadlocked more by the question of northern Cyprus and fears of increased Turkish immigration into the EU than by the difficulties of seeking a better deal for the Kurds. There is a strong sentiment among many senior Turks that the EU is not really interested in accepting Turkey as a fellow member and it may be better for Ankara to cultivate closer ties with Syria and Iran, than to be preached at by the Europeans. One Kurdish journalist in north-east Turkey commented recently, 'The EU talks were only a shield.'[15] If they should break down, one can only assume that Turkish Kurds will be very vulnerable once more.

Conclusion

A meaningful measure of *de jure* autonomy looks an unlikely early prospect for two of the three major Kurdish communities we have discussed, and this bodes ill for the future of the diaspora as a whole. It seems improbable that either the Turkish or the Iranian government will do any more than allow a separate cultural identity to be established and maintained, and even that is a best-case scenario. As explained above, Turkey, as long as it is a candidate for EU membership, is under pressure about its human rights record and will need to adopt a more enlightened attitude towards its ethnic minorities if it is to satisfy its many critics in the Union. European politicians have to take account of the views of a significant number of Kurds, many of them highly militant, forming part of the Kurdish diaspora that is scattered throughout the Union. This is unlikely to lead to autonomy for Kurdistan, but it may eventually result in the establishment of institutions reflecting a separate Kurdish identity. And, of course, a new factor is the major role being played by Iraqi Kurds. Their accomplishment of a wide measure of autonomy within Iraq will encourage their Turkish counterparts to agitate for similar concessions, which could also become central to the negotiations with Brussels. But there remains a danger of all-out conflict. If the PKK becomes too enamoured with the Iraqi model and continues to agitate against Ankara from its base in northern Iraq, military intervention by the Turkish army might become inevitable. And this would be a serious problem for many interested parties, not least the United States, which would have to find a way to balance relations between a NATO ally and a client Iraqi state.

In Iran, the Islamic regime has inherited from its monarchist predecessors the belief that ethnic disintegration would be a very real possibility if the central authority of Tehran were loosened and the Kurds granted autonomy.

There is still a great need for a united and visionary Kurdish leadership to evolve in order to represent effectively the interests of the various Kurdish communities without, it must be hoped, resorting once again to the self-defeating and divisive option of armed struggle. One hopes that a post-Ocalan PKK can pursue a peaceful struggle. By the same token, Turkish and Iranian governments will also need to show understanding of the more reasonable and moderate aspirations of their Kurdish communities. A near-federal solution in Iraq, which the new constitution prescribes, should still offer the prospect of maintaining the territorial integrity of the state and enshrining democratic rights for the Kurds that could, eventually, be emulated elsewhere. The Kurdish Regional Government of Iraq enjoys executive powers in cooperation with a National Assembly whose members are popularly elected. There remains an intent, signalled in 2007 by Masoud Barzani, that the Kurds will not easily surrender their autonomy in a country at war with itself. Clearly the demands of the Kurdish people have not faded with the demise of the Ba'athist regime, and any future Iraqi administration should resist the temptation of trying to turn back the clock.

7 War in the Gulf

Iran and Iraq, 1980–9

It is tempting to portray the Iraq–Iran conflict predominantly in terms of a recent manifestation of a historical enmity between the Arabs and the Persians. Or, and indeed as well, as a religious and political struggle between Sunni and Shi'a. But both descriptions are misleading and incomplete. This was a thoroughly modern inter-state war for thoroughly modern reasons of national interest and regional hegemony in which ideology, ethnic rivalries and religious fervour played their parts but were not central to the main issues.

The war itself was also modern in its nature in terms of armaments and *matériel*: missiles, aerial bombardment and the use of weapons of mass destruction. While neither country had a nuclear capability, they both deployed sufficiently lethal chemical weapons to cause thousands of deaths and casualties. Estimates vary, but probably up to one million people were killed or injured in this decade-long conflict – with 60 per cent of those casualties sustained by Iran. The war also cost US$200 billion directly and another $1,000 billion indirectly, according to most estimates. By the end of the war each side had more than 1.3 million people under arms – half of all Iraqi men and a sixth of all Iranian men of military age.[1] Both sides somewhat stretched the definition of 'military age', using both teenage conscripts and equally immature 'volunteers' as cannon fodder, especially in the later stages of the conflict.

As Yapp has pointed out, although the Iraq–Iran War has generally been known as the Gulf War, the Gulf itself, whether prefixed as 'Arab' or 'Persian', was neither the bone of contention nor the main theatre of operations.[2] We have stuck to the usual description because, from the perception of non-combatants, especially the Gulf monarchies and the superpowers, the Gulf was the major focus of concern, irrespective of where the main fighting actually took place. As we describe later, worries about the effect of hostilities (attacks on shipping and mining) on the flow of oil and other trade through and from the Gulf (from where a sixth of the West's oil imports originated) made external involvement inevitable – as did fears that the Iranians were intent on 'exporting' their revolution via the subversion of minority Shi'a communities in Gulf Cooperation Council (GCC) countries, in addition to other considerations to do with maintaining the stability and security of the region.

It is difficult to identify a single *casus belli*, unless it was simple Iraqi miscalculation. There were points of friction aplenty between the two countries. From the overthrow of the Hashemite monarchy in Baghdad in 1958, up to the collapse of the Shah's rule in 1979, relations between the two regimes had rarely been better than correct, and often much worse. Republican, self-styled revolutionary, anti-Western Iraq was instinctively chalk to the cheese of the equally self-styled 'imperial' Iran, westward leaning and perceived to be Washington's natural partner, if not its client state, in the northern Gulf. This mutual antagonism was compounded by rival ambitions for political and economic hegemony in the region. The Iranians, even unprompted by Washington, saw themselves as the guardians of Gulf security following an announcement in 1968 of the British withdrawal in 1971. Iran considered this necessary to safeguard oil exports and offshore oil installations. By contrast, Iraq cast itself as the principal proponent of the concept of the 'Arab' Gulf. The Iranians, although not Arab, were more akin in political ethos to the traditional, also Western-aligned, Arab Gulf monarchies than was republican Iraq – an Arab 'brother' but an uncomfortably big one.

The Iranians demonstrated their military reach as a regional power by sending troops to Oman in 1972 to assist the Sultan in suppressing a nationalist revolt. They had also alienated much of the Arab world a year previously by seizing two strategic islands (the Greater and Lesser Tunbs) off the coast of the UAE and had imposed control on a third – Abu Musa – extracting a joint sovereignty agreement with the ruler of Sharjah through *force majeure*. Baghdad had led the anti-Iranian pack on that occasion (breaking relations with Tehran) and stridently opposed foreign intervention in Oman. But whatever the rhetoric, and despite the evidence of Iranian aggrandizement, the Arab Gulf monarchies continued throughout the 1970s to be instinctively more comfortable with Iran than with Iraq. The latter, with its radical posture on Arab–Israel in an attempt to assume Arab leadership from Egypt and its close ties with the Soviet Union (despite the regime's advocacy of non-alignment), on whom it mostly relied for arms, alienated the moderates and conservatives in the area. They, of course, had vivid memories of Iraq's aggressive stance towards Kuwait in 1961, when the newly independent emirate had come under threat of attack from General Qasim's regime.

Territory was the major issue for dispute between Iraq and Iran from the early 1960s onwards. The important Shatt al-Arab waterway (from the

Map E – Iran/Iraq and the Northern Gulf

confluence of the Tigris and Euphrates to the Gulf) had been under Iraqi control since a treaty of 1937 placed the border on the Iranian eastern bank low watermark. In 1969 Iran defied Iraqi instructions by using warships to escort Iranian flagged vessels in the Shatt, asserting a claim, by dint of *force majeure*, to a right of navigation along the *thalweg* – the middle of the deepest shipping channel. Iran's military superiority at the time forced a humiliated Iraq to accept *de facto* use of the waterway by Iranian ships.

Further aggravation was inevitable, especially against the background of substantial Iranian assistance for Iraqi Kurds in the north in their revolt against Baghdad – flaring intermittently from the early 1960s onwards – which nearly led to an all-out military confrontation following a series of border skirmishes.[3] It was during this period that both countries, realizing the vulnerability of installations in the Shatt to hostile acts, took strenuous action to relocate strategic facilities, such as oil terminals, away from this narrow waterway. This was easier for Iran, with its long length of eastern Gulf coast, than for Iraq, with its limited access to open sea. Consequently, Iran built ports in the Gulf to lessen dependence on its principal oil terminal at Abadan, while the Iraqis sought to use overland pipelines to export their oil from the Gulf area. This was not altogether a successful strategy as the trans-Syrian pipeline was subject to intermittent closure because of internal political upheaval. Pipelines built later across Saudi Arabia (TAPLINE) and Turkey in the 1980s during the Gulf War proved more reliable until put out of commission following the Iraqi invasion of Kuwait in 1990.

The 1975 Algiers Agreement between Iran and Iraq confirmed the border along the *thalweg*. In exchange for getting their way on the border, the Iranians stopped assistance to the rebellious Kurds, who accepted a ceasefire and agreed a truce with Baghdad. However, although the treaty led to a suspension of hostilities and a lessening of tension, the Iraqis never really accepted the *thalweg* as a *de jure* frontier, and a return to control of the waterway as enshrined in the 1937 agreement remained a central Iraqi objective.

The Iranian revolution of 1979 under the leadership of Ayatollah Khomenei started the countdown to conflict. The downfall of the Shah more or less coincided with the emergence of Saddam Hussein as President of Iraq and chairman of the ruling Ba'ath Party's Revolutionary Command Council (RCC). Saddam, as secretary-general of the party, had pulled most of the strings from behind the scenes for several years but now felt the need to entrench his position in the public eye. He immediately claimed the unearthing of an attempted coup in which he alleged that the Syrians were implicated. This led to a ruthless purge of opponents within the RCC and an abrupt end to recently formulated plans for a union with Syria, thus once again reopening the long-standing rift with the other wing of the Ba'ath Party, which had ruled in Damascus for several years. Saddam also cracked down on the Iraqi Communist Party (ICP) and distanced himself from the Soviet Union (and dependence on Russian weapons), whose invasion of Afghanistan in late 1979 he publicly condemned.[4] This indicated a tilt to the West, a tactic which was to benefit him during the coming conflict with Iran. Relations between Saddam's Iraq and Khomeini's Iran deteriorated rapidly. The Iraq Sunni leadership of a predominantly secular state was concerned that the appeal of Shi'ite revolutionary Iran ('exporting the revolution', it was soon to be called) might inflame anti-regime sentiments among Iraq's Shi'a majority, estimated at 55 per cent of the population at the time. The Iraqi Shi'as, since the formation of the modern state, had perceived themselves as something of an oppressed majority – second-class citizens under-represented in the government hierarchy and within the senior ranks of the armed forces. There were therefore ample long-standing grievances within the community to be exploited by aggressive co-religionists advocating resistance to Sunni oppression throughout the region.

In an increasingly hostile war of words the Iraqi and Iranian leaderships exchanged accusation and counter-accusation linked to territorial claims. Iraq, as part of its bid for recognition as the paramount power in the Gulf, called for the liberation of the Tunbs and Abu Musa. Tehran blamed Baghdad for demands for autonomy by the majority Arab community in Iran's province of Khuzestan (called 'Arabistan' by Arabs). Border incidents proliferated once again and Saddam Hussein probably calculated that revolutionary Iran was in such turmoil, and its army so weakened by purges, that it would not be able to resist a massive attack, albeit one confined to achieving limited territorial gains along Iraq's south-eastern border. Thus he could reverse the humiliation of conceding to Iran over the Shatt and, using captured territory as a bargaining counter, make border adjustments in Iraq's favour to other disputed areas, including winning concessions over Khuzestan, thereby demonstrating that Iraq, not Iran, was the power to be reckoned with in the Gulf. The overthrow of Khomeini, if not the main war objective (as some writers have claimed[5]), would certainly be a welcome bonus.

Whatever Saddam Hussein's intentions, once open conflict erupted it was soon evident that he had badly miscalculated the effectiveness of the Iranian response. The initial invasion was launched on 22 September 1980 on a 300-mile front. This had been preceded by a formal Iraqi abrogation of the Algiers Agreement on the pretext that Iran had failed to make a border readjustment as agreed in 1975. Despite considerable early territorial gains in the south-east, much fiercer than expected Iranian resistance ensured that the Iraqi advance soon halted. Indeed, in spring 1982 an Iranian counter-offensive regained most of the territory occupied by Iraqi troops, including

Khorramshahr in May. Both sides were now deadlocked in an immobile war of attrition.

The Iraqi leadership had rightly estimated that the Iranian armed forces had been seriously disrupted by purges immediately following Khomeini's assumption of power, but against all expectations they managed quickly to reorganize and fight back. Saddam Hussein had given an ideological spin to his campaign by naming it the 'Battle of Qadisiyya', recalling the Arab victory over Sassanid Iran (and its subsequent conversion to Islam) in AD 637. But the Iranians more effectively summoned up past spirits of deeply rooted hostile and equally ideological images of Arab Sunnis who had oppressed Persian Shi'as for centuries.[6] Saddam had also underestimated Khomeini's ability to unite and inspire his people to resist and defeat Iraqi aggression, motivating his troops with religious and nationalistic fervour. As the war progressed many eyewitness accounts contrasted the often suicidal fanaticism of the Iranian soldiers, apparently eager to die in battle in human-wave attacks, with the more conventional tactics of the obviously less committed Iraqis. By June 1982 it was clear to Saddam that the new Battle of Qadisiyya had failed. He recognized this by pulling his forces out of what little territory in Iran still lay under Iraqi control. Indeed, it was apparent to some observers even at this early stage that this war would not be decided on the battlefield.

Space does not permit a blow-by-blow chronological account of the next seven years of ultimately futile war,[7] but some features and distinct phases are worth detailing briefly. Iraq was on the defensive in the land war from 1982 onwards. By contrast, Iran was occupying nearly 800 square kilometres of Iraqi territory by October 1983. Indeed, until the last stages of the war, Iran had much the better of land engagements, also capturing Fao in 1986. Never in any real danger of defeat, the Iranians doggedly stuck to their apparently immutable position of no peace negotiations in the absence of massive reparations, admission of guilt by the Iraqis and the removal of Saddam Hussein from the Iraqi leadership. This obliged Iraq to embark on a policy of seeking to inflict such unacceptable damage on the enemy that the regime would be forced to the negotiating table. So, from 1984 onwards, Iraq used its superior air power, including the most sophisticated French-supplied Super Etendard fighters and Exocet missiles, to target Iran's petroleum export industry. Previously both sides had used missiles to attack each other's towns in what became known as 'the war of the cities'. Iraq also declared an exclusion zone in the northern Gulf and attacked vessels going to and from the main Iranian terminal at Kharg Island, and thus succeeded in making the export of Iranian oil hazardous and expensive.

Saddam also sought to 'internationalize' the conflict and attract as much external support as possible. In this he was assisted by increasing Iranian intransigence in refusing to negotiate a settlement, with the Iranians brushing aside numerous attempts by the UN and others to mediate. Before the war Saddam's regime had courted financial backers among the Gulf states, such as Kuwait and Saudi Arabia, arguing that Iraq would act as a first line of defence against any threat posed by Shi'a militants in Tehran. Aware of their own uneasy relations with the native Shi'a populations in their own states, the rulers of both countries were prepared to be generous with financial support for Baghdad throughout the war: Kuwait provided loans of over US$6 billion while Saudi Arabia was even more generous, and both states sold oil on behalf of Iraq. By the end of the conflict some estimates puts Baghdad's total indebtedness to Kuwait at $15 billion and to Saudi Arabia at a staggering $34 billion! Other Arab Gulf states chipped in, too, with the United Arab Emirates (UAE) being especially forthcoming. With Iraq's Gulf ports of Basra and Umm Qasr under threat, its neighbours also helped with opening up land transit routes for oil exports. Aqaba, in Jordan, in effect became Iraq's largest seaport. Generally speaking Arab countries were solid in their backing for Baghdad, and Egypt's strong support (some of its troops even fought alongside the Iraqis) did much to restore its position in the Arab world following ostracism after Camp David. Only maverick Libya and anti-Saddam Syria refrained from any form of support for their Arab brother.

As the conflict dragged on the two superpowers were also inclined towards Iraq. The USA initially found both regimes repugnant and tended to remain aloof. But its attitude to Iran was particularily strongly coloured by the humiliation of the seizure of the US Embassy in 1979 and the subsequent failure of a military operation to rescue the staff held hostage. Despite strains in the relationship over Baghdad's treatment of the ICP, the Soviets were instinctively inclined to support a long-standing client. Crucially, both superpowers had a common concern: the effect of an Iranian victory on the stability of the region. Any 'export' of what was perceived as a subversive form of aggressive Islamic 'fundamentalism' not only had the potential to inflame Shi'ite minorities (a majority in Bahrain) in GCC countries but to excite Islamic communities in nearby regions of the Soviet Empire. The USSR accordingly became, once again, the principal arms supplier to Iraq. European states such as France and Britain also benefited from satisfying Iraqi arms demands, and the People's Republic of China was another major weapons provider to both sides, but more so to Iraq.[8] We shall describe below how the superpowers and their allies became more directly involved in the protection of their interests as the area of conflict expanded.

Iran experienced considerable problems both militarily and diplomatically. The lack of air power and enough modern armour prevented a successful frontal assault towards central Iraq. And its willingness to stir up the Iraqi Kurds was initially inhibited by fear of repercussions among its own Kurdish community, should the Iraqis retaliate similarly, although this was a card that was played in desperation in the latter part of the war. Thus Iran concentrated its efforts on the south, where it was hoped (vainly, as it happened) that Shi'a Iraqis might join in – capturing Fao, cutting on occasion the main Basra–Baghdad road, but never managing to seize Basra itself. Here too the land war remained in stalemate, sapping the morale of the forces, although in 1986 it seemed possible that the Iranians might win a major victory in the south.

Iran's other option was to attack shipping in the Gulf belonging to (or using ports of) states sympathetic to Iraq. Kuwait was a particular target: between October 1986 and April 1987 fifteen ships going to and from Kuwait were attacked and in some cases cargoes seized. To these maritime attacks were added occasional (if haphazard) launches of Chinese-supplied Silkworm missiles targeted on Kuwait City. Iran also made liberal use of mines in the narrow sea-lanes of the Straits of Hormuz. However, much of this proved self-defeating. The Kuwaitis cleverly manipulated the major powers into protecting its oil tankers by having them reflagged with either the 'Stars and Stripes' (in the case of eleven vessels) or British colours (on four more). Other tankers were leased from the USSR and remained Soviet-flagged vessels. Thus external parties were obliged to provide protection for 'their' ships. A Western naval presence was anyhow in place to try to maintain normal commercial activity, deterring both Iraq and Iran, and minesweepers became increasingly involved in keeping the sea-lanes open. This multinational task force (US, UK and France, mainly), known as 'the Armilla Patrol', was a substantial naval presence by the end of the war and seen by the Iranians as mostly directed against them. The Iranians threatened retaliation and promised to sink US warships if provoked, but, ironically, it was the Iraqis who ultimately attacked a US frigate, USS *Stark*, killing thirty-seven sailors. The Iraqis claimed the attack was an 'error' and apologized, but suspicions remain that it was in retaliation following media revelations that Washington had secretly supplied arms to Iran in the so-called 'Irangate' affair.[9] There were also press allegations that the USA had supplied false intelligence to both sides to ensure a stalemate in the war: the argument being that it suited Washington's strategic interests to have Iraq and Iran at each other's throats so as to counter any threat that either regime might otherwise present to the Gulf monarchies.

There were various attempts at mediation throughout the war, and the UN managed the odd success, such as brokering a cessation of attacks on civilian targets by both sides in June 1984. This, however, was subsequently ignored by Iraq, which resumed air attacks in March 1985, having been frustrated by continued stalemate on the ground. Further unilateral suspensions offered by Iraq to induce Iran to negotiate failed to achieve the desired result. Other attempts to bring Iran to peace talks continued to founder on

Iranian insistence on unacceptable conditions, such as claiming $350 billion war reparations at one point. This attitude increased Iran's international isolation, limiting its diplomatic options; but pariah status did not seem to influence (or worry) the regime. Saudi Arabia, Iraq's principal financial backer, made strenuous behind-the-scenes efforts to bring about a ceasefire, having improved its own relations with Tehran through pragmatic negotiations over restoring and then maintaining the price of Gulf-sourced oil. Then the UN Security Council's efforts took on a new urgency with the prospect of the USA being drawn into a direct military confrontation with Iran over its threats to attack US warships in the Gulf 'if provoked'. Attacks on vessels in the Gulf by both sides escalated sharply throughout 1987, and the damaging of a US frigate by a mine allegedly laid by Iran resulted in a US retaliatory attack on an Iranian naval base. Security Council Resolution (SCR) 598, adopted unanimously on 29 July 1987, called for an immediate ceasefire and withdrawal of forces to international borders, and sought Iranian and Iraqi cooperation in seeking a settlement. Iraqi acceptance (conditional on Iranian agreement) was negated by Iran's condemnation of the resolution as unfair, because Iraq was not identified as the aggressor and the USA was maintaining its naval presence in the Gulf as 'Iraq's ally'.

Iran continued to resist pressure from the international community to accept SCR 598 and agree to a ceasefire, presumably because the regime felt that the war could yet be won. However, then the tide of battle turned in favour of Iraq. Iran had enjoyed some success in the land war in early 1987, penetrating Iraqi territory in several places along the 1,200-kilometre war front, but by early 1988 Iraqi counter-offensives had caused heavy casualties (the Iraqis, in particular, made effective use of chemical weapons, such as mustard gas), taking their toll on an increasingly war-weary Iranian military infrastructure. Volunteers were not coming forward as before and there was apparently disagreement over strategy and tactics in the higher echelons of the Iranian government. A Kurdish offensive (the largest since 1974–5) hoping to exploit Iraq's involvement on a broad front and in support of Iranian forces, although initially successful, came to a tragic end with an Iraqi chemical attack on Halabja in March 1988, killing 4,000 Kurdish civilians. Many more were allegedly killed by poison gas in a subsequent campaign after the Gulf conflict had apparently ended.[10] With their forces in retreat on most fronts, and with Iraqis on Iranian soil for the first time for some years, the Iranians unexpectedly announced their unconditional acceptance of SCR 598 on 18 July 1988. Here again Saudi Arabian influence may have played some part, and it is believed that they may also have persuaded the Iraqis to agree to a ceasefire despite their recent military successes. (This was shortly after a US warship accidentally shot down an Iranian civilian airliner, killing 270 people.) A ceasefire came into effect a month later. Apart from a few subsequent minor alarums and excursions, the Iraq–Iran war was at an end.

The Iraqis declared themselves the victors in the contest. Certainly they had had the best of the last few months of fighting, liberating all their own territory and occupying parts of Iran. But in truth this wretched war, the greatest inter-state conflict in the second half of the twentieth century, ended as a draw. Most of the goals scored were 'own'. In terms of casualties, damage (to fifty large towns or cities) and bleeding of resources, both countries were losers. Aburish called it 'an aimless war,'[11] but 'pointless' is perhaps a more fitting epithet. Saddam, preoccupied with Kuwait in August 1990, quietly conceded all points of difference with Iran in that month when seeking a formal peace with the old enemy. He thus tacitly acknowledged that Iraq had achieved none of its war aims. Neither side had established a clear hegemony in the region. The international community – the UN and the major powers – had only just managed to contain the conflagration within acceptable limits; the stability of the rest of the region was maintained and a temporary loss of oil production managed without significant disruption to the market. But it had failed to halt the war until the combatants themselves were prepared to call it quits, thus demonstrating the limitations of international intervention even when both superpowers were, more or less, pulling in the same direction. However, it has to be said (for reasons described in Chapter 3) that the Soviet Union was beginning its withdrawal from substantial involvement in international issues towards the end of the 1980s, and so was not a major player in the Gulf for the latter part of the conflict.

The longevity of the conflict was primarily down to the determination and stubbornness of the two main protagonists, Saddam Hussein and Ayatollah Khomeini. Neither was prepared to give way and both managed to gain and retain sufficient control to ensure they got their way. Despite the evident futility of the war, especially as it appeared to foreign observers, neither leader's position was even seriously threatened by the indecisive outcome of the conflict. Indeed, for some years the war against old enemies was popular in both countries. Small successes could be presented domestically as major national triumphs. The ebb and flow of the contest gave both nations hope of ultimate victory from time to time. It also suited both regimes to have an external enemy to take people's minds off domestic discontents. Moreover, as the war dragged on and became bogged down, both leaderships probably hesitated at calling a halt to hostilities, given the difficulty of explaining to their people how so much effort and bloodshed had achieved so little. This was especially so as the casualties mounted; very few families in either country were left personally untouched by the carnage of war. But, in the final analysis, public opinion counted for little in both countries. And even if one of the two protagonists had clearly been seen as the loser, it is unlikely that the defeated regime would have been swept away, so efficient (and ruthless) were both countries' mechanisms of repression. In the Iranian case, the Islamic republic effectively adapted and refined the instruments of control invented under the Shah.

Throughout the war both regimes felt they were playing for big stakes. Each saw the other as a formidable obstacle to their ambitions. Khomeini remained intent on the export of his revolutionary ideals via co-religionists throughout the Gulf. Saddam's desire for his regional hegemony to be recognized and his position in the wider Arab world to be appreciated drove him on. Both leaders glimpsed fleeting opportunities of victory – Iran in the land battle, Saddam via the air war. This helped to keep them going. Saddam also felt that the apparent support of the international community, with both superpowers more hostile to Iran, might in the end prove decisive. Ultimately, as stalemate set in, both leaderships recognized that the chances of decisive victory were illusory and that there were limits, even in autocracies, to what could be expected of exhausted and demoralized armed forces. Morcover, both economies were badly damaged by nearly ten years of conflict. Although Saddam may have been tempted to carry on when his army started to get the better of the land war in the dying months of the war, he was probably reluctant to push his troops much further. So, in the end, grim determination and the mutual personal hatred that motivated both leaders were not enough for one to see off the other.

One conflict spawned a second. Iraq, with the damage done to its economy and with fears about the long-term effects that this might have on popular support for a regime severely dented by the war, needed a quick fix to its problems. This at least seemed to be Saddam's perception. How important a factor it was as a cause of part two of the Gulf War – the Iraqi invasion of Kuwait – we will discuss in the next chapter.

8 The Kuwait crisis

Brother versus brother

The Iraqi invasion of Kuwait began in the early hours of 2 August 1990 and ended after a few hours of sporadic fighting with the occupation of the entire emirate by 100,000 troops. This was the start of a crisis that was to lead to conflict and the comprehensive rout of the Iraqi occupying forces six months later – but only after the assembly of a massive military coalition, over 700,000 strong, under US leadership and with contributions from over thirty countries, ten of them Arab. Never before in the history of the region had so many Arab countries gone into battle against an Arab brother, one who not much more than a year previously had enjoyed widespread fraternal support against the Iranian (Persian) enemy. Never before had the United Nations authorized the use of force against a member state with the consenting votes of both superpowers. A decade later, divisions in the Arab world opened or exacerbated by this conflict remained largely intact. By then, the United States had no serious international challenger within the region. And Iraq, still under Saddam Hussein, remained a pariah state, subject since 1990 to the most draconian sanctions regime implemented in the history of the United Nations.

The complex circumstances surrounding Saddam Hussein's second serious miscalculation – his invasion of Iran in 1980 being the first – need to be examined in the wider international context.[1] As we described in Chapter 3, the start of the 1990s saw a dramatic decline in Soviet influence and involvement in the Middle East. President Gorbachev's twin policies of glasnost (greater openness and a measure of democratization) and perestroika (restructuring and liberalizing the economy) – the so-called 'new thinking' – started to loosen the grip of Moscow over the Soviet Empire, a process that was to reach its inevitable conclusion under his successor, Boris Yeltsin.[2] Soviet preoccupation with domestic upheaval and the need to encourage economic assistance from the West led to a scaling down of Cold War rhetoric and a willingness (opposed by old-style hardliners within the Soviet leadership) to seek cooperation rather than confrontation with the

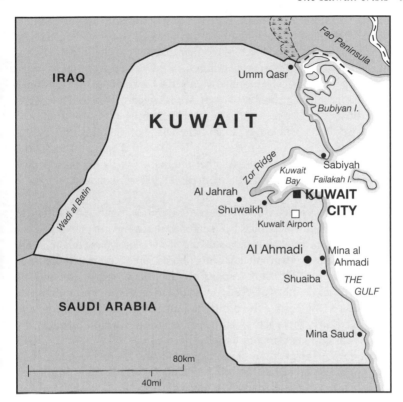

Map F – Kuwait

United States. Following the Soviet disengagement from Afghanistan in 1988, Moscow, although still maintaining great power pretensions, became increasingly reluctant to take on new foreign commitments and was, indeed, unable to honour existing ones. This partial withdrawal from the world stage had serious implications for former traditional clients in the Middle East. Syria, Iraq, South Yemen and the PLO in particular could no longer look to the Soviet Union for economic and military aid, nor, as time went on, for effective diplomatic support.

The United States and its allies were also absorbed by developments within Eastern Europe throughout the first half of 1990, as influenced by evidence of dramatic change in Moscow. Despite political and economic turmoil within the Soviet Union and the increasingly obvious and seemingly inevitable decline of Soviet influence, Washington was not yet in a position to proclaim the existence of a 'new world order' – a now hackneyed expression referring to a structure of international politics dominated by one major global player instead of two. But as Soviet power waned within the Middle East there were signs of Washington preparing to fill an impending vacuum through new contacts with Moscow's former 'clients', such as the PLO leadership and Syria. This was in preparation for a new attempt to kick-start the peace process, once again in abeyance against the backcloth of the Palestinian Intifada (described in Chapter 2). Not all Arabs welcomed the relentless rise of American influence at the expense of Soviet involvement. Many believed that Israel would be the main regional beneficiary of Washington's peace-brokering, which, with the eclipse of the USSR and the end of bipolarity, could operate unchallenged by any other international player, thus leading to the imposition of an unjust settlement on the Palestinians and their Arab supporters.

The Kuwait crisis has probably become the most analysed conflict in recent history, about which it has been claimed that more ink than blood has been spilt. One recurring theme in academic discourses is that contemporary observers, especially governmental ones, should have anticipated the invasion.[3] Surely, given Saddam's record of precipitate aggression and his rhetoric in the early months of 1990, Iraqi military action against the emirate was inevitable? But, despite the proliferation of hints and (with the benefit of hindsight) fairly strong indications, most people were still taken by surprise. We need to discuss briefly why this was so.

As described in the previous chapter, Saddam and his regime ended their pointless war against Iran as the self-proclaimed victors. But in truth Iraq had emerged from a close contest only marginally ahead on points. It had also been bankrupted by the conflict and for much of the period was largely dependent on very generous assistance from the Arab Gulf states, especially Saudi Arabia and Kuwait.[4] Iraq's pretensions as a regional superpower had foundered on the rock of Iranian opposition. There had been considerable popular internal opposition to a military adventure that had brought no measurable benefits to the country, and certainly not enough to compensate for the nationwide distress caused by thousands of casualties, considerable war damage and the crippling of the economy. Saddam, although pursuing plans to liberalize the political system partly to encourage more involvement by the Shi'as and to open up the economy, remained totally dependent on the support of an entrenched oligarchy and the regime's instruments of state oppression to maintain power. He survived at least one serious coup attempt between the end of the Iraq–Iran War and the invasion of Kuwait, and, despite his brutal crushing the Kurdish separatists in 1988–9, he realized that further trouble from that quarter was only a matter of time.

Unabashed by his failure to persuade his neighbours to recognize Iraqi hegemony as the dominant regional power, though, Saddam began to strut on a bigger stage, seeking the leadership of the radical pack in the Arab world. There followed vehement and strident attacks on Israel, coupled with a war of words with the USA, culminating in a resolution passed by the US Congress to impose sanctions on Baghdad because of Iraqi plans to manufacture weapons of mass destruction, including chemical weapons as used against Iran and the Kurds.

Saddam also encouraged the external PLO leadership (based in Tunis) to look upon him as a major patron and to establish an important regional office in Baghdad, and exploited Iraq's membership of the Arab Cooperation Council (ACC) – a four-country grouping also including Jordan, Egypt and Yemen that was established in February 1989. Saddam used this platform to play to a wider Arab audience, turning up the volume on his anti-Israeli rhetoric and simultaneously seeking to outflank his long-standing Ba'athist rivals in Damascus, who had themselves for many years been predominant radicals.

Alarm bells started ringing in the Gulf and in the West when the extent of Iraq's crash rearmament programme became apparent in 1989 and early 1990. Despite severe economic problems exacerbated by depressed oil prices, the regime was spending vast sums of money on the purchase of sophisticated weapon systems, mainly from France and the USSR, and also seeking to acquire the technology to develop an in-house capability to produce its own. The Israelis in particular had expressed concern about Iraq's nuclear potential,[5] and its ability to produce and use chemical weapons was well documented. The regime's arrest and execution of an Iranian-British investigative journalist drew international attention to the existence of advanced armament-manufacturing facilities in Iraq,[6] as did the interception of items of technology from Western companies thought to be integral to the development of sophisticated long-range missiles and weapons of mass destruction. The Iraqi regime, courting Arab approval, made no secret of its ambitions to produce advanced weapon systems, saying they were necessary to combat the threat from Israel.

This policy was indeed widely supported throughout the region because of popular resentment against perceived Western, especially American, double standards: pressurizing Iraq, an important Arab country, to desist from enhancing its military capability while saying nothing about Israel, a country well believed to be in possession of nuclear weapons. Even Syria, Iraq's arch rival, publicly supported the latter's right to defend itself against an Israeli nuclear threat.

Increasingly, throughout the early months of 1990, Iraqi rhetoric had another target: its neighbour Kuwait. Relations had deteriorated since the end of the Iraq–Iran War. Even during the conflict Iraq had been angered by the refusal of its Kuwaiti ally to lease, or otherwise hand over, the two strategic islands of Warba and Bubiyan at the mouth of the Shatt al-Arab waterway, which would have been of considerable military value against

Iran. Iraq also demanded a renegotiation of the border with the emirate, claiming that, besides the erection of military installations on Iraqi territory, Kuwait was illegally exploiting the Rumeila oil field (partially straddled by the international frontier) – which, in its view, rightly belonged to Baghdad – and had 'stolen' US$2.4 billion worth of Iraqi oil. The most serious charge was that both Kuwait and the United Arab Emirates (UAE) were over-producing oil, well beyond the quotas laid down by OPEC, and had done so since 1981, thus drastically and deliberately reducing Iraq's income. This was perceived in Baghdad as another act of robbery by Kuwait and the UAE. Baghdad also indicated that it expected its Gulf War financial backers to release Iraq from the huge debts it had incurred in 'defending them from Iranian aggression'. In mid-July 1990, just prior to an important OPEC council meeting, Iraq warned that it might take military action against any countries that continued to exceed oil quotas. Simultaneously, two Iraqi divisions (30,000 troops) were moved up to the border with Kuwait.

Most analysts agree on Saddam Hussein's motives for this aggressive posture.[7] Apart from a bid to assume a leadership role, they were primarily economic. He desperately needed to increase his oil income, well nigh Iraq's sole source of quick money in what amounted to a 'one-crop' economy, to finance his rearmament programme and address the damage caused to the Iraqi economy by eight years of war. Certainly, there was no way he could consider repaying the debts run up with Kuwait and his other Arab Gulf creditors. Strategic considerations also applied. One lesson learned from the war with Iran was that Iraq needed better territorial access to the Gulf to secure the sea approaches to the Shatt al-Arab. Readjustment of the border to include Warba and Bubiyan, plus the added economic bonus of absorbing the entire Rumeila oil field under Iraqi sovereignty, was an attractive proposition. These were powerful motivations, but did they justify going to war?

It seems unlikely that we will ever know for certain precisely when and exactly why Saddam decided to launch his invasion of Kuwait. Undoubtedly he was angered by Kuwait's stubborn refusal to bow to Iraqi pressure. The emirate insisted on repayment of Iraq's Gulf War debt as a precondition to discussing the border. It had announced plans for the development of Bubiyan. It continued to overproduce beyond the OPEC quota, only agreeing to toe the line at the OPEC meeting in July. And it was publicly robust in countering the Iraqi propaganda campaign. To some analysts, the extent of Kuwaiti robustness was surprising. Did the Amir have secret assurances of American military support? To others, Kuwaiti 'intransigence' – the refusal to concede an inch to Iraq's demands despite the increasingly urgent attempts by mediators to reach a compromise – served only to humiliate Saddam and provoke him into intemperate action.[8]

In the absence of authoritative primary-source Iraqi material, uncertainty will continue to surround Saddam's decision to order his forces into Kuwait. Was it long premeditated or an act of sudden impetuosity? Against the background of increasing Iraqi military build-up on the border with Kuwait there had been an apparently successful OPEC summit on 25 July (which raised the price of oil as demanded by Iraq). Nevertheless, the Iraqi tanks started to roll within twelve hours of an inconclusive meeting chaired by King Fahd of Saudi Arabia on 1 August between the Kuwaiti Crown Prince and the deputy chairman of Iraq's Revolutionary Command Council (RCC).[9] But one thing does seem probable: Saddam surely would not have attacked unless he believed he was going to get away with it.

It is on this point that conspiracy theories abound. Analysts have made much of a meeting between Saddam and the US Ambassador to Iraq, April Glaspie, on 25 July. Did she give a virtual green light to Saddam to pursue his quarrel with Kuwait without fear of US intervention?[10] She evidently believed from Saddam's reaction, which she reported to Washington, that there was no immediate danger of military action, as she promptly departed Iraq on leave.[11] Our view is that Saddam completely miscalculated the likely Western and indeed Arab governments' response to his act of aggression, believing that no one would reckon Kuwait was worth a fight. Or, if they did, that they would hesitate to take on the might of the Iraqi armed forces, said to be the world's fourth largest, with more than a million men under arms. He may well have intended to teach the Kuwaitis a lesson and withdraw his forces after achieving a readjustment of the disputed frontier in Iraq's favour, following the installation of a puppet government and the writing off of his debt. Subsequent manoeuvres seem to indicate that this was his intention, but it was frustrated by developments that Saddam had simply failed to anticipate.

Space does not permit a detailed account of events from the Iraqi seizure of Kuwait on 2 August 1990 to its liberation as a result of Operation Desert Storm on 28 February 1991. There are, however, several features that are worth highlighting – notably the unprecedented nature of the international response to Saddam's aggression. It came as no surprise that Washington reacted swiftly and angrily. Iraq possessed the second-largest oil reserves in the world (perhaps 10 per cent of the total), a position significantly enhanced by its seizure of Kuwait (nearly another 10 per cent) and its prolific oil fields. The United States relied on imports for about 50 per cent of its oil requirements and it was unacceptable for it to be potentially held to ransom by a maverick autocrat like the Iraqi leader. Moreover, it seemed possible in early August that Saddam, with his forces poised on the southern Kuwaiti border, was contemplating adding the even larger oil fields of Saudi Arabia to his conquests. American allies in the West were also highly alarmed and needed little persuasion to join forces with Washington in confronting the Iraqi regime – initially via the UN Security Council and subsequently in the Desert Shield/Desert Storm military coalition.

It was the Arab reaction to the attack by an Arab on a brother that dramatically changed the traditional pattern of regional alliances. For the first time since the creation of the Arab League, conservative regimes such as the Gulf monarchies made common cause with radical states like Syria and Libya.[12] Normally conservative monarchist Jordan, influenced by enthusiastic popular support for Saddam, refused to join in the condemnation of Iraq and opposed US and other Western involvement, calling for an 'Arab solution' to the crisis. In the circumstances of total disarray in the Arab world this was oxymoronic, to say the least. Two emergency meetings of the Arab League illustrated the lack of common purpose. The first, on the day after the invasion, saw six out of the twenty-one members voting against the resolution to condemn the invasion and insist on Iraq's unconditional withdrawal (Jordan, Mauritania, Sudan, Yemen, the PLO and Iraq itself), while Libya abstained. At the second summit meeting on 10 August, twelve of the participants voted to send a deterrent force to Saudi Arabia to support the build-up of primarily American troops preparing to defend the kingdom against possible Iraqi attack. On this occasion Libya declined to send soldiers, but called upon Saddam to withdraw his forces.

Official hostility to Iraq, as reflected by the actions of a majority of Arab governments, was not an accurate reflection of popular sentiment in many of these states. Two factors influenced the public mood. First, there was a widespread lack of genuine sympathy for Kuwait. The emirate was widely disliked for its perceived arrogance, its unconvincing pretensions to non-alignment and patronizing use of its great oil wealth. Its treatment of resident guest workers and the large Palestinian community as third-class citizens also raised hackles. Kuwait's refusal to show any flexibility in its dispute with Iraq engendered a common feeling that it had done much needlessly to provoke Baghdad. Second, Saddam, despite his surprise at the robustness of the international response, demonstrated considerable skill in mobilizing Arab street opinion in his support.

Saddam originally claimed he had sent forces into Kuwait in response to an appeal by patriotic insurgents who had overthrown the 'corrupt' Sabah regime. However, having failed to establish a client regime consisting of credible Kuwaitis he proceeded to Plan B, he announced that Kuwait had been 'reunited' with its motherland Iraq; in other words, annexed to become Baghdad's nineteenth province. Iraq had thus reclaimed its birthright, and one of the artificial borders created by colonialists had been liquidated in the interests of pan-Arab unity.[13] He also sought to attract regional support by creating major linkage between his Kuwait operation and the wider Middle

East dispute. In effect he proposed an Iraqi withdrawal from Kuwait in exchange for, at the very least, an international conference on Palestine. However, this proposal was rejected out of hand by the United States and its Western allies, who wanted nothing to do with any idea that might be seen to reward Iraqi aggression and enhance its standing in the region. It struck a populist chord, however, especially in Jordan, the West Bank and Gaza and the Maghreb states. As the crisis developed, the Iraqi leader continued to play to a popular gallery by posing as the new Arab champion prepared to stand up to Western bullies, the traditional supporters of Israel, against overwhelming odds. Subsequent 'Scud' missile attacks on Israel after the outbreak of war immensely enhanced his standing in many Arab streets. He also sought through his rhetoric to add an Islamic dimension to the conflict, invoking an image of a new Saladin fighting a jihad against the Crusader West. As part of this campaign he added the phrase 'Allah Akbar' (God Is Great) to the Iraqi flag. Given the perceived overwhelmingly secular nature of the Iraqi establishment, this was probably the least successful of his ploys.

But, despite his manoeuvring, Saddam made little impression on the wider international community. The UN Security Council quickly established the most comprehensive regime of sanctions ever imposed on a member state, passing a raft of unopposed resolutions. Iraq's invasion of Kuwait served as a catalyst to draw the American and Soviet former rivals together, and there was no clearer indication that some kind of 'new world order' had been created than the disappearance of references to 'East' and 'West' from the discussion of international crisis management. However, such harmony was more of an indication that the Soviet star was on the wane and more pre-occupied with domestic issues than any real meeting of minds in Washington and Moscow.

Although the international community, including the Security Council, called for a peaceful outcome to the crisis, seeking unconditional Iraqi withdrawal, the build-up to military confrontation was inevitable. By the beginning of 1991, 700,000 Desert Shield coalition forces had assembled – mostly in Saudi Arabia – far outnumbering the half a million Iraqi troops thought by then to be in Kuwait. A multinational armada of 200 naval ships had also been sent to the Gulf. Reports of Iraqi brutality in Kuwait, Saddam's abuse of civilian hostages trapped in the country and plans to use them as potential 'human shields' to deter military attack, plus his refusal, despite many attempts at mediation, to withdraw from the emirate on acceptable terms hardened international opinion against him. Moreover, the US leadership stepped up the pressure for military action, fearing that a long stalemate (which sanctions seemed unlikely to end) would erode public support for armed conflict. The legal basis for going to war was provided by Security

Council Resolution (SCR) 678 of 29 November 1990, which authorized 'all necessary means' to liberate Kuwait. Last-minute mediation attempts, notably by the Soviet Union, failed to prevent the outbreak of hostilities, codenamed 'Operation Desert Storm', on 16–17 January 1991. The war was nasty, brutal and short. The forty-day air campaign consisting of over 90,000 missions wreaked havoc on Iraq's military and industrial infrastructure. Iraq's only effective counter – the use of the Scud missile – was nearly successful in widening the war by involving Israel, which was restrained from direct retaliation only by massive US military assistance. Of course, if Israel had been provoked into attacking Iraq, this would have gravely threatened the cohesion of the Arab–Western alliance. The overwhelmingly one-sided aerial assault, with more bombs dropped than during the Second World War, was followed by the 100-hour rout of the land campaign, which led to the liberation of Kuwait. This campaign inflicted heavy casualties on the fleeing Iraqi contingents of what proved to be a paper tiger of a military machine quite incapable of fighting the 'Mother of all Battles' proclaimed by their leader.[14]

Saddam had not committed the 'crack' Republican Guard to the defence of Kuwait (nor did he deploy biological or chemical weapons) – wisely, as it transpired, as it was needed to crush revolts in the predominantly Shi'a south of Iraq and by the Kurds in the north. The US-led coalition was criticized in some quarters for neither pressing on to Baghdad to remove Saddam nor assisting these rebellions. But the first was not within the mandate of SCR 678 and the USA with memories of Vietnam, was reluctant (in both cases) to be involved in what could become long-term messy campaigns. This was despite US President George Bush's apparent encouragement of the uprisings when he addressed the Iraqi people following the ceasefire, although it seems unlikely that either the Shi'as or the Kurds needed much prompting to take advantage of what must have seemed a good opportunity to assert themselves. Moreover, Washington did not wish to see Iraq disintegrate. Eventually the Americans and British provided some protection for the Shi'as and the Kurds via the establishment of 'no-fly zones' in the south and north of Iraq. They later also created a safe haven for the Kurds, barring Iraqi aircraft from both sectors.

In the decade following Desert Storm little of real substance changed in the region. Above all, the same divisions in the Arab world were still apparent; although, admittedly, the Jordanian and Palestinian leaderships eventually managed to mend most of the fences damaged by their stance during the crisis. The Jordanians also successfully absorbed 300,000 Palestinian–Jordanian refugees expelled or refused permission to return to Kuwait, where they had been long-term residents. But there was no Arab or indeed wider international consensus on how to deal with Iraq. Popular attitudes and the views of elites and regimes remained far apart. And more than a decade of draconian sanctions linked to the dismantling of Iraq's arms industry damaged, but probably did not destroy, Saddam's capacity to produce weapons of mass destruction. (Although it remains a mystery when and where they were destroyed.) Up to the Allied invasion of 2003, he remained entrenched in power with little apparent prospect of departure. The sanctions were widely perceived to have been more damaging to his people than harmful to the regime, and led to widespread public sympathy, in the West as well as in the Arab world, for the ordinary Iraqis who failed to benefit from the humanitarian provisions of the sanctions legislation. The UN, including governments previously supportive of the coalition, grew increasingly divided over confronting and punishing Iraq, especially on the issue of how to enforce an effective arms inspection and monitoring regime. Two intensive (Anglo-American) air campaigns after 1991 to enforce Iraqi cooperation with the UN both failed to achieve their objectives. And subsequent aggressive enforcement of the no-fly zones by US and British warplanes attracted widespread international criticism, even though they probably protected the Kurds from serious Iraqi government interference. Ultimately, when George W. Bush's administration launched its full-scale attack on Iraq in March 2003, it did so without the endorsement of the UN.

Hopes in the West that one outcome of the defeat of Iraq would be significant democratization in the region have largely been dashed. In 1991, US and other Western commentators expressed unease about going to war on behalf of monarchical regimes that seemed almost as autocratic as their Iraqi enemy. Although the National Assembly was restored in Kuwait, its narrow, male-only franchise remained unchanged until the emancipation of women voters in 2005 – and only then after stiff resistance from conservative elements. There has also been timid liberalization in Qatar and Oman, and more so in Bahrain (even after the Amir elevated his status to that of King), but Saudi Arabia and the UAE remain monolithically undemocratic. Significant constitutional liberalization in Jordan began in 1989, a year before the start of the first Gulf conflict, but continued popular support for Iraq was a factor in renewed authoritarianism by the late King Hussein and his successor. One positive outcome was the relaunch of the Middle East peace process, but that reflected the new unchallenged predominance of the USA as the main external player in the region, as well as Palestinian impotence, rather than any recognition of the validity of Saddam's 'linkage' between the Gulf and developments in the Levant. As Cordesman argued in the wake of the coalition's victory, 'Like it or not, the US is the only nation that can assemble and project enough power to meet any aggressor. While Americans may not want to be the world's policeman, they must consider what it could be like to live in a world without any policeman at all.'[15]

Indeed, the very visible dominance of the United States is the most striking legacy of the part that Washington played in orchestrating and prosecuting Desert Storm at the beginning of the 1990s. Without continual US pressure it is unlikely that the countries of the region, with the exception of Kuwait and Saudi Arabia, would have made their peace with Iraq by the turn of the century. US insistence also held together the sanctions regime, ragged at the edges though it eventually became. North American commercial interests riding on the back of US military and political influence substantially increased their share of an already lucrative market. Washington never ceased to remind its friends and allies in the Arab Gulf that its ready help at times of trouble merited commercial recompense, whether through yet more purchases of military hardware or by the award of very large civil contracts to US companies.

Nor was Washington reluctant to remind the Gulf monarchies of its role as protector of last resort in the face of the threat that Saddam Hussein was still believed to present to the region despite his crushing defeat in 1991. Sanctions could help to keep Saddam in his cage but only the USA had the muscle to put him back behind bars whenever he might try to break out. So, to a great extent, as some cynics have argued, it suited the USA before 9/11 to have the neighbourhood bully still at large, thus justifying its position as the policeman on the block. By the end of the twentieth century, Saddam had shown no signs of an early departure from a scene he had dominated so long. However, the start of the new millennium and the arrival of a new US administration, headed by veterans of the first Gulf War, appears to have initiated, after the dramatic events of 9/11, a countdown towards the inevitable conflict we describe in Chapter 10. Even without the events of 9/11, many believed that it was only a matter of time before the administration of George W. Bush finished the business with Iraq that had been started by his father a decade earlier. Such an argument has even been proposed by the ex-Treasury Secretary of the Bush administration, Paul O'Neill, who claimed in 2004 that 'from the very beginning [of the Bush government, in 2001] there was a conviction that Saddam Hussein was a bad person and that he needed to go'.[16] As we see in the next two chapters, Bush had at least achieved this, if little else of a positive nature, by the beginning of 2007.

9 The politics of conflict and failure of peacemaking

It is a safe prediction that conflict in the Middle East will never be fully resolved, nor for that matter will it be fully resolved anywhere else. Nevertheless, levels of conflict and how they interrelate can be reduced or controlled, and in some cases removed. However, the most important point to be made about conflict and peacemaking since 1945 in the Middle East is that it was not until the early 1990s that substantial progress towards the formal conclusion of peace treaties was achieved within the region.

Conflict resolution as a meaningful process has taken the best part of fifty years to emerge as something in which the parties to conflict can effectively engage. This is not to ignore Kissinger's shuttle diplomacy of the 1970s or the Egyptian–Israeli Peace Treaty of the same era, nor the numerous plans and proposals outlined by successive US administrations since their increasing involvement in the region following the decline of Britain and France after the Second World War. Rather, it is to put such efforts into historical context, a context that actually militated against any serious attempt to address the real issues at the heart of so many conflicts in the region. Indeed, we believe that in many respects it was only with the ending of the Cold War and superpower competition in the Middle East that progress could be made in the major arena of conflict in the region, the Arab–Israeli and Palestinian–Israeli conflicts. We would caution, however, that without a more comprehensive approach to conflict resolution and appropriate linkages to other political and economic issues in the region, there is still a serious likelihood that conflicts such as those in Iraq could undermine the wider goals of peacemakers. Such an approach, however, also requires a major adjustment of the Western mindset towards the region's majority Muslim population, which is currently perceived as part of a suppurating mass of Islamic violence, repression and primitivism that threatens Western interests in the region.

In September 1993, when Israeli Prime Minister Itzhak Rabin and PLO President Yasser Arafat shook hands on the lawn of the White House at the conclusion of the Declaration of Principles, the rest of the world declared that peace had at last been achieved in the Middle East. The white dove with its olive branch had finally shown up in a region where conflict had become a way of life for citizens and of politics between states. Many may have rubbed their eyes in wonderment at two battle-hardened combatants finally, if grudgingly, grasping the prize of peace. Indeed, both Rabin and Arafat were formerly regarded as men of war, each with battle experience under his belt, each the declared enemy of the other. Now heralded as a 'peace of the brave', the ability of military men to put the past behind them and grasp the hand of friendship was promoted by pundits and commentators alike as a symbol of how far along the path to peace the leaders of the Israelis and Palestinians had come. Such figures added a legitimacy to a difficult process of peacemaking.

But on the same day, far away from the White House in the Middle East itself, a different picture emerged. There was very little celebration, an absence of euphoria, no dancing in the streets, no victory parades and parties, no national days of rejoicing. Instead, there was a recognition that the first, not the last, difficult step on a long road had been undertaken by participants who were largely cajoled and pressurized into peacemaking by outside players and major powers. For many, the famous picture of the Rabin–Arafat handshake was too much to absorb. Generations within the region had battled with each other, being fed on national images demonizing the enemy with atavistic abhorrence. Yet now the 'peace of the brave' was declared from on high. Peacemaking became a daunting, novel prospect, and the familiar certainties of conflict remained all too alluring for leaders whose authority and survival in the region depended on the military.

To argue that many in the Middle East might have a stronger stake in conflict than in peace and stability might sound perverse. However, many of the region's political systems have been dominated for decades by antagonisms around which political power, economic decisions and regional alliances have been constructed. The political and economic elites of many states within the region have prospered on the back of conflict and its associated commerce in arms. In the case of Jordan, for instance, its position as a front-line state in both the MEPP and Iraq contexts attracts considerable financial and other support from the USA and its allies. Internal political divisions and discontents have often been suppressed through appeals to national unity in the face of the enemy from outside, not within. The prevalence of the military in the political systems of the region, as was discussed in the introduction to this book, is immense, even in democracies like Israel where, as Arian has remarked, 'the boundaries between the civilian and the military . . . are not clear . . . With the army being so esteemed, so prominent, and so important, it is not surprising that it is also so powerful.'[1]

Arms spending in the region has always been prolific, higher than that in any other area of the developing world, and with little evidence of decline as yet. Thus, those who may be said to have a stake in conflict are admittedly few in number, but they form the core elites in many states so their perspective matters. These political leaders are rhetorically bound into the cycle of what appears to be interminable conflict; this is an image they project at national as well as regional and even global level. Breaking out of such habit-forming behaviour appears almost impossible. In striking the pose of conflict, it is no wonder that so many have viewed the Middle East through the kaleidoscope of war, conflict, bloodshed, soldiers, terrorism and guns, and that so many have talked about the region in terms of a cycle of war, conflagration and antagonism.

At the beginning of the twenty-first century, signs of major conflict or full-scale war had been absent for a decade. Lebanon, Israel–Palestine, Israeli–Arab, Iran–Iraq, Kuwait and Yemen could all be cited as arenas where major conflict and war had subsided or dissolved into 'complex political emergencies'.[2] Indeed, the closing decades, and particularly the events of the last decade, of the twentieth century contributed to what many called new patterns of conflict transformation and peace-building. Less than a decade later, though, major conflict gripped parts of the region again: Lebanon, Iraq, Israel–Palestine and Israeli–Arab conflagrations were all apparent. Complex political emergencies still raged, too, and the recourse to war once again appeared irresistible to political leaders both inside and outside the Middle East. The regional arms race, particularly the nuclear capacity of at least Israel and Iran, has played its part as an issue of regional escalation rather than preventive strategy for ruling out the kind of major wars that characterized the region for so many decades. Nuclear deterrence was not working when external parties were prepared to deal with the issue in a piecemeal manner. The futility of developing economies dedicated to arms spending, arms production and arms procurement is still barely recognized among the elites of Arab capitals across the region and beyond. The race to acquire or develop ever-more sophisticated weaponry systems, and the willingness of Western governments and others to supply arms, continues apace. Newspapers and specialist reports consistently cite the extent to which states within the region as well as others outside it are willing to fund an escalating arms race, often citing 'mutual deterrence' as the pretext for funding and allowing the shipment of thousands of arms and billions of bullets into contested arenas. As one Gazan asserts, 'For a gun, a piece of bread and the promise of a job tomorrow everyone is a gun for hire when there is hunger and extreme poverty on our streets.'[3]

Since 1945 attempts at peacemaking within the region have been perceived as largely unsuccessful. Indeed, the standard response to a conflict seemed to be extra effort in exacerbating the problem rather than seeking its peaceful resolution. For many years, the most that was hoped for in the field of peacemaking were internationally mediated ceasefire agreements. In addition, the politics of peacemaking were not viewed positively in the national and regional arenas from which political leaders took their cues. Political legitimacy was all too often tied to aggression, belligerence and a vocabulary of conflict. The nature of leadership within the region was, for many decades, predicated on the notion of strength through aggression and conflict. President Nasser of Egypt, probably the greatest Arab leader of the twentieth century, underpinned his leadership of Egypt and his bid for the regional crown by promoting an agenda of belligerence, in particular against Israel but also in his relations with Jordan, Iraq and Syria, and on the side of one of the parties in the civil conflict in Yemen in the late 1960s. His roots lay in the Egyptian military, and the *coup d'état* launched by the Egyptian Free Officers in 1952 which led to the establishment of the Egyptian republic was but one episode in a phenomenon that characterized the region throughout the 1950s and 1960s. Israel is another example where the military and conflict mentality has dominated the conduct of diplomacy and regional relations for decades. Even when Israel has succeeded in concluding peace with its closest neighbours, that peace has been largely diplomatic and has not extended to the citizens of either party to it. Thus, it is fair to assert that mutual loathing and animosity has been the key characteristic behind many of the key relationships within the region, whether between Israel and Lebanon, Syria and Iraq, Iraq and Iran, Egypt and Libya, Syria and Jordan, Iran and Israel, or Saudi Arabia and Egypt. So does all of this mean that peacemaking is doomed to perpetual failure in the region?

In short, no. Although, as the new millennium witnessed the almost complete collapse of the MEPP, as well as the invasion of Iraq, it is tempting to be more pessimistic. Nevertheless, peacemaking has developed in a variety of ways. Major political changes in the late 1980s occurred regionally and globally to create a new platform from which peacemaking could be launched. Peacemaking – or perhaps more accurately 'conflict transformation' – has finally, albeit with great difficulty in some quarters, entered the vocabulary of policy-makers and political leaders across the region.[4] The futility of conflict has sometimes been recognized independently but mostly through the role, coercive or otherwise, of external actors or mediators. Indeed, it would be foolhardy in the extreme to ignore the impact that external third parties and the internationalization of conflict have had on attempts at conflict resolution in the Middle East. It would, for example, be impossible to understand the dynamics of the Middle East peace process in the 1990s without factoring in the role of the USA and its position as a hegemonic global superpower. In addition, the impact that the United Nations has had in attempting to resolve the conflict, rather than just condemning actors through Security Council resolutions, needs to be acknowledged. Finally, the growing or potential import of other transnational bodies, such as the European Union, must be acknowledged when examining the thorny issue of external involvement in conflict transformation in the region. Indeed, Rupesinghe has argued that 'the chances of successfully resolving a dispute are much higher if national and international agencies and organisations can be persuaded to combine their efforts'.[4]

Many factors, however, need to be critically assessed to determine the required minimum to maintain the momentum for peace in the region. Such factors include the changing pattern of global politics and the end of super-power rivalry in the Middle East, economic issues linked to globalization and the region's poor performance in global markets, the impact of oil prices on world markets, and the religious dimension of some conflicts in the region which concern millions of adherents to one faith or the other across the globe. This last issue in particular was brought into sharp relief during the Palestinian–Israeli negotiations on Jerusalem in summer 2000 and the sub-sequent crisis of violence and conflict in the autumn of that year. The status of Jerusalem ignited violence not only between Israelis and Palestinians in the Holy Land, but in New York, London, South Asia, Yemen and elsewhere. Violent protest, conflict and mutual antagonism underscored the import of the issue to Muslims and Jews across the world.

Conflict resolution, the methods by which wars and other conflicts are ended and resolved, has also changed.[5] Traditional methods and roles remain in some contexts, but in others they have been diminished by new ways of making peace, which include indigenous and regional-based solutions. Indeed, there is evidence of an increasing resistance in many quarters to external mediation of processes of conflict resolution in the region and an increasing reliance on local, traditional methods of dispute resolution which are more inclusive of religious elements, tribal leaders and other elements in society.

The types of conflict resolution and successes associated with them have also varied considerably. Major long-term conflicts have been resolved through peace treaties brokered by international actors, predominantly the USA. Civil conflict in Lebanon has been resolved as a result of regional actors bringing the warring parties to the negotiating table. They may yet have to persuade the Lebanese to stop the descent to war again. Countries in the region such as Saudi Arabia were also responsible for promoting an end to inter-factional conflict and violence between the Palestinians in February 2007. The UN has been responsible for helping to forge peace between Iran and Iraq, and European efforts have been conspicuous in attempts to resolve the Algerian conflict. So what accounts for the renewed interest in peacemaking and conflict resolution within the region? Before this question is answered it is important to make some distinctions. Peace-building, peacemaking, peace processes, conflict resolution and conflict transformation are all separate but related activities. Peace is not something that can be achieved overnight in the Middle East. Nor should the formal cessation of hostilities in the form of signed agreements be viewed as an end to conflict. It is not even enough to presuppose that the conclusion of peace treaties between states means that peace has truly been achieved between the citizens of those states. Unfortunately, 'cold peace' is all too familiar a concept in the region.

The first seismic shift in global politics to impact on the prospects for peacemaking in the Middle East was the end of the Cold War and the collapse of the Soviet Union from 1989 onwards. While the immediate results of this were clearly discernible in the Gulf crisis and the decline of Soviet support for radical Arab states such as Syria, the impact on the politics of peacemaking was not so clear. In many respects the change can only be ascertained by a retrospective focus. For example, the nature of peacemaking between Israel and Egypt in the late 1970s, following the war of 1973, was utterly altered by superpower rivalry in the region and the battle for hegemony between the United States and the Soviet Union. The détente relationship had been severely tested in this theatre of the Cold War and extended to peacemaking brokered by the superpowers. With the absence of the Soviet Union, would the USA play a different role within the region when it came to the realm of peace politics?

The change in the balance of power and an increasing perception of US hegemony in the region led many to believe that US national interest – as represented through its foreign policy – would shape the future of the Middle East, with capitulation the order of the day in a series of Arab capitals that had traditionally been hostile to the USA. It was expected that Syria, for example, bereft of its Soviet patron, would be propelled into the arms of the American State Department. In reality Washington has discovered that there is a limit to its influence in the region, particularly in pushing traditional enemies together and persuading them to negotiate peace. The first round of multilateral peace conferences in 1991, which brought Syrian and Israeli negotiators together for the first time, was misleading because the Syrian President Hafez al-Assad would travel only so far along the road to peace. In addition, the State Department in Washington faced a hostile Congress that maintained that Syria was a 'terrorist state' to which no concessions, even in the name of peace, could be countenanced. Similar accusations are now being made again in the wake of regime change in Baghdad, with members of the US 'hard right' implying that the Syrian regime should be next in line. America's traditional allies, however, have continued to benefit from a 'special relationship' which is able to withstand the pulls and pushes of everyday politics in the region. Yet, as Halliday reminds us, 'To ascribe all of the region's ills to Washington's actions or inaction is facile. To argue consistently that alternative possibilities are preferable and practicable is not.'[6] Evidence of consideration of these new approaches is to be found not only in those spheres of the American orbit in the Middle East such as the Palestinian–Israeli peace process but in those orbits where other actors have a greater interest or influence, such as the Lebanese peace process, where Arab and European actors have played greater roles.

Out of a changing political climate, with America achieving a greater profile in the Middle East yet also determined to ensure that European and other actors play roles when necessary, the new economic landscape has yet to be evaluated. Making war is an expensive business and turning guns into ploughshares has the potential radically to alter and improve living standards in a number of states across the region. In addition, there is a prevalent belief in aid, development and diplomatic circles that with peace a new stability will be generated across the region that will promote greater economic unity and suitable economies of scale, and decrease dependency and indebtedness. Thus, not only will peace mean that the governments of the region devote less of their resources to the military and more to welfare and education, but that improved diplomatic relations will promote inter-regional trade agreements that will assist liberalizing economies. In Israel, for example, if peace agreements are reached with Syria, the Palestinians and Lebanon, not only will the government have to devote less to its standing army and arms industry but the potential markets of the Arab world will be realized for Israeli goods, particularly those in the technology sector.

Another indication that economics matters is the willingness of the international community to promote peace and sponsor peace processes and confidence-building measures through aid and loans. In the late 1980s and early 1990s, King Hussein of Jordan faced mounting economic pressures in his country that sparked public unrest and riots. But with the underpinning of his peace deal with Israel by American aid, and loans from the World Bank and the International Monetary Fund, risking the wrath of his vehemently anti-Israeli citizenry became a realistic proposition. Nor can there be any doubt that without the promise of a peace dividend within the American-sponsored orbit Jordan would not have climbed aboard the peace train that culminated in a treaty with Israel in November 1994. Yet while many believed that Israel would deliver the bulk of the economic dividend, the reality was that the international community – through bilateral and multilateral assistance, loans and direct aid – would shore up the economy and help it to withstand popular discontent at the King's political gamble. The same was true in Lebanon, where, following the end of Israel's occupation of the south in May 2000, the international community reiterated its commitment to assist the process of peace and reconstruction through aid and loans. On the other hand, after 1990 Iraq's population suffered under the regime of internationally imposed sanctions as a result of the conflict with Kuwait. If the UN-imposed sanctions were designed to bring the regime of Saddam Hussein to its knees and prevent further military escapades then they failed; instead, they had the effect, thanks to cynical manipulation by the Iraqi regime, of raising rates of infant mortality, disease and malnutrition and penalizing the most vulnerable and helpless sectors of Iraqi society. The resumption of the weapons inspection programme, the rupture of international opinion, a crisis wrought on the head of the United Nations, and a further pre-emptive military action in which hundreds of thousands of American and other troops were amassed in the Gulf in early 2003 was the way in which certain quarters of the international community sought to achieve the kind of regime change that had not taken place in 1991. Along the way the legitimacy of war was severely scrutinized and immense disquiet was palpable in the majority of Arab capitals.

In Middle East peacemaking talks economic considerations loom like a spectre at the feast at the negotiating tables. Economic issues, therefore, even in the wealthier states of the Gulf, have compelled policy-makers and political leaders to consider new ways of conducting inter-state relations and regional competitions for leadership. Even Saudi Arabia and Kuwait, two of the wealthiest states in the world, were forced to rethink peace strategies in the wake of the 1990 debacle with Iraq. With a decline in oil prices, growing dependency on imports and expanding populations, the leaders of these states were compelled to assess the cost of conflict, and this was largely reflected in national plans that emerged in the latter part of the 1990s.

In the wake of the Gulf crisis, with the collapse of old Arab–Arab and Arab–Iranian relationships and the decline in the importance of maverick leaders like Hafez al-Assad (of Syria) and Muammar Gadaffi (of Libya), some new patterns formerly associated with the politics of conflict have emerged. Such patterns are nascent and it would be premature, for example, to declare that a new era of Arab unity mirroring that of the 1960s or 1970s can be discerned. This also presupposes that such unity was ever achieved in reality anyway. Nevertheless, the rhetoric and postures of hostility, mutual suspicion and antagonism that characterized so many regional relationships within the Arab orbit, as well as in the Arab–Israeli, Iranian–Israeli and Iranian–Arab spheres, show signs of decline or change. Much sabre rattling in the name of Arab unity has been replaced by new statements about unity through partnership and peace. War-weary Iranians, Syrians, Saudis, Lebanese, Iraqis, Kurds, Shi'as and Islamists have developed novel strategies for achieving their goals which increasingly involve negotiation, compromise, peace-building and power-sharing. The importance of such initiatives lies not in their achievements but in the new dialogues emerging in some Arab circles. The role of the Arab League in helping to broker an end to the civil war in Lebanon in 1990 highlighted new approaches. The Ta'if Accord was negotiated by several Arab actors: the Arab League, the governments of Saudi Arabia and Syria, and a tripartite commission of the kings of Morocco and Saudi Arabia and President Chadli Benjedid of Algeria. In this context the tireless efforts of Arab diplomats and political leaders in both the regional structure of the Arab League and the individual mediator states resulted in an end to what was generally considered to be intractable conflict that had destroyed the very fabric of Lebanon over a fifteen-year period. The success of these efforts, however, was explicable only in the context of the new global balance of power and the willingness of the USA to allow the Arabs to negotiate their own way out of this particular conflict.[7] Whether this formula can be repeated in the aftermath of the Israeli confrontation with Hizballah in 2006, which has led to dangerous instability in a country previously apparently on the mend, remains to be seen. Once again the USA will need to step aside from a situation complicated by Washington's hostility to Syria and its obsession with alleged Syrian interference in Iraq and its support for 'international terrorism'. Traditionally, the Americans have always sided with those elements within Lebanon which want an end to Syrian influence and interference.

Negotiation – albeit stalled, erratic, fuelled by emotion and political rhetoric – has become a new political game in the conduct of conflict transformation at an inter-state level in the region. Negotiation processes, however, can take many forms, including: pre-negotiation negotiations; bilateral or multilateral talks; first-, second- and third-track negotiations; and issue-specific negotiations. Formal and informal dialogue and processes characterized relations within the region, particularly around the issue of the Arab–Israeli conflict and associated conflicts throughout the 1990s. Approaches to negotiating processes, therefore, need to be understood and contextualized in terms of the rules of this game.

While negotiation was perceived as a form of externally imposed capitulation, weakness from within, and an acknowledgement that the conflict could not be won by other means, it had little value in the Middle Eastern context. For, after all, these conflicts allowed people to live insular, community-based lives eschewing major episodes of contact with the other as an acknowledgement of their existence. It was a mindset that allowed no room for the enemy. The recognition that negotiation entailed dialogue as well as acceptance or recognition of the enemy was an important feature in conflict transformation in the Arab–Israeli and Palestinian–Israeli conflicts throughout the 1990s. In addition, trust-building as both a prerequisite and a primary feature of such processes was essential, yet at the same time most difficult to achieve. The difficulties were encountered within the first months of the twenty-first century, and any trust that had developed was ruptured by the events that followed the outbreak of the second Palestinian uprising in September 2000. Those involved in the Oslo process failed to surmount the final obstacles and garner support for trust and concession as frantic final status talks were convened by the Clinton administration.

Negotiation, then, became meaningful only when recognition, trust-building, compromise and compensation entered the vocabulary of the peacemakers. Problem-sharing is the key to problem-solving. As Flamhaft illustrates in the Israeli–Palestinian context, three factors determine the point at which the time is ripe to negotiate: 'the combatants' conclusion that the continuation of the status quo would only worsen their situation, their simultaneous desire to reach an agreement . . . [and] the domestic support for a negotiated solution'.[8]

The Oslo process, which followed the very public failure of the Madrid Conferences (1991–3), was shrouded in secrecy and involved, for the first time, direct recognition of the PLO and contact between the Israeli government and PLO officials. The failure of Madrid, where Yitzhak Shamir had refused to recognize the PLO as the legitimate representatives of the Palestinian people and had engaged in a public strategy of stalling and intransigence, had served only to reinforce mutual suspicion and mistrust. Secrecy, on the other hand, was the key to the success of the Oslo talks: negotiators were free from external pressures and interference – exactly the type of interference that had characterized the American- and Russian-sponsored Madrid process. The bedrock of the Oslo process, however, was recognition and trust-building. On the Israeli side indirect recognition occurred in two ways. First, the secret talks were to be held directly with a member of the PLO and not through a delegated conduit, such as the Jordanians. Second, in January 1993 Israeli law repealed the ban on contacts with the PLO. As Abu Odeh highlights, 'Rabin was the first Israeli leader to recognize the Palestinians as a peace partner to be approached rather than as an obstacle to be bypassed. The DOP [Declaration of Principles] attests to that.'[9] The ground rules outlined at the first meetings in January 1993 reveal much about the processes of pre-negotiation and negotiation. The two sides agreed that there would be 'no dwelling on past grievances, total secrecy, and retractibility of all positions put forward in the talks'; from this point constructive dialogue and then negotiation could take place.[10]

Secrecy, trust-building and recognition, however, cannot guarantee any peace process, and the stalled timetabling of such processes illustrates the

impact that time and motion can have on the so-called momentum for peace.
The achievement of peace treaties, agreements and timetables for future
negotiation and resolution of outstanding issues is admirable, but remains
conspicuous by its absence in the context of the Middle East; these are
national governmental and non-governmental strategies that engage citizens
in inter-state peace-building measures. To date, much of the peacemaking
and confidence-building that has occurred in the region has been limited to
the elite. There are no indications as yet of a generational change in attitudes
towards the futility of major conflict, acts of political violence and harm to
each other despite the emergence of a dynamic, motivated younger generation of citizens who are increasingly aware of their position, not just in the
region but within the global system. For, as Halliday has suggested, 'relations
between the states of the region themselves remain dominated by suspicion,
conflict and latent (when not overt) confrontation'.[11] Certainly, externally
imposed solutions to conflict in the region will ultimately fail to address core
national interests and citizens' rights in a global era. Externally imposed
solutions, while professing even-handedness, neutrality and mediation rather
than intimidation, are nevertheless motivated by economic and strategic
concerns about maintaining the global balance of power both politically
and economically in the Western orbit. Wars to 'bring democracy' to the
region fail to convince subject populations that the intentions of such
liberators are as honourable as they claim to be. For this is the point when
the collective historical memory which is so important to so many in the
region comes to the fore. For the Iraqis, for instance, when British Prime
Minister Tony Blair declared that the war on their country in March 2003
was about 'liberating the Iraqi people', not conquering them, the bitter
memory of Britain's less-than-glorious previous meddling in Iraq was
revived. For the same promises had been uttered by the British General
Maude during the First World War when he conquered Baghdad, promising
the people: 'Our armies do not come into your cities and lands as conquerors
or enemies, but as liberators . . . Your wealth has been stripped off you
by unjust men . . . The people of Baghdad shall flourish.'[12] Less than five
years later the British, as one of their spoils of war, had created Iraq as a
mandate territory, a highly artifical construction subject to their authority
and to that of a puppet monarch, and not reflecting the aspirations of the
local people.

There is a residual fear in the region of history repeating itself – this time
with America replacing Britain or France as the imperial power keen
to secure its economic and strategic interests at the expense of the rights of
the native people. However, the tentative emergence of local methods
of conflict dispute, such as religious- or tribal-based conciliation processes,
offers some hope that the region may emerge from its conflicts to establish

new relationships of peace-building rather than slipping back into the atavistic grip of a Hobbesian state of war, to which so many in the West have ascribed the region in the past. To assume the former rather than the latter is to credit the citizens of the region with the same human values of compassion and peace as are found anywhere else in the world. Accepting the latter, however, might also imply that while so many states of the region remain dominated by authoritarian leaders and their military machines, the ordinary citizens will remain immobilized by oppression and conflict. Additionally, however, the prospect of liberation, by any means, does not necessarily promise automatic upgrading to freedom, equality and liberty.

In the twenty-first century, as much as at any other time in the Middle East's history, one is reminded of the words of Agatha Christie, who remarked in a different context that one 'is left with a horrible feeling now that war settles nothing; that to win a war is as disastrous as to lose one'. The challenge is to exert as much effort and put as many resources into peace-making in the region as have been devoted to militarization and conflict. This challenge has never been greater than now, as we shall describe in our final chapter.

10 No end to the storm
9/11 and the war in Iraq

And after these things I saw another angel come down from heaven, having great power; and the earth was lightened with his glory. And he cried mightily with a strong voice, saying, Babylon the great is fallen, is fallen, and is become the habitation of devils, and the hold of every foul spirit, and a cage of every unclean and hateful bird. For all nations have drunk of the wine of the wrath of her fornication, and the kings of the earth have committed fornication with her, and the merchants of the earth are waxed rich through the abundance of her delicacies.

Book of Revelation, XVIII, King James Bible

Post-1945, the day the world appeared to pause and understand again the frailty of human life was 11 September 2001, when members of an Islamist terror organization named al-Qaeda (the Base) led by Usama bin Laden launched a series of attacks on New York and Washington. Hundreds lost their lives on the three planes that were hijacked and crashed by the hijackers into buildings that symbolized American military, economic and political power. Thousands in total died as a result of the attack. The American people experienced a direct sense of terrifying vulnerability, but the shock waves were felt worldwide.

The instant judgement on the terrorist attacks was that they 'changed everything'.[1] The twentieth-century tradition of nation-states in conflict had been, at a stroke, transformed into the twenty-first-century fear of a new world disorder, with the prospect of the 'evil' forces of fanatical transnational terrorism challenging the established basis of civilized society on an un-precedented scale. In this instance, the shadowy network of al-Qaeda was perceived as taking on 'the West', as represented by the United States of America. In this sense 'the West' was understood as representative of values that bin Laden and his cohorts contested. The locus of the new conflict, the seed-bed of Islamist hate, the region that spawned the callous suicide-bombers, was the Middle East.

The 'Middle Eastern and Islamist connection' to the attacks, assumed from the outset, resonated strongly throughout such Western capitals as Washington, London and Rome. In this respect the Middle East was once again perceived in many quarters as a harbinger of conflict, with Islamic dimensions to boot. This revived notions of a clash of civilizations, with Islam and the West facing each other across an ever-widening chasm. Under this notion the West led and Islam trailed in the wake of the progressive, democratic and plural values of the new world order shaped by non-Muslim power. Indeed, following the attacks, Italian Prime Minister Berlusconi declared, 'We must be aware of the superiority of our civilization, a system that has guaranteed well-being, respect for human rights and – in contrast with Islamic countries – respect for religious and political rights.'[2]

The response from quarters of the international community made vulnerable by al-Qaeda's attacks was to declare a 'global war on terrorism'. In an address to the American nation after the attacks, US President George W. Bush outlined the scale of the conflict with terrorism, declaring that, 'This is not, however, just America's fight. And what is at stake is not just America's freedom. This is the world's fight. This is civilization's fight. This is the fight of all who believe in progress and pluralism, tolerance and freedom.' Thus the war on terrorism was declared and President Bush outlined in stark terms the American position to states in the international order, including those of the Middle East: 'You're either with us or against us in the fight against terror.'[3] The mood in Washington, or more specifically within the dominant elements of the Bush administration, now mattered more than ever in terms of the prospects for conflict and peacemaking in the Middle East. It has been noted that, 'Since the al-Qaeda attacks Americans have thought differently about their vulnerability, their power and the need to use that power in faraway places in order to feel safe at home. Because America has changed, the world has changed too.'[4] The greatest change, with major implications for the Middle East, was the feeling in Washington of confidence, almost triumphalism, springing from the success of the initial stages of the war on terrorism. The campaign against the Taliban government and al-Qaeda in Afghanistan was launched within three months of 9/11 and waged by a US-led coalition allied to anti-Taliban elements within the country itself.

Self-congratulation was perhaps not out of place at that time. The rapid removal of the Taliban regime from power, with negligible loss of Allied lives, was a remarkable accomplishment. It was achieved despite concern that the Allied coalition could, like the Russians before them, be sucked into a long, bloody campaign with the odds stacked against them. With the ejection of the Taliban as the governing force and the installation of a new, broad interim governing force (the Loya Jirga), the main task appeared to have been achieved in terms of Afghanistan being understood as the seat of terror in this region. Usama bin Laden also lost out on a wider front. Despite his appeals, there were no uprisings against moderate Muslim regimes with close links to the West, which he stigmatized as being part of a 'Zionist–Crusader alliance'. The jihad, as a form of conflict undertaken by ordinary Muslims in the Middle East, never materialized. The anti-Western demonstrations that were staged in a number of Muslim countries were few in number and lacked the fervour for which bin Laden must have hoped. (Nevertheless, the fact that they took place at all contributed to a sense of disquiet and alarm in the United States of America.) Countless Muslim leaders and preachers, as well as ordinary people, condemned bin Laden's act as terrorism, not jihad, and accused him of bringing the name of Islam into terrible disrepute. Even elements of radical Islamism distanced themselves from such deeds and refuted claims that *their* struggles, *their* resistance, even if undertaken by violent means, could be equated with the atrocities perpetrated by al-Qaeda on American targets. However, the reaction to the 2003 invasion of Iraq was on an entirely different scale.

As we noted in Chapter 3, the perceived success on the Afghan front encouraged elements of the Bush administration to widen the war on terrorism. 'Axis of evil' references to Iraq, Iran and North Korea in Bush's statements jarred in the Middle East and he was widely ridiculed for his jingoistic 'OK Corral' presentation. But this was not just chest thumping. The jungle drums conveyed a serious message. The epithet 'axis of evil', reminiscent of President Reagan's memorable description of the former Soviet Union as an 'evil empire', together with deliberate leaks of a US Pentagon 'hit-list' of nuclear targets in a number of 'rogue' or potentially rogue states signalled Washington's resolve to deal severely with any government that it assumed presented a grave threat to its security.[5] A threat to security was taken as meaning, among other things, unconcealed or clandestine support for movements such as al-Qaeda, or a whole host of other groups from the Middle East region designated as 'terrorist'. In this respect most states of the region, and a significant number of non-state actors, would fall under the scope of the USA.

Indeed, by 2003, the FBI list of foreign organizations designated as 'terrorist' by the USA featured twenty-eight names, of which eighteen originated or were based in the Middle East. Also officially threats to security were any states thought to be in possession of or developing weapons of mass destruction (WMD), which, because of the disposition of the regimes in question, could find their way into the hands of terrorists. There was a particular fear of an 'un-Holy' alliance between transnational terror elements such as al-Qaeda and the regime of Saddam Hussein in Iraq. In this case, and at that time, there was a lack of hard intelligence specifically linking the Iraq ruling clique to bin Laden, and the ideological chasm between a religiously motivated extremist and a secular regime tended to be overlooked. However, as has been the case elsewhere among disparate radical groups, the one issue that was presumed to unite such unlikely bedfellows was their anti-Americanism. It was bin Laden's supposed links with Saddam Hussein that President Bush had primarily in mind as he asserted on 11 March 2002: 'the war will not be over when the terrorist networks are disrupted, scattered and discredited but when the sources of the weapons of mass destruction they are seeking to obtain have been removed as well'.[6] This pronouncement represented a new focus on the Middle East. Finding friendly governments in the region that would be ready to prosecute the war on terrorism alongside the USA would be important. Yet, the prospect of an increased American presence in the Arab world, irrespective of the intent, alarmed many Arab leaders. Only the leadership in Israel seemed to find solace in the prospect that the USA could take up arms in the region and prosecute military conflicts against some of its main enemies. Even on this front, however, there were tensions as the American administration urged restraint in the Israeli government's attitude to the Palestinians, while busily courting Arab support for an international coalition against the Taliban and al-Qaeda.

One of the more immediate manifestations of new conflicts in the Middle East – between an actor external to the region and state and non-state actors within it – occurred in Yemen. There the USA turned to the governing authorities and applied pressure on them to cooperate in the war on terrorism. Since late 2001 hundreds of US special forces have been stationed in Yemen (and neighbouring Djibouti), undertaking the training of Yemeni special forces as well as manning their own missions against suspected Islamist elements. This has led to the government being targeted by anti-American and Islamist elements as 'stooges' of the USA and generated new tensions in an already fractious region. Yemeni political stability has never been taken for granted and, only a decade on from the reunification of the country, destabilization was an ever-present prospect. Continued American involvement could create new problems in the not-too-distant future.

The US government was also anxious to build and maintain a long-term international alliance against terrorism. When the Taliban had been routed (albeit temporarily) in Afghanistan, the Iraqi President Saddam Hussein and his regime came into the frame as 'Public Enemy Number One' in the US hit-list of 'rogue states'. President Clinton's policy of containment in respect of Iran and Iraq was now replaced with one of active and aggressive confrontation. With that came consideration of pre-emption. Elements within the US administration who had been deeply engaged in the events of 1990–1, such as Donald Rumsfeld, now seemed determined to finish what had been started by the first President Bush. Figures such as Paul Wolfowitz, who had served as Under-Secretary of Defense for Policy during Desert Storm and helped to shape US policy, outlined their position on Iraq as self-confessed 'hawks' who made clear their determination to achieve regime change in Baghdad. The neo-conservatives, the hard men of the American right and in alliance with the 'Christian Zionist' fundamentalists, were to have a profound effect on US policy towards the Arab world. To what extent this aligned with the broader goals of the war on terrorism, the notion of threat to American security or economic and strategic considerations and ambitions as they related to the Middle East would become clear as the case for military action against Iraq was proposed by the US administration (along with British Prime Minister Tony Blair) to the court of world opinion. However, much as the USA wanted to carry a respectable body of international support with it, especially in the Islamic world, the bottom line appeared to be that if its traditional friends could not or would not help (including a largely unconvinced UN Security Council), it was prepared to do the job itself.[7]

At first it appeared that old alliances would endorse the US spearhead against Iraq. Through astute diplomatic endeavour, the USA and UK were able to secure a unanimous Security Council resolution (SCR 1441) on 8 November 2002, in which the UN stipulated that Iraq must disarm, with provision for further UN action in case of non-compliant Iraqi behaviour. The resolution was designed to restart the UN weapons inspections and disarmament process that had halted in 1998. The other dimension to this was to increase pressure for the maintenance of the UN sanctions regime against Iraq. UN data itself demonstrated that the sanctions, or rather (as some would argue) how they had been implemented by the Iraqi regime, had made conditions for ordinary Iraqis similar to those in a poorly resourced refugee camp. But, in the event, SCR 1441 was not the 'green light' for military action that many in the Anglo-American camp believed it to be. Encouraged by the adoption of SCR 1441, the case for war was being furiously constructed in Washington and London, with regime change, weapons of mass destruction, human rights abuses and other issues cited as reasons for seeking a pre-emptive conflict on Iraq and the regime of Saddam Hussein. As diplomatic pressure grew and UN Security Council members such as France and Russia remained unconvinced by the case for war against Iraq, Dr Hans Blix, heading the UN weapons inspection team, also asked for more time. Yet, by early March 2003, Britain and the USA (along with other, much smaller contingent Allied forces) were strategically located in the Middle East, with only the reluctance of Turkey to allow a US military presence on its territory hampering the war plans. At the UN the failure to obtain the necessary votes dissuaded Britain and the USA from pursuing a Security Council resolution sanctioning military action under the auspices of the United Nations.

By 17 March, preparations for war were well advanced and the prospect of sustaining peace in the Arab Gulf waned as UN personnel were ordered out of Iraq. Thousands of British and American troops took up positions in northern Kuwait, diplomats packed their bags and the massed ranks of the international press corps arrived in Doha and Kuwait City. Whether the war would be short or long, would bring the region to the brink of international crisis, would lead to the toppling of regimes and the visible increase of American power in the Middle East were all questions that were then unanswerable. There were fears that if Saddam Hussein possessed weapons of mass destruction of a biological or chemical variety, then he would employ them – precisely the same fears which were expressed over a decade earlier as the land war of February 1991 got under way. There were also worries that America would end up engaged in a long-term conflict that would become increasingly unpopular at home, in which their military superiority would be undermined by local guerrilla tactics, as had happened in Vietnam. Moreover, there was a conviction in some quarters that a war against Iraq would do more to engender conflict in the Middle East – and *from* the Middle East, as perpetrated by terrorist elements – than ever before. This vision was outlined by the Vatican, which declared:

> One can foresee the destabilisation of the entire Middle East because the more politicised Islamic masses, which already harbour a deep hate for the West, will see it as an act of war against Islam and against Arab and Muslim countries . . . The gravest consequence of a war against Iraq, however, would be a flare-up of terrorism against the United States and against allied Western countries.[8]

These were prophetic words indeed. Four years on, Iraq was immobilized by insurgency and civil war and was still occupied by thousands of foreign troops. And terrorists claiming the invasion of Iraq as a primary motive had perpetrated atrocities in Spain, the UK and elsewhere.

Nevertheless, on 19 March 2003, the USA took the initiative, launching missile strikes against targets in Baghdad, and in the first weeks of the war Allied military gains were made at some cost to the civilian population as well as Iraqi military conscripts. There was a moment of disquiet in the second week of the war when it appeared that, after taking Umm Qasr and Basra to the south of the country, military victory in the rest would not be swift. In reality, though, there was merely a military pause before the assault on Baghdad. Concerns about a new Stalingrad failed to be borne out as the

Iraqi defence of the capital disintegrated, with even allegedly elite units refusing to fight. The only determined opposition come from Ba'ath Party, irregular units and some foreign Arab fighters. The regime's elite seemed to evaporate literally overnight between 9 and 10 April, most tellingly symbolized by the overnight disappearance of the Iraqi Information Minister Mohammed Sahaf, the infamous voice of the regime. Even as Baghdad burned before his eyes and with US tanks less than a kilometre away, he announced to the global media that the city was safe. He had labelled the British and US leadership 'an international gang of criminal bastards, bloodsucking bastards, ignorant imperialists, losers and fools'.[9] With the fall of Baghdad a few hours later, and the capitulation of the northern cities of Mosul, Tikrit (the hometown of Saddam Hussein and many others in the regime) and Irbil within the week, military war was all but over.

Yet the fall of Baghdad, the capture of Kirkuk and the end of the regime of Saddam Hussein did not mean that the campaign had successfully run its course, as we shall see later. Its repercussions in the Middle East were keenly felt. First, the implications of regime change pursued and achieved by America began to sink in. As David Frum, a former presidential speechwriter, noted: 'an American-led overthrow of Saddam Hussein . . . would put America more wholly in charge of the region than any power since the Ottomans, or maybe the Romans'.[10] Indeed, the sense that America was enjoying unprecedented authority over a number of regimes in the Middle East was overwhelming, with important implications for future conflicts and peacemaking. Within weeks of the fall of Baghdad the American spotlight was falling on Damascus, with demands on President Bashar al-Assad to crack down on certain elements within his country. Then there was news that American troops would now be deployed out of Saudi Arabia, with many cynics pointing to Iraq as the new location for a US military presence in the Gulf. One conflict in particular, the Palestinian–Israeli dimension of the Arab–Israeli dispute, would once again come to the forefront of many minds in the region. The extent of power, as held in American hands, would now assume new dimensions. However, in reality, the next four years would expose both that power's limitations and its abuse, in Iraq, in Lebanon, in the Israeli–Palestinian arena, in Yemen, and indeed in Afghanistan.

The extent to which the ordinary people of Iraq and the country in general have suffered since the fall of Saddam Hussein's regime and the American-led war against the country can be summed up by reflecting on a variety of statistics as well as human stories. Since 2003 over 3,000 American troops have been killed in Iraq and many more have been injured. Some might argue that such casualties are to be expected during war but not in the rebuilding of the Iraqi state. Clearly concern over this issue motivated American voters to elect the Democrats to the US Congress in 2006. The death toll of Iraqi civilians post-war, however, simply defies belief. The most conservative current estimate runs at 100,000 deaths, but a study in the highly respected medical journal *The Lancet* concluded that this figure had been reached as early as October 2004 (*The Lancet*, 28 October 2004). Two years later, Johns Hopkins University (cited in the *Washington Post*, 10 October 2006) estimated that 655,000 Iraqis had died since the end of the war in 2003. Over 1.8 million Iraqis have undeniably become refugees (including many key professionals, such as doctors and engineers) and a further 1.6 million are internally displaced from their homes, their families and their livelihoods. Fear and paralysis of the state infrastructure and economy mean that the country has fractured and the state is imperilled. The infrastructure, devastated by the war and by the subsequent insurgency, has not been restored to its pre-war state; although electricity generation is at about 2003 levels, there are frequent power cuts. In oil-rich Iraq petrol is in short supply, with motorists having to queue for it for hours. And the government elected as a result of remarkably well-supported elections – given the lack of security and much intimidation – has a remit which barely runs outside the capital. Perhaps inevitably, politics and government are now a sectarian affair. There may be a democratically elected Iraqi government, but without the support of coalition forces, predominantly US, it would struggle to survive, having seen its authority seriously eroded by a sectarian conflict that it seems wholly unable to bring under control. The anti-regime insurgency has been fuelled by about 3,000 foreign militants, from whose ranks it is believed that most of the seemingly inexhaustible supply of suicide-bombers originate. But the insurgency is not a one-sided affair, with both Sunni and Shi'a elements mounting attacks against the coalition forces and their contractors across the country. Total collapse of the government (a serious possibility) would probably lead to a disintegration of the Iraqi state into areas of Sunni, Shi'a and Kurdish influence, with all the further ethnic cleansing this would inevitably entail. This in turn would raise the spectre of intervention from other regional players: Iran, Turkey and Saudi Arabia among them. Such fears have already prompted these external actors to seek to influence the situation within Iraq.

With the deterioration of the situation in Iraq, support for the war among coalition member countries continued to fall. Disillusion with US/UK policy in particular dated from the eventual revelation that Saddam did not possess weapons of mass destruction, certainly in 2003, so the assault against Iraq was both an illegal and a pointless campaign. The supposed existence of Iraqi WMD had been the primary *casus belli*. In Washington, the report by the Baker–Hamilton Iraq Study Group,[11] commissioned by President Bush and published on 6 December 2006, displayed a belated realization that the war was not being won. However, the President's response to calls for an urgent exit strategy was to insist that the only reasonable policy was to 'stay the course', although it was difficult to see how this could be achieved by an administration which had lost its Republican majority in the Senate and House in the mid-term elections of late 2006. With no bipartisan support for plans to increase the number of US forces, the so-called 'surge' planned for 2007, especially in Baghdad, involving one final push to defeat the insurgents and stop the inter-factional hostilities while accelerating the training of more Iraqi security forces to take over from the coalition and allow its withdrawal or redeployment, seemed unlikely to succeed.

The much predicted mess that the war has made of Iraq has truly imperilled the chances for peace and stability in the region. With the wisdom of hindsight, it can be seen that the US-dominated coalition made a number of serious mistakes following its military victory. The dismantling of almost the entire Ba'ath Party infrastructure, including much of the civil service, armed forces and police, for basically doctrinaire reasons put many desperately needed people on the streets immediately and left them at odds with the new administration. This meant having to rebuild the security forces and much of the civil service from scratch while attempting to control an emerging insurgency. It is now also apparent that the Americans from the outset, did not have a proper post-war reconstruction plan or the number of troops to control the country effectively. The occupation administration, the Coalition Provisional Authority (CPA), which was in power before the installation of an Iraqi government, was clumsy and lacked vision, with the occupiers seemingly unwilling to try to understand Iraqi civil and religious society. An obsession with combating 'Islamic radical fundamentalism' unnecessarily made enemies of powerful groups, such as the followers of Moqtada al-Sadr, a prominent Shi'a cleric who, despite being a major-power broker, was studiously ignored by Paul Bremner, the US 'proconsul' who headed the CPA and should have recognized Sadr as a natural ally following the overthrow of an oppressive Sunni minority regime. The lack of American expertise and the fact that the military seemed to call most of the shots ensured that the CPA failed to find any answer for a society in turmoil. With a strong central government removed at a stroke, all the old centrifugal tendencies of a largely artificial entity resurfaced, exacerbated by factional infighting – the dispossessed (from political power) Sunnis increasingly at odds with the triumphant, resurgent Shi'as, so long oppressed by Saddam and his predecessors. Added to this was an increasingly effective and popular insurgency, with a number of al-Qaeda elements, many of them from outside Iraq, delighted to be given the chance to get at the Western occupiers of an Arab country at such close quarters.

As for the Americans, in popular perception at least, they seemed to be intent more on bolstering their strategic position in the Arab world while *inter alia* safeguarding US access to Arab oil and establishing permanent bases for their forces than putting Iraq back on its feet. Billions of US dollars were earmarked for development and reconstruction, but the UN and other agencies, often the targets for insurgent hostility, were increasingly unwilling to expose their staffs to the dangers of working outside the Green Zone, while commercial civil contractors faced similar problems that severely curtailed their effectiveness. There are suggestions that much of this money has yet to be accounted for and there is little enough to show for it on the ground. Nor was the American image helped by its inactivity in the Middle East peace process and seeming complicity with Israeli excesses on the West Bank. The Baker–Hamilton Report recommended that the USA should engage with Iraq's neighbours, Syria and Iran, to elicit their help in trying to resolve the conflict. But President Bush still resorted to the old rhetoric decrying Syria for its alleged assistance to the insurgents in Iraq and its support for Hizballah in its anti-Israeli activities. Iran was similarly fingered for arming and encouraging Shi'a militants in Iraq, and for supporting groups fighting Israel, whether Palestinian or Lebanese. But the big issue for Washington became Iran's nuclear programme, which was believed to be for the production of weapons rather than power generation. Nevertheless, Washington may yet come to see that Damascus and Tehran need to be engaged, not only to help the USA extricate itself from the Iraqi morass but to kick-start the peace process. As we have reiterated a number of times, deal positively and fairly with the Palestinians and Israelis within the framework of a two-state solution and much of the heat of anti-Americanism will evaporate in the Arab world. But this is a tall order for what is increasingly a lame-duck administration.

Iraq is not the only problem George W. Bush has faced during his time in office. A significant casualty of the 9/11 attacks has been the Middle East peace process. Before September 2001, the second Palestinian Intifada had already erupted. Palestinian violent resistance to the continued occupation of the West Bank and the hopeless stalemate in negotiations resulted in increasingly aggressive Israeli government military action, leading to unprecedented, mostly civilian casualties. Palestinian suicide-bombers were becoming a familiar phenomenon, inflicting horrific carnage mostly against Israeli civilians – and these acts inevitably led to instant, severe military retaliation.

Then came 9/11. The Israeli government, sensing a major tactical advantage, was quick to align Israel with the USA in the war on terrorism. Palestinian political violence was increasingly conflated with the threat posed by al-Qaeda.[12] Israel, and the powerful Israeli lobby in the USA, enthusiastically embraced and endorsed a simplistic view prevalent mostly on the American (and Israeli) right, with neo-conservatives and Christian Zionists to the fore, that indiscriminately lumped together many dissident elements, mostly with Islamic connections and, for the main part, Arabs. As Camille Mansour has put it: 'Sharon immediately concluded that the new situation allowed him to claim that he was in the front line against terrorism. He now had *carte blanche* to set the rules of the game in the Palestinian–Israeli sphere . . . while loudly proclaiming that Arafat was Israel's Bin Laden.'[13] The most striking manifestation of Israeli policy post-9/11 was the effort to marginalize Arafat and to degrade his security apparatus. Later, Sharon even tried to drive him into exile: from December until early May 2002, Israeli tanks besieged the PLO leader, confining him to his office complex in Ramallah. Punitive Israeli air strikes targeted Arafat's security forces and destroyed much of the Palestinian Authority's infrastructure. At the same time, though, the Israelis demanded that the neutered Palestinian authorities rein in radical elements like Hamas and Islamic Jihad. In pursuing these tough tactics, Sharon appeared to be acting with US acquiescence, if not active support. On the Palestinian side, suicide attacks deep into Israel and guerrilla raids on Jewish settlements and military outposts increased as part of the spiral of violence and counter-violence.

These conflagrations, covered on prime-time television, forced a reluctant US intervention in the form of Colin Powell, the US Secretary of State. This high-profile regional swing was a watershed for the Bush administration with regard to the Palestinian–Israeli conflict as the USA had previously adopted a hands-off approach to conflict management rather than resolution.[14] The Israeli reoccupation of the West Bank in April 2002 changed that. Many Arab capitals erupted in anti-Israeli and anti-US demonstrations in support of the Palestinians, and the potential for destabilization forced the USA to act. As far as many in the administration were concerned, the Middle East peace process was a lower priority than dealing with Iraq, but even the hardliners realized there was no hope of any Arab support for a new confrontation with Baghdad – even from traditional friends in the region – unless the USA could be seen to be actively involved in reviving it. The degree of US even-handedness mattered little. The onus was inevitably placed on the Palestinians to undertake a series of changes and reforms (some much needed) in a climate of daily Israeli measures against their civilian population. In the spring of 2003 the promise of a 'roadmap' for peace was announced by the USA. This built on the American-supported UN Security Council Resolution 1397,[15] which for the first time specifically endorsed a 'vision' of a Palestinian state alongside an Israeli one. In Bush's words, that vision is

of a day when two states, Israel and Palestine, will live side by side in peace and security. I call upon all parties in the Middle East to abandon old hatreds and to meet their responsibilities for peace. The Palestinian state must be a reformed and peaceful and democratic state that abandons forever the use of terror. The government of Israel, as the terror threat is removed and security improves, must take concrete steps to support the emergence of a viable and credible Palestinian state, and to work as quickly as possible toward a final status agreement. As progress is made toward peace, settlement activity in the occupied territories must end.[16]

So, to what extent, post-9/11, are there new 'lines in the sand' with regard to the prospects for conflict and peace in the Middle East? Will Middle Eastern and Western (as well as other) governments need to reorder their priorities dramatically in the light of the war on terrorism? Lights still burn late in many capitals of Western Europe, the former Soviet Bloc, the Middle East and beyond looking at this question, and have done ever since September 2001. Our judgement is that the attacks of 9/11 have altered the balance of power in the Middle East, with the most immediate consequences being felt in Afghanistan, among radical Islamist elements, in the Palestinian–Israeli matrix and in Iraq. In the medium to long term, American re-engagement in the region, which has given preference to pre-emptive military (rather than diplomatic) power, has major implications for relations within the region as well as for other international actors. There is now much more emphasis on security issues, such as military training, sale of sophisticated defence equipment and the exchange of counter-terrorist intelligence with friendly countries. Arms sales, trading and militarization of the region are unlikely to decline. There may well be a realignment of the American military presence, but Iraq is unlikely now to be the route out of Saudi Arabia for US forces. Rather, the upper Gulf presents a more welcoming environment, but much still depends on any US confrontation with Iran. It is difficult to predict whether this will result in conflict prevention of a major order and/or the promotion of localized conflicts within states. However, it is safe to say that bilateral and multilateral involvement by Western governments in aid programmes aimed at alleviating poverty in the poorer Arab countries will not be substantially increased. And peace-building will be difficult to sustain if that is the case.

A major priority will be monitoring potential internal threats in those countries with close ties with the West, where there is known to be sympathy for al-Qaeda and some of whose nationals have been involved in the terrorist network. Saudi Arabia is probably the most worrying case. Despite the tight control that the House of Saud maintains over its citizens, there is a real threat from dissident elements with radical Islamist associations. Some of these will also reflect the schisms within Islam and the tensions that

Saudi promotion of Wahhabi fundamentalist ideology has created within the Muslim domain. For it is not only young Saudi radicals who are turning to Islam out of disgust with their regime's close ties with the West – especially the USA, with its support for Israel – and out of despair at the inability of regimes like their own effectively to help the Palestinians. Stories of corruption on a vast scale among the princely elite fuel similar emotions in a country where the economy is weak and unemployment is rising among a young workforce. There was some evidence that bomb outrages in 2003 and 2004 that were blamed on expatriates were in fact the work of home-grown elements seeking to destabilize the country, and the bland assurances of senior Saudis that all was well were not convincing. Since then, the Saudi authorities have had a number of successes against the home-grown militants, but there is still a failure to grasp the fact that the absence of adequate political and social rights generally, especially in the context of close official ties with the West, encourages support for radical dissident elements in a number of 'moderate' Arab countries. Poverty, abuse of human rights, striving for security at the expense of liberty and an absence of democratic or pluralistic institutions all create the conditions for political violence and terrorism, and thus conflict.

The problem is that there is considerable ambivalence throughout the Arab world over the question of political liberalization. Many political elites recognize the need to allow more popular participation, if only as a political safety valve, but others (especially those who appear to be calling the shots), perhaps mindful of what happened to the Soviet Union after Gorbachev, are concerned that liberalization or democracy will quickly undermine their authority and even oust them from power. Indeed, evidence of opposition from Islamist groups influenced by philosophies that are also embraced by Usama bin Laden may be used by some of these regimes as yet another pretext for resisting the democratic impulse expressed among their people. They may be genuinely anxious about the degree of fundamental opposition – from a variety of social forces and elements – to their rule and prefer repression to liberty. And it is not only in the Gulf countries that ruling authorities have ordered security crackdowns on the grounds of tackling terrorism: in less evidently autocratic regimes, like Jordan, Morocco and Egypt, threats, real and imaginary, have provided the pretext for new attacks on fundamental liberties.

Admittedly, in the Gulf some cautious steps permitting participation in state legislatures were taken in the wake of the Gulf War of 1990–1. Votes for women in Kuwait, albeit in a very limited franchise, were a case in point. This can be considered as a form of internally driven conflict prevention by the ruling elite. There is also awareness, in such circles, of the importance of economic reform to meet the rising expectations of expanding populations. Yet support for economic liberalization and diversification away from total reliance on oil and gas and their derivatives has not proved a resounding economic or political success.[17] In 2002 there was recognition in reports from organizations such as the United Nations Development Programme and the World Economic Forum that the states of the Middle East risked further regional instability and conflict because of their failure to modernize. The natural resources of the region, including water, oil and gas, have not been effectively harnessed. Corruption, stagnating economies, poor levels of basic education and high population growth rates (in some cases they are the highest in the world) generate conditions that undermine the prospects for peace and prosperity for the citizens of this region. Economic greed motivated many past conflicts within the region, and they in turn were often linked to strategic considerations allied to external powers and actors. Additionally, there is scepticism that economic reform policies, which were advocated and promoted without much success throughout the late 1980s and 1990s, will work any better second time around.

After the occupation of Iraq, there is a perception in the region, rightly or wrongly, of the threat of further Western military intervention to enforce regime change. Heavy hinting about possible US-led action against Syria and Iran inevitably could be a serious destabilizing factor should it become a consistent *leitmotif* of US rhetoric. Indeed, recent moves by US military units, especially a naval build-up in the Gulf, have raised fears that the Americans are once again about to go beyond the rhetoric. And there will continue to be dissonance between Western-led global capitalism and resistance to it within much of the region. A UNDP report was forthright in its conclusions, arguing that the refusal of political and other leaders in the region to grant women more rights, open up the political process, improve education and crack down on widespread corruption left it incapable of pulling itself out of a two-decade slump.[18] Additionally, the geopolitics of the region, focused as they are on the negative recurrence of conflicts, have left little opportunity for policy-makers and bureaucrats to concentrate state resources and energies on growth, prosperity and peace. The example of Israel demonstrates this, for even with major economic assistance from the USA in the form of direct aid and loans, the Israeli economy has been driven into crisis as a result of conflict with its Palestinian neighbours, 9/11 and fear of instability in the region, depressing economic activity and discouraging foreign investment. A return to peace will promote economic recovery for Israel and help it regain global competitiveness. Regional peace will provide an even greater aid to recovery. Indeed, it is worth remembering that the peace dividend for Israel, in terms of inward investment and so on, from the Oslo accords were higher than for any Arab party, and this imbalance needs to be taken into account in the new equations for peace in the region. Unfortunately, the asymmetry of power – political, economic or otherwise – militates against a lasting peace.

So, in the current highly charged atmosphere it will need a major effort by the international community to revive any peace process. The grievances of the Palestinians and how they are addressed will remain the touchstone of how the Arabs view the policies of the West. Following the inconclusive Israeli–Hizballah confrontation in 2006, Israeli politics are in a state of flux, with a government lacking credibility, popular support or an effective leadership. Meanwhile, the Palestinians have never been so divided. And recent policies of the Israeli government, plus the seeming inability of the international community to alleviate the poverty of many Palestinians, are not making it easy for the latter wholeheartedly to opt for peace.

A fair, just and comprehensive peace – tragically still a distant prospect – will do more than anything else to dissipate support for al-Qaeda and other extremist groups. Despite the ambitions of British Prime Minister Tony Blair to lead the march for peace as part of his 'legacy' before leaving Downing Street, or the agendas of France and Russia, it is only American leverage, pressure, military or diplomatic power that can put the Palestinian–Israeli peace process back on track. This is not, however, the same as applying such pressure in other areas of conflict in the region. American leverage did not work and is unlikely to work in the future in Lebanon or Algeria. Iraq has hardly been a conspicuous success, either. Nor, given its present circumstances, can it hope to answer the challenges arising from the wider manifestation of Islamist politics, including their extremist offshoots. The path to peace, rather than to military pacification, throughout the region will have to be envisioned entirely differently.

Short glossary of terms and organizations

Aliyah Jewish immigration. The first Aliyah was between 1882 and 1884, with another between 1890 and 1891, when immigrants came to Palestine from Russia and Eastern Europe. Four further Aliyahs between 1905 and the 1930s were stimulated by events in Europe, the most significant being the rise of the Nazis in Germany.

Amal Groups of the Lebanese resistance. An anti-Israeli Shi'a radical organization based in southern Lebanon founded by Imam Musa al-Sadr in 1974. Post-1980, the Islamic section of Amal propagated Ayatollah Khomeini's views. It developed into **Hizballah** ('the Party of God'). Amal enjoyed support from Syria and Iranian Hizballah, thus splitting the Shi'a radical movement in Lebanon into two rival groups.

Arab League The League of Arab States founded in 1947 by Egypt, Lebanon, Iraq, Syria, Transjordan, Yemen and Saudi Arabia. Since then all independent Arab countries have joined, as has 'Palestine', as originally represented by the PLO.

Ba'ath Party From the Arabic for 'Renaissance'. A pan-Arab socialist party originating in Syria in 1947. It had considerable influence in Jordan, Lebanon and Iraq, and came to power in both Syria and Iraq.

Black September Name given by Palestinians to events in Jordan in September 1970 which initiated a civil war leading to the defeat of the PLO leadership by King Hussein. Following the Palestinian defeat in Jordan Fatah created a terrorist organization of this name. It was responsible for the killing of the Jordanian Prime Minister in 1971 and of eleven Israeli athletes at the Munich Olympics in 1972.

Deir Yassin Palestinian village where, in April 1948, 245 Palestinian civilians, including women and children, were massacred by Zionist forces. Palestinians claim that this was an act of ethnic cleansing sanctioned by the new Israeli leadership to encourage Palestinians to flee. The majority of Israelis refute the Palestinian claim as propaganda.

Diaspora Originally referred to the dispersal of Jews around the world following the destruction of Jerusalem by the Romans in AD 135. Now also applied to worldwide Palestinian communities exiled since the war of 1948.

Eisenhower Doctrine Proclaimed by President Eisenhower in 1957, this promised US assistance to Middle Eastern states threatened by 'international communism'. Cited to justify US assistance to Jordan and military involvement in Lebanon in 1958. Ideological basis for US support for the Central Treaty Organisation (CENTO), involving Turkey, Iran and Pakistan.

Al Fatah Reverse acronym from the Arabic *Haraka Tahriir Falistiin*, a movement to liberate Palestine. Established in 1957 and brought to prominence by Yasser Arafat, it remains the largest Palestinian movement.

Fatwa Muslim edict issued by religious leaders.

Fedayeen Arabic term for resistance forces, particularly those of the PLO.

Golan Heights Strategically important Syrian highlands dominating the Sea of Galilee and the northern Jordan Valley. Occupied by Israeli forces in 1967 and 'annexed' in 1981. Now the home of a number of Jewish settlements. Remains the main bone of contention between Syria and Israel.

Green Line Line in Beirut dividing Christian and Muslim communities established during the civil war of 1975 to 1990. Also the armistice lines between Israel and neighbouring Arab countries drawn up in 1949 following the first Arab–Israeli War.

Gulf Cooperation Council (GCC) Formed in May 1981 by the six Arab gulf monarchies of Saudi Arabia, Bahrain, Qatar, Oman, Kuwait and the United Arab Emirates. Framework for cooperation among the member states in a number of areas, including defence and external relations.

Halabja Iraqi Kurdish area attacked by Iraq with chemical weapons in March 1988.

Hamas Acronym from the Arabic *Harakat al-Muqawama al-Islamic* (Movement of the Islamic Resistance). Radical Palestinian Islamic movement opposed to peace with Israel and to the Oslo accords. Emerged during the **Intifada** and has conducted a number of terrorist attacks on Israelis, including suicide bombings.

Hizballah (Party of God) Lebanese Shi'ite radical organization. Rival of **Amal**. Enjoys financial backing from Iran. Instrumental in enforcing the Israeli withdrawal from south Lebanon in 2000.

Intifada Palestinian popular uprising that erupted in December 1987 against the Israeli occupation of the Gaza Strip and the West Bank.

Islamic Jihad Palestinian Islamist organization which gave first impetus to the **Intifada**, calling for a return to Islamic values as well as taking the fight to Israel. Also name for members of Khomeini's Islamic Revolutionary Movement operating with **Amal** and **Hizballah** from the Beqaa Valley in Lebanon under the command of the 'Council of Lebanon'.

Jihad Literally 'struggle'. Obligation of Muslims to engage in defensive battle in the face of foreign occupation or unjust rule.

Knesset Israel's parliament.

Law of Return Law passed by **Knesset** in 1950 giving Jews throughout the world the legal right of immigration to Israel.

Levant Translates as 'rising' (sun). Originally the eastern Mediterranean landmass from Greece to Egypt. Now commonly refers only to Syria and Lebanon.

Likud Israeli right-wing parliamentary bloc formed in 1973.

Maghreb 'West' in Arabic. Used to describe the North African countries of Morocco, Algeria, Tunisia and Libya.

Majlis Arabic (and Farsi) word meaning 'assembly'. Used for parliaments throughout the Arab world and in Iran.

Mandate System of administration authorized by the League of Nations for former German colonies and Asian parts of the Ottoman Empire at the end of the First World War. Intended for the tutelage by the more advanced nations of peoples considered unready for independence. In the Middle East Britain was awarded the mandates for Palestine, Transjordan and Iraq; France for Syria and Lebanon.

Mossad Israeli external intelligence service.

Nasserism Arab nationalist sentiment focused on President Gamal Abdel Nasser of Egypt throughout the 1950s and 1960s as the main exponent of shaping a distinctive Arab identity and social progress.

Occupied Palestinian Territories The areas occupied by Israel following the 1967 war: the **Golan Heights**, taken from Syria (and annexed by Israel in 1981); the West Bank, conquered from Jordan; the Gaza Strip and the Sinai peninsula, seized from Egypt; and East Jerusalem, taken from Jordan and illegally annexed.

Palestine Liberation Organization (PLO) Founded in 1964, the umbrella organization for a number of Palestinian political and guerrilla organizations.

Palestinian National Authority (PNA) Originally chaired by Yasser Arafat, the legislative and executive body responsible for exercising powers devolved to the autonomous Palestinian areas following the Oslo accords with Israel.

Pan-Arabism Movement for Arab unity as one Arab nation.

Phalangist Party (Kataib) Main political party of the Maronite right in Lebanon with a history of fascist tendencies.

Republican Guard Elite Iraqi troop unit which spearheaded the Ba'athist coup of Baghdad in 1968.

Sephardi Commonly refers to Jews of Middle Eastern or North African origin.

South Lebanon Army A Christian militia force which acted as an ally and proxy of Israel during its occupation of south Lebanon.

UNIFIL United Nations Interim Force in Lebanon, established in 1978 as a result of UN Resolution 425 as a peacekeeping force.

Zionism Political ideology for the establishment of a Jewish state.

Notes

Introduction

1 Orientalism refers to the tradition of antipathy and hostility to the Middle East and Muslim world that grew out of the political motivations of colonial intervention in the Middle East. The debate about Orientalism is discussed further in Chapter 4. See E. Said, *Orientalism*, Harmondsworth: Penguin, 1995 (second edition).

2 S. Bromley, *Rethinking the Middle East*, Cambridge: Polity, 1994, p. 116.

3 Arthur Balfour was the British Foreign Secretary who in 1917 issued a declaration announcing support for the Zionist cause in Palestine. See Chapters 1 and 2 for further explanation (also notes for Chapter 1).

4 S. Fischer, D. Rodrik and E. Tuma (eds), *The Economics of Middle East Peace: Views from the Region*, Cambridge, Mass.: MIT Press, 1993, p. 2.

5 E. Picard, 'Arab military in politics', in G. Luciani (ed.), *The Arab State*, London: Routledge, 1990, p. 192. According to A. H. Cordesman, the 'Middle East remains the most militarised region in the world by virtually every measure of effort' (A. H. Cordesman, *The Military Balance in the Middle East – An Overview*, Washington, DC: Centre for Security and International Studies, 1998, p. 3).

6 A. Richards and J. Waterbury, *A Political Economy of the Middle East*, Boulder, Colo.: Westview Press, 1990, p. 359.

7 F. Halliday, 'The Middle East at the millennial turn', *Middle East Report*, Winter 1999, p. 5.

Chapter 1

1 Quoted in A. Gresch and D. Vidal, *An A to Z of the Middle East*, London: Zed Books, 1990, p. 210.

2 E. Sahliyeh, 'Beyond the Cold War: the superpowers and the Arab–Israeli conflict', in S. L. Speigel (ed.), *Conflict Management in the Middle East*, Boulder, Colo.: Westview Press, 1992, p. 381.

3 Many members of south Lebanon's Shi'a population had originally welcomed the Israelis, believing they would rid Lebanon of the PLO, which by that point had not only become embroiled in Lebanon's civil war but was universally accused of exacerbating and creating new dimensions to it.

4 E. Monroe, *Britain's Moment in the Middle East*, London: Chatto & Windus, 1963, p. 66.

5 The Balfour Declaration issued on 2 November 1917 outlined a British government pledge to support the Zionists. It announced, 'his Majesty's Government views with favour the establishment in Palestine of a national home for the Jewish people'. The League of Nations mandate for Palestine awarded to the British government in 1923 urged Britain in Palestine to 'be responsible for placing the country under such political, administrative and economic conditions as will secure the establishment of a Jewish national home'.

6 M. Rodinson, *Israel and the Arabs*, Harmondsworth: Penguin, 1982, p. 45.

7 M. Gilbert, *The Arab–Israeli Conflict: Its History in Maps*, London: Weidenfeld & Nicolson, 1984 (fourth edition), p. 46.

8 King Hussein of Jordan, for example, was pressurized into a war that he knew he could not win. See B. Milton-Edwards and P. Hinchcliffe, *Jordan: A Hashemite Legacy*, Reading: Harwoods, 2000.

9 T. Fraser, *The Arab–Israeli Conflict*, Basingstoke: Macmillan, 1995, p. 86.

10 The main principle behind SCR 242 was 'Land for Peace', in which it was hoped that Israel could be persuaded to trade the Arab land it occupied for the promise of recognition and peace from its Arab neighbours.

11 D. Gerner, *One Land, Two Peoples: The Conflict over Palestine*, Boulder, Colo.: Westview Press, 1994, p. 120.

12 D. Gilmour, *Dispossessed: The Ordeal of the Palestinians*, London: Sphere, 1980, p. 224.

13 The extent of Israeli losses in Lebanon became a major factor in motivating public opinion in favour of a withdrawal. From 1982 onwards more than 1,000 Israeli soldiers lost their lives as a result of the occupation of south Lebanon. Their local proxy, the South Lebanon Army, also incurred losses at the hands of Hizballah resistance fighters and others which ran into the hundreds.

Chapter 2

1 M. Tessler, *A History of the Arab Israeli Conflict*, Bloomington and Indianapolis: Indiana University Press, 1994, p. xi.

2 A. Gresch and D. Vidal, *An A to Z of the Middle East*, London: Zed, 1990, p. 221.

3 D. Gerner, *One Land, Two Peoples, The Conflict over Palestine*, Boulder, Colo.: Westview Press, 1994, p. 15.

4 E. Karsh (ed.), *Between War and Peace: Dilemmas of Israeli Security*, London: Frank Cass, 1996, p. 1.

5 See I. Pappe, *The Making of the Arab–Israeli Conflict 1947–1951*, London: I. B. Tauris, 1994. Also B. Morris, 1948 and after: Israel and the Palestinians, Oxford: Clarendon Press, 1994.

6 By 1999 there were 195 Israeli settlements in the West Bank (including Jerusalem) and the Gaza Strip. Since 1967 the Israeli authorities have confiscated 750,000 acres of land from the 1.5 million acres in the West Bank and Gaza Strip. According to Miftah (a widely respected Palestinian lobby group), the 'very existence of Israeli settlements is a direct violation of internationally binding agreements and regulations; international humanitarian law explicitly prohibits the occupying state to make permanent changes that are not, in the first place, intended to benefit the population of the occupied' (<www.miftah.org/factsheets/sheets/settlements.html>).

7 See: Y. Sayigh, *Armed Struggle and the Search for a State*, Oxford: Oxford University Press, 1980.

8 Ibid., p. 624.
9 See E. Ya'ari and Ze'ev Schiff, *Intifada, the Palestinian Uprising – Israel's Third Front*, New York: Simon & Schuster, 1989, pp. 263–64. Also D. Peretz, *Intifada: The Palestinian Uprising*, Boulder, Colo.: Westview Press, 1990.
10 R. Khalidi, *Palestinian Identity, the Construction of Modern Consciousness*, New York: Columbia University Press, 1997, p. 201.

Chapter 3

1 Chomsky goes on to remark that 'While it is true that the US would not tolerate Soviet moves that threatened to provide the USSR with a significant role in Middle East oil production or distribution, this has rarely been a realistic concern – which is not to say that ideologists have not come to believe the fantasies they conjure up to serve other needs' (N. Chomsky, *Fateful Triangle: The United States, Israel and the Palestinians*, London: Pluto Press, 1999 (updated edition), p. 17).
2 M. Rodinson, *Israel and the Arabs*, Harmondsworth: Penguin, 1968, p. 115.
3 D. Lesch (ed.), *The Middle East and the United States: A Historical and Political Reassessment*, Boulder, Colo.: Westview Press, 1996, p. 2.
4 Quoted by B. Reich, 'The United States and Israel: the nature of the special relationship', in ibid., p. 233.
5 Interviewed on *Today*, BBC Radio 4, November 2006.
6 These figures, along with others are quoted, in A. Richards and J. Waterbury, *A Political Economy of the Middle East*, Boulder, Colo.: Westview Press, 1990, p. 362.
7 N. Chomsky, op. cit., p. 19.
8 E. Alin, 'US policy and military intervention in the 1958 Lebanon crisis', in Lesch, op. cit., p. 160.
9 Ibid., pp. 148–62.
10 J. Stork, N. Aruri and F. Moughrabi, *Reagan and the Middle East*, Belmont, Mass.: AAUG, 1983, p. 31.
11 As Reich notes, Reagan actively courted Israel, 'he saw Israel as an important ally and an asset in the struggle against the Soviet Union . . . [and] the US–Israeli relationship during the eight years Reagan held office was generally characterized by close positive ties' (Reich, op. cit., p. 238).
12 D. McLaurin, *The Middle East in Soviet Policy*, London: D C. Heath, 1975, p. 126.
13 A. Dawisha and K. Dawisha (eds), *The Soviet Union in the Middle East: Policies and Perspectives*, London: Heinemann, 1982, p. 77.
14 G. Mirsky, 'The Soviet perception of the US threat', in Lesch op. cit., p. 409. See also Dawisha and Dawisha op. cit.
15 R. Fisk, 'Myth of "Pax-Americana"', <http://www.thenation.com/issue/961014/1014fisk.htm>, 1996, p. 1.
16 George W. Bush, State of the Union Address, 29 January 2002.
17 George W. Bush, Radio Address to the American People, 22 March 2003.

Chapter 4

1 S. Huntington, 'The clash of civilisations?', *Foreign Affairs*, Summer 1993, p. 25.
2 See E. Said, *Orientalism*, Harmondsworth: Penguin, 1995 (second edition).

3 E. Said, *Covering Islam: How the Media and Experts Determine How We See the Rest of the World*, London: Vintage, 1997, p. 163.
4 J. Miller, 'The challenge of radical Islam', *Foreign Affairs*, Spring 1993, p. 33.
5 B. Lewis, 'The roots of Muslim rage', *Atlantic Monthly*, Vol. 266:3, February 1990, p. 53.
6 Mubarak at the 'Summit of the Peacemakers', 13 March 1996.
7 J. Esposito, *The Islamic Threat: Myth or Reality?*, Oxford: Oxford University Press, 1992, p. 139.
8 For more on the cause of the Algerian crisis, see M. Willis, *The Islamist Challenge in Algeria: A Political History*, Reading, Mass.: Ithaca Press, 1996. Also G. Joffe (ed.), *North Africa: Nation, State, and Religion*, London: Routledge, 1993.
9 A. Taheri, 'Algeria's democratisation process: a frustrated hope', *Third World Quarterly*, Vol. 16:2, 1995, p. 219.
10 H. Amirouche, 'Algeria's Islamist revolution: the people versus democracy?', *Middle East Policy*, 1 January 1998, p. 2.
11 D. Rapoport, 'Fear and trembling: terrorism in three religious traditions', *American Political Science Review*, Vol. 78, 1984, pp. 662–84.
12 A. Taheri, *Holy Terror: The Inside Story of Islamic Terrorism*, London: Sphere, 1987, p. 1.

Chapter 5

1 From Albert Hourani, *Political Society in Lebanon: A Historical Introduction*, Centre for International Studies, Cambridge, Mass.: MIT, 1986.
2 For greater historical detail on pre-1920 Lebanon, see M. Yapp, *The Making of the Modern Near East*, London and New York: Longman, 1987, pp. 128–37. See also the clear and concise essay by Y. Choueiri on the history of the Lebanon in *Middle East and North Africa 2000*, London: Europa, 1999, pp. 776–77.
3 F. Massoulié describes this episode in *Middle East Conflicts*, New York: Interlink, 1999, p. 137.
4 This agreement was a secret arrangement between the French and British governments, in effect, to carve up the Ottoman Empire between the European victors of the war in the Middle East against the Ottomans spearheaded by the Arab Revolt. It was thus in conflict with assurances given by the British to Sherrif Hussein of Mecca to support the formation of an Arab kingdom in much of the area to be liberated from the Turks – with the help of Hussein's tribal armies.
5 'Little Lebanon' in 1913 had a population of 415,000, of which 330,000 (79 per cent) were Christians. By 1923 'Greater Lebanon' – the area of the present state – had over 600,000, of whom 47 per cent were Muslims. The smaller entity was largely Christian–Druze while the post-1920 mandated territory was a patchwork of religious communities and included the largely Sunni coastal towns and the Shi'ite Beqaa Valley.
6 A recent (1998) estimated breakdown gives Shi'a Muslims at 33 per cent, Sunni Muslims 20 per cent, Maronite Christian 20 per cent, Greek Orthodox 8.3 per cent, Druze 8 per cent, Greek Catholic 6.0 per cent, Armenian Christian 4 per cent, and other 0.7 per cent (C. C. Held, *Middle East Patterns, Places, Peoples and Politics*, Boulder, Colo.: Westview Press, p. 221).
7 Farid el-Khazen describes how Lebanon's 'plural society' differs from other communally divided countries, such as Belgium, Switzerland, Canada, the former

Czechoslovakia, Malaysia, Sri Lanka, India and the Sudan. It is an excellent book for someone wishing to study Lebanon in more depth: F. el-Khazen, *The Breakdown of the State in Lebanon*, London and New York: I. B. Tauris, 2000, especially pp. 32–33).

8 So sensitive did the question of population become – especially to Christians who realized that they were being steadily overtaken by Muslims – that 1932 was the last official census undertaken by the Lebanese government. Any new census would certainly demonstrate a marked decline in the Christian communities.

9 D. Stoten, *A State without a Nation*, Durham: University of Durham Centre for Middle Eastern and Islamic Studies, 1992, especially pp. 78–82.

10 For further reading on pre-1957 Lebanese politics, see M. E. Yapp, *The Near East since the First World War*, Harlow: Longman, 1996, pp. 110–15.

11 Farid el-Khazen, *The Communal Pact of National Identities*, Oxford: Centre for Lebanese Studies, 1991. See pp. 5–7 for more detail on the negotiations also involving the French, British and Egyptians which led to the adoption of the pact.

12 Massoulié, op. cit., p. 139.

13 Yapp, *The Near East*, op. cit., p. 265.

14 The civil war has spawned many books, some of the more graphic by Western victims of the spate of kidnapping (see Bibliography). For a well-written and atmospheric (if journalistic) account, see Robert Fisk, *Pity the Nation*, London: Athenaeum, 1990.

15 G. Luciani and G. Salamé, *The Arab State*, London: Routledge, 1990, p. 402.

16 UNRWA statistics in 1998 show a figure of 364,551 registered Palestinian refugees. Their situation is in marked contrast to the 1.3 million in Jordan, many of whom are fully integrated into Jordanian society.

Chapter 6

1 There is a wide variation of estimates of the Kurdish population worldwide. P. G. Kreyenbroek and S. Sperl (eds), *The Kurds: A Contemporary Overview*, London and New York: Routledge, 1992 puts the figure at nineteen million. The estimate of twenty-six million comes from David McDowell's *The Kurds*, London: Minority Rights Group International, 1996. Accuracy is difficult, given the tendency of Kurdish nationalists to inflate the figure and for host governments to minimize the statistics (or up to recently in the case of Turkey to disallow the use of the label 'Kurd' at all). McDowell's breakdown on p. 7 of the MRGI publication is likely to be as accurate as any.

2 Some scholars have argued that the Kurds are a nation and rather more than an ethnic group, although one without a state. G. M. Kirisci and K. Winrow (eds) discuss this in *The Kurdish Question and Turkey: An Example of a Trans-state Ethnic Conflict*, London and Portland: Frank Cass, 1998. This is a very useful and balanced account of the Kurds within Turkey.

3 McDowell's report, op. cit., p. 6 refers to the fact that modern Kurdish nationalists tend to exaggerate the exact extent of historical Kurdistan. In some areas 'claimed' by the Kurds, such as the environs of Irbil (which has an almost exclusively Kurdish population), Arabs have always been in a large majority.

4 Kirisci and Winrow, op. cit., p. 26. They point to the possible sense of multiple identity felt by some Kurdish Turks (or Turkish Kurds!) depending on their tribal identity, primary dialect group, religion or social class. The context would

often determine which identity such persons might wish to stress at any one time.

5 The issue of Sèvres and the aspirations of the Kurds is discussed in great detail in David McDowell's seminal work, *A Modern History of the Kurds*, London and New York: I. B. Tauris, 1997. This is probably the best comprehensive historical study of the Kurds in English and is easily accessible to the general reader. However, McDowell has considerable sympathy for the Kurds so his objectivity is occasionally open to challenge.

6 According to McDowell, recent research has uncovered such an idea emanating from Atatürk (see Kreyenbroek and Sperl, op. cit., p. 18).

7 Jon Lee Anderson, 'Mr Big', *New Yorker*, 5 February 2007, p. 55.

8 In safeguarding the interests of a 'recognized minority' the British had undertaken to replace their own officials with Kurds and to maintain Kurdish as the language of administration and of education. McDowell, *The Kurds*, op. cit., pp. 23–24 provides an excellent and concise summary of this period.

9 Translated as 'those who face death'. A romantic title for the Kurdish nationalist fighters!

10 Accurate figures for Kurdish losses at this time are impossible to obtain. According to R. Lawless in his 'Essay on Iraqi History', in *The Middle East and North Africa 2000*, London: Europa, 1999, pp. 522–23, over 3,000 out of 4,000 Kurdish villages were razed during the Iraq–Iran War alone and one-third of the Kurdish area depopulated. The figure of 200,000 dead comes from McDowell, *The Kurds*, op. cit. – from Kurdish sources – and may be exaggerated. Other authorities quote 100,000 plus.

11 Reported in *Hurriyet*, 5 November 2006.

12 Gül quoted in *The Economist*, 11 November 2006.

13 Quoted in the McDowell, *The Kurds*, op. cit., p. 18.

14 The then Minister of Justice is quoted in McDowell, *The Kurds*, op. cit., as saying, 'I believe that the Turk must be the only lord, the only master of this country. Those who are not of pure Turkish stock can only have one right in this country, the right to be servants and slaves' (Mahmut Esat Bozhurt, 22 September 1930).

15 Quoted in *The Economist*, 27 January 2007, p. 38.

Chapter 7

1 These estimates are from M. E. Yapp, *The Near East since the First World War*, Harlow: Longman, 1996.

2 Ibid., pp. 427–32 provides a readable and succinct account of the war. Professor Yapp's conclusions are particularly convincing. Indeed, his history makes an excellent supplementary companion to this work.

3 Pirouz Mojtahed-Zahed, *Security and Territoriality in the Persian Gulf*, Richmond: Curzon, 1999. Despite some pro-Iranian partiality, pp. 44–52 provide good background to the Iraq–Iran confrontation of 1969 to 1975.

4 Richard Lawless, 'Essay on Iraqi History', in *The Middle East and North Africa 2000*, London: Europa, 1999. See pp. 549–56 for a detailed but concise account of the build-up to and main events of the war.

5 Ibid. claims that 'most commentators' agree that Saddam Hussein was seeking the toppling of the Iranian regime as the primary war aim. By contrast, Bassam Tibi, in his *Conflict and War in the Middle East*, Basingstoke: Macmillan, 1998, p. 156, convincingly outlines a range of Iraqi objectives on the lines we have

described in this chapter. See also Yapp, op. cit., p. 428. For an admittedly prejudiced Iranian perspective, see Farhang Rajaee (ed.), *The Iran–Iraq War: The Politics of Aggression*, Gainesville: University Press of Florida, 1993. For a differing view, see L. Freedman and E. Karsh, *The Gulf Conflict 1990–1991*, London and Boston, Mass.: Faber & Faber, 1993. They argue that Saddam was reacting to Iranian provocation and had very limited war aims confined to deterring Khomeini and occupying small areas of Iran of strategic importance for Iraq's access to the Gulf.

6 Tibi, op. cit., pp. 156–57. He coins the phrase 'potent socio-psychological synthesis between Shi'a Islam and Persian nationalism' to describe the unifying force in Iran in the early stages of the Gulf War.

7 In addition to Lawless's coherent account of the ebb and flow of war (see n. 4) there is a detailed annotated chronology in *The Longman Companion to the Middle East since 1914*, London and New York: Longman, 1998, pp. 145–48. A. Ehteshami and G. Nonneman's (eds) comprehensive study *War and Peace in the Gulf*, Reading, Mass.: Ithaca Press, 1991 also has an excellent chronology. This is one of the best studies for the specialist reader.

8 Lawless quotes a *Washington Post* report to the effect that the Chinese sold Iraq arms worth $3,100 million between 1981 and 1985. Sales to Iran were $575 million in the same period. Soviet supplies to Iraq included SS-12 missiles. These were more sophisticated than the Chinese 'Silkworm' missiles used by the Iranians, which basically used the same technology as the German V2 rockets of 1944–45. For comprehensive statistics on arms transfers see especially Ehteshami and Nonneman, op. cit., ch. 4.

9 It emerged in November 1986 that despite a formal position of neutrality the USA had supplied arms to Iran – three shipments since 1985. Washington had been strongly discouraging any arms transfers to Iran. The primary purpose was to enlist Iranian help for freeing American hostages held by Shi'a militant groups in Lebanon. One further scandalous aspect was that it transpired that profits from these consignments were secretly siphoned off by officials to fund Nicaraguan rebels – the Contras – thus evading congressional prohibitions on such operations. This, together with allegations that the CIA had provided intelligence (much of it said to be falsified) to both combatants (blamed by the Iraqis for the loss of Fao), raised doubts as to the aims of US policy towards the war. One theory was that Washington was trying to ensure that neither side could gain a decisive advantage.

10 For more detail about the Kurdish involvement in the Gulf War, see Chapter 6. A detailed if partisan account of the chemical attacks on Halabja and subsequently in the campaign are given in D. McDowell's *A Modern History of the Kurds*, London and New York: I. B. Tauris, 1997.

11 Said K. Aburish, *Saddam Hussein: The Politics of Revenge*, London: Bloomsbury, 2000 gives an interesting analysis of Saddam's motives and conduct of the war (pp. 190–222). It is very biased against the Iraqi leader but a good read none the less.

Chapter 8

1 M. E. Yapp's *The Near East since the First World War*, Harlow: Longman, 1996 gives a good overview. Pp. 499–501 cover the run-up to the Kuwait crisis.

2 For a detailed account of the 'new thinking' in the Soviet Union up to, during and immediately after the Kuwait crisis, see R. O. Freedman, *The Middle East*

after Iraq's invasion of Kuwait, Gainesville: University Press of Florida, 1993, ch. 3. This book also has excellent essays on the policies pursued by the other main players, and the opening chapter, 'The Gulf War: a political and military assessment', is a valuable analysis of the conflict.

3 For examinations of this argument, see A. Ehteshami and G. Nonneman (eds), *War and Peace in the Gulf*, Reading, Mass.: Ithaca Press, 1991. Pp. 71–75 provide an especially concise and clear account of the developing crisis in 1990. The whole book is a very worthwhile and accessible (to the general reader) analysis of the war, including documents such as Iraqi statements and UN resolutions. For more detail of the war itself and the immediate aftermath, see L. Freedman and E. Karsh, *The Gulf Conflict 1990–1991*, London and Boston, Mass.: Faber & Faber, 1993.

4 According to Ehteshami and Nonneman, op. cit., Iraq's indebtedness by August 1990 amounted to $34 billion to Saudi Arabia and about $15 billion to Kuwait. This included the proceeds of oil sold by both countries on behalf of Iraq as well as the huge debts run up during the war with Iran.

5 In June 1981 Israeli warplanes attacked a building complex outside Baghdad suspected of being an Iraqi nuclear installation.

6 This was Farzad Bazoft, on assignment for the *Observer* newspaper, who had been arrested near a defence industry complex in March 1990. His subsequent trial and execution for spying led to a marked deterioration of relations with the UK.

7 An excellent analysis of Iraqi conduct and motivation is in Bassam Tibi's *Conflict and War in the Middle East*, Basingstoke: Macmillan, 1998 (2nd edition), especially ch. 9.

8 See, for example, Said K. Aburish, *Saddam Hussein: The Politics of Revenge*, London: Bloomsbury, 2000. His account of the Arab League summit of 30 and 31 May 1990 illuminates vividly the attitudes of the main players as the crisis deepened.

9 There are persistent reports that although the Kuwaitis showed some inclination towards considering Iraqi demands, Sheikh Sa'ad bin Abdullah, the Kuwaiti Crown Prince, had been very insulting about Saddam personally, thus triggering the invasion.

10 See, for example, Sami Yousef, 'The Iraqi–US War: a conspiracy theory', in Haim Bresheeth and Nira Yuval-Davis (eds), *The Gulf War and the New World Order*, London and New Jersey: Zed, 1991. Like some other writers (mostly Arab), Yousef believes that Washington lured Saddam into attacking Kuwait so that the USA could set him up as the regional 'bogeyman'.

11 April Glaspie told one of the authors that she felt sure she had left Saddam Hussein in no doubt that the US government would not accept Iraqi aggression against Kuwait (conversation with Hinchcliffe in Amman, July 1996).

12 Four members of the Arab League had sent troops to Kuwait in 1961 to take over from the British forces that had responded to a request for assistance from newly independent Kuwait following a claim by Iraq of sovereignty over the emirate. The Arab League's principal motivation was to end the embarrassment of having troops from the former colonial power intervening in the region rather than facing a real prospect of fighting Iraq. A subsidiary factor was the contest for leadership in the Arab world between Baghdad and Cairo. The United Arab Republic strongly supported British claims that the Iraqis had designs on Kuwait. An excellent account is given in M. M. Alani, *Operation Vantage: British Military Intervention in Kuwait 1961*, Surbiton: Laam Press, 1990.

13 The claim to Kuwait had been maintained by successive Iraqi regimes: Kuwait was an artificial, neo-colonialist creation of the British carved out of the Ottoman province of Basra, which became Iraq, and rightfully formed part of its territory. This argument was broadened to include all colonial-imposed frontiers as serving imperialist interests and being obstacles to the Holy Grail of pan-Arab unity.
14 See Ehteshami and Nonneman, op. cit., especially pp. 81–83.
15 Anthony H. Cordesman, *Kuwait: Recovery and Security after the Gulf War* (Washington, DC: Centre for Strategic and International Studies, 1997), p. 129.
16 Paul O'Neill interviewed on *60 Minutes*, CBS, 11 January 2004.

Chapter 9

1 A. Arian, *Politics in Israel: The Second Generation*, London: Chatham House Press, 1989 (revised edition), pp. 218–19.
2 For further discussion, see J. Goodhand and D. Hulme, 'From wars to complex political emergencies: understanding conflict and peace-building in the new world order', *Third World Quarterly*, Vol. 20:1, 1999, pp. 13–26.
3 M. al-Masri, interview with Beverley Milton-Edwards, Gaza City, November 2006.
4 See K. Rupesinghe (ed.), *Conflict Transformation*, Basingstoke: Macmillan, 1995. Also L. Kriesberg, T. A. Northrup and S. J. Thorson (eds), *Intractable Conflicts and Their Transformation*, Syracuse, NY: Syracuse University Press, 1989.
5 K. Rupesinghe, *Civil Wars, Civil Peace – an Introduction to Conflict Resolution*, London: Pluto Press, 1998, p. 115. For further debate of conflict resolution theory, see C. Mitchell and M. Banks, *Handbook of Conflict Resolution, the Analytical Problem-solving Approach*, London: Pinter, 1996, and L. Kriesberg, *Constructive Conflicts, from Escalation to Resolution*, Lanham, Md.: Rowman & Littlefield, 1998.
6 F. Halliday, 'The Middle East at the millennial turn', *Middle East Report*, No. 213, Winter 1999, p. 6.
7 See J. Maila, 'The Ta'if Accord: an evaluation', in D. Collings (ed.), *Peace for Lebanon: From War to Reconstruction*, Boulder, Colo.: Lynne Rienner, 1994.
8 Z. Flamhaft, *Israel on the Road to Peace – Accepting the Unacceptable*, Boulder, Colo.: Westview Press, 1996, p. 183.
9 A. Abu Odeh, *Jordanians, Palestinians and the Hashemite Kingdom in the Middle East Peace Process*, Washington, DC: USIP, 1999, p. 274.
10 D. Makovsky, *Making Peace with the PLO: The Rabin Government's Road to the Oslo Accord*, Boulder, Colo.: Westview Press, 1996, p. 22.
11 Halliday, op. cit., p. 5.
12 B. Milton-Edwards, 'Iraq, past, present and future: a thoroughly modern mandate', *History and Policy*, May 2003, pp. 1–6.

Chapter 10

1 'The day the world changed'. This cover headline in *The Economist* of 15 September 2001 typified the Western media reaction to 11 September.
2 Italian Prime Minister S. Berlusconi, 24 September 2001.
3 George W. Bush, Address to Joint Session of Congress, 20 September 2001.
4 'Six months on: a balance-sheet', *The Economist*, 9 March 2002, pp. 11–12.

5 The target countries nominated by the Pentagon in the leaked classified document were the 'axis of evil' gang of three, plus China, Russia, Libya and Syria. The Nuclear Posture Review widened the circumstances thought to justify a possible nuclear response and expanded the list of targets.

6 George W. Bush, White House Lawn Address to mark six-month anniversary of 9/11.

7 In contrast to the cool reception US Vice-President Dick Cheney received from a number of Arab countries in his tour in March 2002, and criticism of a possible US attack on Iraq from some other EU leaders, the UK was markedly supportive. At a joint press conference with Cheney on 11 March 2002 British Prime Minister Tony Blair stated: 'There is a threat from Saddam Hussein and the weapons of mass destruction that he has acquired. It is not in doubt at all.' A Downing Street source later said that 'no decisions' had been taken about military action against Iraq (*Independent*, 12 March 2002).

8 *Civiltà Cattolico*, January 2003 (official publication of the Vatican).

9 Sahaf on BBC, 8 April 2003.

10 D. Frum, *The Right Man: The Surprise Presidency of George W. Bush*, New York: Random House, 2003, pp. 232–33.

11 <http://www.google.co.uk/search?hl=en&ie=ISO-8859-1&q=Baker +Hamilton+Iraq+Study+Group&btnG=Search&meta=>.

12 See <www.STRATFOR.com>, 24.6.02, *The Palestinian strategy*: 'The Palestinian strategy makes no sense except in the context of alignment with al-Qaeda . . . the goals of the Palestinians and those of al-Qaeda have converged.'

13 Camille Mansour, 'The impact of 11 September on the Israeli–Palestinian conflict', *Journal of Palestinian Studies*, Vol. 31:2, Winter 2002, p. 13.

14 Aluf Benn, *George Bush: Ariel Sharon's Most Powerful Weapon*, <www.salon.com/news/features/2002/03/08/weapon>.

15 SCR 1397, adopted on 12 March 2002, affirms 'a vision of a region where two states, Israel and Palestine, live side by side within secure and recognised borders'.

16 President George W. Bush, White House Address, 14 March 2003.

17 *The Economist*, 23 March 2002, has an excellent survey on the social and economic problems faced by the Gulf monarchies.

18 UNDP, 'Arab Human Development', September 2002, summarized in Middle East Quarterly, Fall 2002 (<http://www.meforum.org/article/513#_ftnl>).

Bibliography

Aburish, S. K. (2000) *Saddam Hussein: The Politics of Revenge*, London: Bloomsbury. His account of the Arab League summit of 30 and 31 May 1990 vividly illuminates the attitudes of the main players as the crisis deepened.

Achcar, G. and Warschawski, M. (2007) *The 33 Day War: Israel's War on Hezbollah in Lebanon and its Consequences*, Boulder, Colo.: Paradigm.

Alani, M. M. (1990) *Operation Vantage: British Military Intervention in Kuwait in 1961*, Surbiton: Laam Press. For anyone interested in the earlier Kuwait crisis.

BBC News, *The Day that Shook the World*, London, BBC Worldwide, 2001. Correspondents' reports on worldwide reaction to 11 September 2001, written in the weeks following the al-Qaeda attacks.

Ben-Ami, S. (2006) *Scars of War, Wounds of Peace: The Israeli-Arab Tragedy*, New York: Phoenix. Dynamics of the Palestinian–Israeli conflict and its historical dimension.

Blandford, N. (2006) *Killing Mr Lebanon: The Assassination of Rafik Hariri and its Impact on the Middle East*, London: I. B. Tauris. Compelling account of the internal dynamics of post-war Lebanon.

Bresheeth, H. and Yuval-Davis, N. (eds) (1991) *The Gulf War and the New World Order*, London: Zed. Comprehensive collection of articles written at the time of the crisis with particular emphasis on anti-war issues and the global balance of power.

Chomsky, N. (2001) *9–11*, New York: Seven Stories Press. Series of short accounts of responses to the al-Qaeda attacks on America and US foreign policy in the Middle East.

Choueiri, Y. (1999) 'Essay on the history of the Lebanon', in *Middle East and North Africa 2000*, London: Europa. Authoritative and concise history.

Clarke, R. (2004) *Against all Enemies: Inside America's War on Terror*, New York: Free Press. Details the ways in which the Bush administration has tackled the war on terror since 9/11.

Cordesman, A. (1996) *Perilous Prospects: The Peace Process and the Arab–Israeli Military Balance*, Boulder, Colo.: Westview Press. Useful text with expert analysis from a military and strategic perspective.

Ehteshami, A. and Nonneman, G. (eds) (1991) *War and Peace in the Gulf*, Reading, Mass.: Ithaca Press. One of the best studies for the specialist reader.

Eickelman, D. and Piscatori, J. (1996) *Muslim Politics*, Princeton, NJ: Princeton University Press. Excellent account of a diverse body of Muslim political voices from across the globe.

Esposito, J. L. (1992) *The Islamic Threat: Myth or Reality?*, Oxford: Oxford University Press. Strong account of the debate about modern Islamist movements and their impact on contemporary politics.

—— (2002) *Unholy War: Terror in the Name of Islam*, New York: Oxford University Press. Authoritative explanation of the many dimensions of Muslim politics made manifest in the contemporary Middle East and beyond.

Fisk, R. (1990) *Pity the Nation*, London: Athenaeum. A vivid journalistic account of the civil war by a correspondent who has lived in the Lebanon for over twenty years. Good on atmosphere.

Fraser, T. (1995) *The Arab–Israeli Conflict*, Basingstoke: Macmillan. One of the best concise historical accounts.

Freedman, L. and Karsh, E. (1993) *The Gulf Conflict 1990–1991*, London and Boston, Mass.: Faber & Faber. The contrary argument to Rajaee's book: Saddam was reacting to Iranian provocation and had very limited war aims confined to deterring Khomeini and occupying small areas of Iran of strategic importance for Iraq's access to the Gulf.

Freedman, R. O. (1993) *The Middle East after Iraq's Invasion of Kuwait*, Gainesville: University Press of Florida. Excellent essays on the policies pursued by the main players, and the opening chapter, 'The Gulf War: a political and military assessment', is a valuable analysis of the conflict.

Gerner, D. (1994) *One Land, Two Peoples: The Conflict over Palestine*, Boulder, Colo.: Westview Press. Lively and well-written text covering the many aspects of the Palestinian–Israeli conflict.

Halliday, F. (2001) *'Two Hours that Shook the World': Sept. 11 2001*, London: Saqi Press. Best 'instant book' on 9/11 and its likely consequences. Readable and perceptive.

Hinchcliffe, P. with Ducker, J. and Holt, Dr M. (2006)*Without Glory in Arabia: The British Retreat from Aden,* London and New York: I. B. Tauris. A comprehensive account (partly an oral history) of the Aden conflict – not covered in this book.

Hourani, A. (1986) *Political Society in Lebanon: A Historical Introduction*, Cambridge, Mass.: Massachusetts Center for International Studies. Excellent scene-setter for the modern Lebanon.

Huntington, S. P. (1996) *The Clash of Civilizations and the Remaking of World Order*, New York: Simon & Schuster. Controversial analysis of a new post-Cold War world anticipating a (predominantly) Western–Islamic confrontation

Jaber, F. A. (ed.) (2006) *The Kurds: Nationlism and Politics,* London, San Francisco and Beirut: Saqi. Essays by different scholars on all aspects of the Kurds. Very valuable for the specialist.

Kettell, S. (2006) *Dirty Politics: New Labour, British Democracy, and the Invasion of Iraq,* London and New York: Zed. Polemical but well-researched and absorbing hatchet-job on UK policy in the run-up to the 2003 Iraq War.

el-Khazen, F. (2000) *The Breakdown of the State in Lebanon*, London: I. B. Tauris. For anyone wanting to study the Lebanon in greater depth.

Kirisci, G. M. and Winrow, K. (eds) (1998) *The Kurdish Question and Turkey: An Example of a Trans-state in Ethnic Conflict*, London and Portland, Oreg.: Frank Cass. A very useful and balanced account of the Kurds within Turkey.

Kreyenbroek, P. G. and Sperl, S. (eds) (1992) *The Kurds: A Contemporary Overview*, London: Routledge. Excellent for further reading on the Kurdish issue.

Lesch, D. (ed.) (1996) *The Middle East and the United States*, Boulder, Colo.: Westview Press. Excellent analysis of US policy on the Gulf crisis and on earlier superpower confrontation.

Makey, S. (2006) *Lebanon: A House Divided*, London: W. W. Norton. A useful introduction and overview of Lebanon's different confessional communities and the civil war.

Massoulié, F. (1999) *Middle East Conflicts*, New York: Interlink. Well-presented and profusely illustrated paperback with some coverage of the Lebanese civil war. A slightly 'tabloid' approach, but readable.

McDowell, D. (1997) *A Modern History of the Kurds*, London: I. B. Tauris. Probably the best and most authoritative historical study of the Kurds in English and easily accessible to the general reader.

Milton-Edwards, B. (1996) *Islamic Politics in Palestine*, London: I. B. Tauris. Overview of a century of Islamic activism in the Palestinian–Israeli arena.

—— (2004) *Islamic Fundamentalism since 1945*, London: Routledge. Concise account of the various factors giving rise to modern Islamic movements and their defining characteristics.

Mojtahed-Zahed, P. (1999) *Security and Territoriality in the Persian Gulf*, Richmond: Curzon. Despite some pro-Iranian partiality, very strong on Iraq–Iran tensions, including the confrontation of 1969–75.

Packer, G. (2006) *The Assassin's Gate: America in Iraq*, London: Faber & Faber. Searing analysis of America's record in Iraq.

Pappe, I. (1994) *The Making of the Arab–Israeli Conflict 1947–1951*, London: I. B. Tauris. Strong and balanced account of the origins of the conflict between Israel and its Arab neighbours, as well as the birth of the refugee issue for Palestinians.

Quandt, W. (1986) *Camp David, Peacemaking and Politics*, Washington, DC: Brookings Institution. Strong analytical record of the forces employed to create peace between Israel and the Egyptians following the 1973 war.

Qureshi, E. and Sells, M. A. (eds) (2003) *The New Crusades: Constructing the Muslim Enemy*, New York: Columbia University Press. Good analysis of important aspects of the debate about Islam and politics.

Rabinovitch, I. (1991) *The Road Not Taken: Early Arab–Israeli Negotiations*, Oxford: Oxford University Press. Useful historical account and analysis of attempts at peacemaking in the region.

Rajaee, F. (ed.) (1993) *The Iran–Iraq War: The Politics of Aggression*, Gainesville: University Press of Florida. The conflict from a strongly Iranian perspective. Lively essays.

Said, E. (1995) *The Politics of Dispossession: The Struggle for Palestinian Self-determination*, London: Vintage. Very good and readable collection of articles and essays covering twenty years of Palestinian personalities and issues. Edward

Said is a leading US-based Palestinian academic and one of the best Arab writers on this topic.

Smith, C. D. (1992) *Palestine and the Arab–Israeli Conflict*, Basingstoke: Macmillan. Good account of the roots of the conflict for a first-time reader.

Tessler, M. (1994) *A History of the Israeli–Palestinian Conflict*, Bloomington: Indiana University Press. Comprehensive and detailed account by foremost historian.

Tibi, B. (1998) *Conflict and War in the Middle East*, Basingstoke: Macmillan. Convincingly argued text on conflict in the region.

Usher, G. (1995) *Palestine in Crisis*, London: Pluto. Strong journalistic account of the post-Oslo era in the West Bank and Gaza Strip under the Palestinian National Authority.

Willis, M. (1996) *The Islamist Challenge in Algeria: A Political History*, Reading, Mass.: Ithaca Press. Strong account of the rise of Islamist forces in Algeria and the descent into civil violence in the 1990s.

Woodward, B. (2003) *Bush at War*, New York: Pocket Books. Insights into the first battles of the war on terror both inside and outside the Bush administration.

Yapp, M. E. (1987) *The Making of the Modern Near East*, London: Longman. Concise summary of post-Second World War Lebanese history. Covers the historical background up to 1957.

—— (1996) *The Near East since the First World War*, London: Longman. Companion text to *The Making of the Modern Near East*, with sound historical focus.

Index